DATE DUE

WALTZING INTO THE COLD WAR

WALTZING INTO THE COLD WAR

The Struggle for Occupied Austria

JAMES JAY CARAFANO

Texas A&M University Press
College Station

The paper used in this book meets the minimum requirements of the American National
Standard for Permanence of Paper for Printed Library Materials, z39.48–1984.
Binding materials have been chosen for durability.
∞

Library of Congress Cataloging-in-Publication Data

Carafano, James Jay, 1955–
  Waltzing into the Cold War : the struggle for occupied Austria / James Jay Carafano.
    p. cm. — (Texas A & M University military history series ; 81)
Includes bibliographical references and index.
  ISBN 1-58544-213-5 (cloth)
    1. Austria—History—Allied occupation, 1945–1955. 2. United States—Military relations—
Austria. 3. Austria—Military relations—United States. I. Title. II. Series.
  DB99.1 .C37 2002
  943.605'23—dc21
      2002002842

For
Jo Ann Hoeppner Moran Cruz, Lois G. Schwoerer, and Diane Lee Schulz
—friends and heroes

CONTENTS

ILLUSTRATIONS

ACKNOWLEDGMENTS

I have many debts. This book would not have been possible without the mentoring, criticisms, assistance, insights, and support of Günter Bischof, Walter Blasi, Siegfried Beer, Jeff Clark, Ed Drea, Wolfgang Etschmann, John Greenwood, Rudolf Jerábeck, David Keltner, Clay Laurie, Stephanie Lanz, David Painter, Aviel Roshwald, Erwin Schmidl, James Shedel, Robert A. Silano, Richard Wiggers, "Bud" Williams, Dale Wilson, and my constant collaborators Diane Schulz and Luke Carafano. I also thank Georgetown University, Phillip Karber, and the Harry S. Truman Library for research and writing awards and grants. Finally, I owe a debt of gratitude to the staffs of the many research libraries and archives I visited for their unmatched professionalism, extraordinary expertise, and kind assistance.

WALTZING INTO THE COLD WAR

THE FIRING STOPS AT MIDNIGHT

S hortly before three in the morning on May 8, 1945, an exhausted
Gen. Dwight David Eisenhower signed the document that ended
World War II in Europe. There was no celebration. The supreme
commander of the Allied Expeditionary Force and his staff had just com-
pleted a marathon negotiating session, working out the final details for the
German capitulation. Before collapsing into bed Eisenhower called Gen.
Omar N. Bradley, the senior U.S. ground combat leader in the theater.
"Brad, I've got good news," Eisenhower said in a tired, matter-of-fact voice,
"the firing stops at midnight."

While historians still debate the quality of U.S. combat generalship,
none question the seriousness of the American effort or the dedication
with which commanders prepared for battle. Eisenhower was typical. A
West Point graduate, "Ike" had been a student of warfare for thirty-one
years before the United States entered the Second World War. He had
served under and been mentored by many of the "old army's" best-known
leaders—including John Pershing, Fox Conner, Douglas MacArthur, and
George Marshall—and he was a graduate of the Command and General
Staff College and Army War College, the army's schools for mid- and
senior-level officers. As a result, he was also a student of the writings of
Prussian military theorist Carl von Clausewitz. In common with many
senior military leaders, Ike could quote the writer's famous dictum that
war is an extension of politics.[1] This principle guided his every decision
throughout the war in Europe.

Eisenhower's generation gave far less thought to the reverse notion that
military forces could exert a powerful influence on foreign policy, particularly
after the battle, when the lines of authority and responsibility might be far
from clear. Postwar tasks thus were something for which the army had little
interest and scant training. Eisenhower would learn much of the unique challenges they presented while serving as the commander of U.S. occupation

forces in Europe and later as army chief of staff, commander of all North Atlantic Treaty Organization (NATO) forces in Europe, and president.

The lack of thought about the military's role as a shaper of international affairs became abundantly clear as the first dawn without war in six years spread across Europe on May 9, 1945. Eisenhower and the rest of the American military soon discovered that their mission was far from over after the firing stopped. The soldiers who had won the battles were now responsible for the fight for peace: conducting the simultaneous occupation of several European territories, including Germany, Trieste, and Austria. This was a task that could turn Clausewitz's maxim on its head, saddling military commanders with new and uncomfortable responsibilities.

Postconflict military operations including disarmament, denazification, intelligence collection, operational planning, combat training, and military assistance had the power to reshape the postwar settlement, reinforcing peace and preempting future conflict or breeding distrust, division, and confrontation. Rather than a mere instrument of policy, these tasks made soldiers agents in creating Europe's new destiny.

Midnight's Child

Austria's occupation offers a remarkable case study. The First Republic was annexed by Nazi Germany in 1938 during the infamous Anschluss. After the war, the United States, Britain, France, and the Soviet Union occupied the country under the mandate of the Moscow Declaration, which called for the reestablishment of an independent state. This would prove no simple charge. The newly established Second Republic faced immense difficulties: enormous wartime destruction; hordes of displaced persons; severe economic dislocation; smoldering ethnic, religious, and political tensions; potentially explosive territorial disputes with Italy and Yugoslavia; and the bad luck of being caught between the disparate interests of the postwar superpowers.

An unwavering American commitment to a protracted and difficult occupation of what had been considered a strategically unimportant country makes this subject even more intriguing. No one appreciated this situation more than the Austrians. Seven years after Eisenhower signed the declaration ending the war in Europe, their country was still controlled by Allied troops when Chancellor Leopold Figl made an official visit to Washington bearing a very different piece of paper: a copy of the first official communication between America and Austria—a 1784 letter from Benjamin Franklin to Joseph II calling for the establishment of diplomatic relations with the Habsburg Empire. Figl intended for the letter to serve as an illustration of a longstanding bond between the two nations, but, in truth, he knew Americans and Austrians shared a thin history. The imperial establishment gave little attention to the young republic, and when the United States finally emerged as a global actor during World War I, the empire was already on the verge of collapse and fragmentation. America's postwar policy toward the new Austrian state was largely indifferent. During the 1930s, the United States granted Austrians less than fourteen hundred immigration visas per year. Preoccupation with the Great Depression further distanced America from the country's troubles. World War II changed matters little. The United States concluded the conflict reluctant to engage in an area where it had few interests.

No component of the government had less desire to remain in the country than the military. Yet, the army would bear the lion's share of occupation duties and soon become the staunchest proponent for engaging in this corner of Europe. In the process, commanders found themselves in unfamiliar roles and partnered in a unique relationship with political leaders whose experience and perspective seemed as different and remote as the typical Austrian's interests were from the concerns of an average American.

Figl, who dealt with the U.S. military often, was as representative of the Austrian leadership as Eisenhower was of senior American officers. Educated as an agronomist, Figl fashioned a career as a political activist in the First Republic. Jailed after the Anschluss, he did not come out of the concentration camps until 1945, when a reputation for moderate political leadership, persecution by the Nazis, and work with the resistance were virtual prerequisites for participating in Austria's postwar government.

It would be the odd fellowship of leaders such as Figl and soldiers like Eisenhower that would reshape the face of Europe. The common mission of rebuilding the country was shared by skilled politicians and trained warriors, victims and victors, survivors and occupiers. Their peculiar partnership, which lasted until the signing of the Austrian State Treaty in 1955 and the withdrawal of Allied troops, was a distinctive feature of the occupation.

While France and Great Britain also played not inconsequential roles, the other great actor in the occupation drama was the Soviet Union. Across the table at many of the discussions on Austria's future sat the most recognizable public face of the Soviet enigma: humorless and inscrutable Vyacheslav Mikhailovich Molotov. Born in 1890 to a middle-class Russian family, he joined the Bolshevik Party in 1906 and rose to Politburo membership in 1926. A veteran of the blood frenzy of the Stalinist purges, Molotov was appointed foreign minister in 1939 despite his lack of diplomatic experience. Molotov honed his international relations skills throughout the desperate years of war, learning to shake hands in turn with Hitler, Churchill,

Roosevelt, Truman, and Eisenhower. He held his post until 1949, and again from 1953–56. Dogmatic, tireless, and a steadfast party loyalist, his prolonged tenure stemmed in large part from his unswerving dedication to advancing the Stalinist postwar agenda, pressed tenaciously during a decade of treaty negotiations and ministerial conferences.

Late in life, Molotov concluded that it was the contrasting visions for the future of Europe that led to the standoff between East and West, although he had little taste for the notion of a Cold War: "The Cold War—I don't like the expression . . . what does the 'cold war' mean? Strained relations. It was entirely their doing or because we were on the offensive. They certainly hardened their line against us, but we had to consolidate our conquests. We made our socialist Germany out of our part of Germany, and restored order in Czechoslovakia, Poland, Hungary, and Yugoslavia, where the situation was fluid. To squeeze out the capitalist order. This was the cold war. Of course, you had to know when and where to stop. I believe in this respect Stalin kept well within limits."[2] Molotov did not impart where Austria fit within these boundaries, and it was certainly not clear to the Americans or the Austrians during the anxious years of reconstruction. Their apprehension over the limits of Soviet ambition and the precautions they took in the face of that fear is the real centerpiece of the occupation story.

The History of Occupation History

The narrative of the U.S. military's uneasy partnership with Soviet occupation troops and complex relationship with Austria's postwar leadership has always been incomplete.[3] There is, for example, no official history. Although the army's Center of Military History planned to produce a series of occupation studies, only the volume on Germany was completed. Distracted by the requirement to write official histories of the Korean and Vietnam Wars, the center never produced a body of narratives on occupation operations comparable to the famous "green books" on World War II.

The history available is largely the product of individual academic research. Here, the army's role as an occupation force constitutes a very minor contribution to the corpus of Cold War literature in Europe and the United States. Until fairly recently, the Austrian canon was little more than a tool for recasting the political identity of the nation lost with the demise of the First Republic in 1938. An educational narrative that bordered on mythmaking, it focused on the country's self-righteous journey from occupation to sovereignty and neutrality.

While political sensibilities slowed the evolution of Austrian historical investigation, since the 1960s they have fired developments in the West producing three major schools of thought, each with its own partisan tinge. American writings have generally been grouped as the orthodox Cold War narrative, the revisionist reinterpretation, and the postrevisionist critique. In varying combinations within these schools, historians drew on assessments of national interests, ideology, and social and cultural imperatives to assess the behavior of states.

Although the major works only briefly mention the occupation, they suggest Austria's place in the literature. The first significant writings interpreted relations between the United States and Soviet Union as an inevitable struggle between competing ideologies, a classic battle of good versus evil. Herbert Feis cited the conclusion of Austria's occupation as a victory for the West.[4] The State Treaty left a democratic country and a productive member of the European community, making it a Cold War triumph.

Revisionists argued that the real root causes of postwar international tension and competition were America's expansionist tendencies. Ideology was a veneer covering a variety of psychological, political, and economic motivations that led the United States to seek worldwide hegemony. Austria represented a defeat, a lost colony. Joyce and Gabriel Kolko viewed the end of the occupation not as a triumph of democracy, but as a Soviet initiative.[5] In the revisionists' view, the State Treaty represented a setback to U.S. imperialism.

John Lewis Gaddis spearheaded a vigorous critique of Cold War revisionism, believing the approach overemphasized economic considerations, ignored domestic politics, and belittled valid concerns about the Soviets' postwar intentions. Gaddis argued that legitimate, vital national interests drove policy decisions. America sought to establish a stable international order to enhance its own security. Gaddis makes only passing reference to the occupation, concluding that the final resolution was an American initiative and contributed to the containment of Soviet power.[6]

Bruce Cumings, a proponent of the revisionist school, countered that Gaddis, rather than offering a corrective to previous scholarship, represented "anti-revisionism."[7] Gaddis's critiques were simply discursive and not based on an analysis of the revisionist treatment of evidence. Cumings labeled his approach unsystematic and reductionist, ignoring the insights provided by postmodern historical techniques. These objections are noteworthy, and Austria is a case in point. Even with the wealth of new scholarship and sources available since the end of the Cold War, Gaddis's 1997 work, *We Now Know: Rethinking Cold War History*, adds nothing to the Austrian Cold War narrative. But Cumings's criticism is more symptomatic of the disease than the cure. His critique was itself discursive and no more or less compelling.

In many respects, particularly concerning Austria, all of these interpretations are unsatisfying—mainly because they lack any real evidence to support their sweeping conclusions. Two factors accounted for this sad state of affairs. The first was secrecy. It was not that the history of the occupation was unimportant. The case was exactly the opposite. As the Cold War unfolded, Austria's fate became inseparable from U.S. plans for the future of Western Europe, and the delicate nature of negotiations over the State Treaty resulted in much of the written record being given the highest security classification. Without the benefit of this hidden history, memories of the struggles over occupied Austria faded as the Cold War dragged on, and American historians largely lost interest.

Secrecy also contributed to the second feature obscuring Austria's place in the Cold War: a lack of appreciation for the absolutely central role new conceptions of national security played in shaping U.S. behavior. National security became a mantra for successive administrations. In the process of defining potential postwar dangers, the United States helped create, shape, and change the threat. Melvin P. Leffler recently argued that by surveying the vast collection of newly declassified records, a more nuanced understanding of the U.S. conception of national security emerges. After World War II, the unpredictability of Soviet behavior and the uncertain course of the continent's social, political, and economic conditions forced leaders in Washington to develop a set of assumptions concerning potential threats. Faced with great uncertainty, the United States defined its national interests broadly. As a result, all potential threats to European stability were viewed as potential risks for America. It was these fears that bred mistrust and confrontation between the superpowers.[8]

The Path to the State Treaty

With regard to Austria, where military security concerns more than national interests or ideology shaped U.S. foreign policies, Leffler's approach has real utility. This perspective and an unprecedented release of classified documents over the last twenty years suggest a new narrative. American policy was, in effect, *militarized*. Security concerns, as interpreted and expressed by professional military officers, played an inordinately significant role in determining the course of affairs. This militarization represented a shift in the role of the occupation force from rehabilitating and reconstructing Austria to enlisting the state as a partner in NATO's defense. The result was an approach that complicated and prolonged the occupation, but also resulted in unprecedented diplomatic and economic support that were vital to rebuilding the country—aid that most likely would not have been forthcoming if the United States had scaled back its presence in Europe after the Second World War as originally planned.

Revisionist historians are likely to reject this thesis out of hand. Dark and terrible motives, they will maintain, must have underlain American interests. Austria's fate mattered not a whit in the relentless quest for hegemonic power. There is, however, scant evidence for such an interpretation. Without question, the military championed policies that were self-serving and at times ill considered, but at their heart they were aimed at securing peace, stability, economic growth, and democracy in Europe. While the tactics may have been questionable and the goals arguable, in a century marred by more than a few genocidal dictators, the army's hopes for the future were more than noble.

Postrevisionist historians will be equally upset with this analysis, objecting to the notion that army leaders militarized U.S. policy. The Soviet Union was, after all, an evil empire. The military's concerns for the future were certainly justified. Anyway, politicians, not generals, make policy. But again, the facts tell a more a nuanced story. Evil though it was, the American military knew very little of the internal workings of the Soviet regime—and virtually nothing of its intended policy toward Austria. Habit and preconception largely drove the military's appreciation of the threat. And while generals did not make foreign policy, their views significantly influenced the options and factors considered by political leaders in Washington. This was a remarkable, though largely invisible, feature of the early Cold War. There is no smoking gun that makes the case for the militarization of occupation policy; the story emerges by following the hidden history from the inception of the mission to the last parade. What follows is the story of what happened after the firing stopped at midnight.

CHAPTER I

THE DISEASE AND UNREST FORMULA

A twenty-six-year veteran, Lester Delong Flory thought he might never see the face of battle. When war broke out in 1917, he left a promising bank job in Wilkes-Barre, Pennsylvania, and entered West Point. Anxious to join the ranks of the American Expeditionary Force, he was thrilled when the academy graduated his class early. But Lieutenant Flory never got to the trenches. Peace was declared while he was on graduation leave. Instead he was ordered back to the academy to finish his education. As for combat, the closest Flory came was when the War Department sent his class to tour the European battlefields and the U.S. occupation zone in the Rhineland.

Like many of his contemporaries, Flory progressed slowly and methodically in the postwar army. Assignments in the Coast Artillery, Panama, the Civilian Conservation Corps, Hawaii, and Brazil occupied most his career. Between tours, Flory earned an electrical engineering master's degree from the Massachusetts Institute of Technology and attended the Command and General Staff and War Colleges. After the outbreak of World War II, he served a tour at the War Department in Washington, gaining a reputation as a logistics expert. In January, 1944—while the Soviets counterattacked on the eastern front, the Anglo-American Allies pressed the Germans in Italy, and American, British, and Canadian forces readied for the assault on Normandy—Flory, promoted to the rank of brigadier general, assumed command of the 63d Antiaircraft Brigade on the dusty plains of Fort Bliss, Texas.

Despite his new rank, Flory's prospects for war service seemed as remote as ever. Then, a year later, the chief of the Civil Affairs Division, Maj. Gen. John Hilldring, recalled him to Washington for a new assignment: Flory would go to Europe and plan the occupation of Austria. His portfolio came with a stunning array of responsibilities, including supervising details of the organization, personnel, and equipment for the planning team;

mapping out requirements for disarmament and demobilization; coordinating with all the agencies involved in military government; and coordinating with other Allied forces.

The assignment appeared even more remarkable considering that, other than his War Department expertise in large-scale logistics planning (a useful skill for postwar reconstruction), Flory had virtually no training related to the mission. His only experience in international affairs occurred during a brief period with the U.S. military mission in Rio de Janeiro, Brazil, where he had spent most of his time sidelined with typhoid fever. To make the task appear even more daunting, when army planners briefed Flory, he learned that they expected to find Austrian society on the verge of collapse. The Allies, they warned him, had to be prepared to prevent the "the disastrous consequences of mass starvations, epidemic and even revolution."[1] The planners were working on what they called a "disease and unrest formula," an antidote for the worst possible conditions imaginable. With this introduction, as he entered his twenty-seventh year of military service, Flory finally left for the front, unprepared and untrained for the challenges ahead.

The Rhythm of Habits

Many of Flory's fellow officers shared his uneasiness over the prospects of assuming a new and unfamiliar charge. To prepare for the occupation, they relied on what they knew: the *habits* of military operations. Their warrior traditions, experiences, assumptions, preconceptions, organization, training, doctrine, and routine practices determined how the United States conducted the fight for peace.

The most powerful force of habit shaping the U.S. effort was a tradition of forgetting. The army had a long history of conducting postconflict occupation duties. American troops also had considerable experience performing constabulary duties on the frontier.[2] Unfortunately, this knowledge was never incorporated into doctrine, education, and professional development programs, or reinforced in the military's memory through its honors and traditions.

The army taught men like Flory and Hilldring nothing about their legacy as peacekeepers. The official report on the Rhineland occupation after World War I noted, "Despite the precedents of military governments in Mexico, California, the Southern States, Cuba, Puerto Rico, Panama, China, the Philippines, and elsewhere, the lesson seemingly has not been learned."[3] Army leaders had to rediscover the skills for postwar missions on each occasion.

When the doughboys withdrew from Europe, interest in such operations again lapsed. Even after the outbreak of a second global conflict, the War Department staff fiercely debated whether the army needed official guidance or special training and formal staffs for occupation duties. Not until 1940 did the service produce a field manual on administering occupied areas. The first military government school was not established until 1942. Hilldring's Civil Affairs Division, responsible for planning and supervising postconflict preparations, was not created until 1943—the same year the army expanded its general staffs (division and higher) to add a civil affairs G5 section.

The War Department was not only late in organizing, but also slow to apply any resources to occupation duties until these tasks were at hand. Hilldring summed up the military view when he wrote to Assistant Secretary of State Dean Acheson on November 9, 1943: "The Army is not a welfare organization. It is a military machine whose mission is to defeat the enemy on the field of battle. Its interest and activities in military government and civil affairs administration are incidental to the accomplishment of the military mission."[4] The service's extensive and protracted history as an occupation force carried no weight.

This reluctance to engage in postconflict missions was reinforced by a doctrinal approach to military affairs that treated peace operations like an outcast relative. Despite the occupation of the Rhineland, the 1923 *Field Service Regulations,* rewritten to codify the lessons of World War I, ignored the occupation period. The manual directed that "the ultimate objective of all military operations is the destruction of the enemy's armed forces by battle."[5] The army overwhelming emphasized focusing effort on decisive wartime objectives. Secondary missions, like peacekeeping, detracted from the military's real purpose.

The armed forces' mode of thinking derived from a rich tradition of Western military theory, drawn in some part from Clausewitz, which emphasized the primacy of winning battles and campaigns and destroying the enemy's conventional troops. The iron imperative of decisive victory was thoroughly ingrained in service directives. *Field Manual 100-5,* the army's capstone doctrinal manual for World War II and replacement for the *Field Service Regulations,* did not even address postconflict missions. Doctrine reinforced the army's predilection to refrain from applying resources to any endeavor that did not contribute directly to winning the war as quickly and decisively as possible.

The extreme poverty of the interwar years, followed by the tremendous resource demands required for building up an operational force to fight World War II, reinforced the War Department's aversion to investing time or effort on peripheral tasks. The generals assiduously followed their war-fighting doctrine, even writing the president to complain about diverting shipping to ferry civil affairs personnel. The soundest and quickest way to prepare for postconflict operations, they concluded, "is to end the war quickly."[6]

Flory's Dilemma

When Hilldring briefed Flory on his assignment the head of the Austria planning team learned that although preparations had been on going for many months, few assets had actually been committed to the operation. The history of the almost yearlong effort that preceded Flory's appointment is instructive. America had planned for and delivered over a million combat and support troops on the beaches of Normandy and from there had established supply lines all across Europe. Progress for the occupation was far less impressive. The corps of civil affairs and military government specialists assigned to spearhead postconflict efforts was ridiculously small compared to the magnitude of its mission, which eventually grew to administering 200 million people at a cost of $1 billion a year.

The service's military government schools produced only a hundred graduates a year—far too few to meet the demand for their skills. The Civil Affairs Division also had low priority on claiming quality recruits. Of the first 250 graduates, one senior officer complained, only thirty were suitable, and they were "nothing to brag about."[7] Hilldring tried to supplement this contingent by commissioning civilians already knowledgeable of public administration and sending them to a one-month school conducted by the provost marshal general at Fort Custer, Michigan, followed by a course at selected universities where men studied their target countries. At its height, this new system ground out seven hundred graduates a month, but the training was largely superficial, and, with occupation plans changing rapidly to match the waxing and waning of Allied campaigns, little of what they learned was of practical value since many wound up in locations different from the areas they had been trained to administer.

The military's late start and tentative investments left Hilldring with few easy choices. Pressed by the worldwide demand for civil affairs troops, the difficulties of gearing-up training and organizing in the face of tremendous uncertainty, and the fierce competition for personnel and resources, there was not much left with which to prepare for the occupation of Austria. Something had to give. Because the scope of the operation had not yet been formally decided, Hilldring was reluctant to assign any men to the mission.

The situation was no more promising overseas. Allied Forces Headquarters (AFHQ), the senior coalition command in the Mediterranean theater, was responsible for planning the occupation. However, already taxed by its military government responsibilities in Italy, there were few assets to spare for future operations. The supreme Allied commander in the Mediterranean, Britain's Gen. Sir Henry Maitland Wilson, was anxious to have planning for Austria's occupation consolidated under his command, but resources were held in London at the direction of the Combined Chiefs of Staff, a loosely organized body consisting of the British and American chiefs responsible for overall joint military planning. The chiefs, particularly the British, were reluctant to begin dispersing responsibilities.

But work was not completely at a standstill. In the European theater, the Supreme Headquarters Allied Expeditionary Force (SHAEF) organized a planning team that could either support its operations or later be transferred to Italy. There was always a possibility that SHAEF troops, rather than AFHQ forces, would be the first to reach Austria. Although the command was preoccupied with the invasion of Normandy and the fight across France, SHAEF's civil affairs staff found enough room and personnel for the Austria Planning Team at the main headquarters in Shrivenham outside of London.

The venture was a modest joint U.S.-British effort. On May 11, 1944, it had only seventeen officers, far fewer than needed. However, assigning more people to the Austria team could only be done by siphoning them from the postwar Germany planning group—and planning for Germany's occupation had a higher priority. Planners at SHAEF were reluctant to raid their staff to speed up the planning for Austria's occupation, which, in the end, was probably going to be an AFHQ responsibility. The Austria team's chief planner, Lt. Col. (later colonel) George McCaffery, was frustrated by the lack of formal recognition that kept him from recruiting the necessary staff, while the planning group for Germany jealously guarded its personnel. As the Allies pushed back the enemy on every front and pressure to advance occupation planning increased, relations between the two organizations grew tense and combative.[8]

Throughout the summer of 1944, as Allied troops cracked the Normandy defenses and headed toward Paris, the Austrian Planning Team, renamed the Austrian Planning Unit, grew to thirty officers. An American, Brig. Gen. Cornelius Wickersham, was named the acting deputy director. Still the organization continued to struggle, woefully underresourced for the rapidly increasing volume of work demanded to draft and coordinate plans and training for military government personnel.

More troubles were on the way. As prospects for the mission rose and fell, support for the team followed suit. At one point, the War Department announced that the Austrian Planning Unit would be disbanded. Wicker-

sham, flabbergasted, penned a stern protest. Breaking up the unit would sacrifice the expertise built up over six hard months. If the decision were made
to maintain a large presence in the country, U.S. troops would be totally unprepared. Caution won out and disbandment was deferred. By October, the
unit was not only still functioning, but it also had been given a new and important sounding title: U.S. Group Control Council/Austria. Planners redoubled their efforts, developing an organizational scheme for the postwar
administrative occupation machinery. They completed the plan by December. The group also continued to slowly build its ranks, growing to fifty
American and sixty-three British personnel. Wickersham was less successful
in getting permission to transfer the team to Italy.[9]

Despite the team's best efforts, when Flory reported to Bushy Park near
London he discovered progress was even more disappointing than he had
expected. There was a tremendous amount of coordination and training still
to be done. On January 4, 1945, Flory and his unit—including McCaffery;
Col. George Carey, the executive officer; and Maj. C. R. Agnew, the chief intelligence coordinator—assembled at Saint Paul's School. Shortly thereafter
they moved their operations to a building on Upper Brook Street in down-
town London. Through a bleak London winter, as the German Ardennes
counterattack in Belgium was beaten off and the Allies poised for the invasion of Germany, the pressure to prepare for the occupation increased.
Among Flory's top priorities was coordinating with SHAEF, a task made
more difficult by the fact that most key personnel had moved to the forward
headquarters in Paris. Flory faced the same problem that had harried his
group from the start: lack of people. He informed SHAEF that "the most immediate problem . . . is the selection of key officer personnel."[10] The team
needed more trained staff, and soon. But SHAEF had few to spare, and every day that forces in the European theater advanced, civil affairs responsibilities grew.

Finally, in February, 1945, Flory and his team headed to Caserta, Italy,
to work directly with AFHQ, now commanded by Gen. Sir Harold Alexander, and its American component, the Mediterranean Theater of Operations, U.S. Army, commanded by Lt. Gen. Joseph McNarney. Here, Flory
encountered another Herculean task: He was to draw the nucleus of his
military government force from civil affairs personnel already serving in the
theater. Responsibility for putting this corps together fell on Brig. Gen.
E. F. Hume, the Fifth Army G5, who had assembled about 150 men. The
quality of this corps was mixed. "Aside from their Italian experience," one
officer recalled, "few of the men were any more suited in experience and
training than the average American for the difficult and delicate task of recreating a foreign country."[11] Flory was finally getting staff in appreciable

numbers, though they were not terribly well prepared for the mission ahead.

One lesson these men had picked up from their duties in North Africa, Sicily, and on the Italian mainland was that occupation duties were complicated and frustrating. As one veteran recalled, men were "usually sent to lonely posts where they found themselves in a world they had studied academically but which looked very unfamiliar under the impact of war."[12] Learning to cope with the challenges of administering military government was only one problem. The trial of cooperating with combat forces was another. "We grew to manhood," one veteran rather flamboyantly remembered, as warriors and governors managed some semblance of cooperation.[13] Although they eventually learned how to harmonize their efforts, there was always constant friction, a concern that did not bode well for the future.

Not War, But Like War

Meanwhile, civil affairs personnel organized into teams and began training. Preparations covered a variety of issues, including the history of the country, denazification, imposing law and order, and methods and policies for creating a free and independent Austria. The teams also received a lecture detailing the many possible threats and dangers of disease and unrest that awaited the troops.[14] All the subjects covered by the training at the military government school in Caserta reflected one imperative: terminate the conflict under conditions that would ensure decisive victory.

The army recognized that some measure of occupation duty was unavoidable, but it saw the task as ancillary to combat. The purpose of a campaign is to allow a commander to impose his will upon the enemy. The need for troops after a battle is only to ensure the completeness of the conquest. Hilldring tried to explain this to Acheson. Occupation operations are important when the "lack of condition of social stability in an occupied area would be prejudicial to the success of the military effort."[15] The purpose of postconflict tasks is to create order and stability, thus allowing the troops freedom to completely crush the enemy.

The experience and education of military leaders reinforced doctrinal beliefs in the proper scope and purpose of occupation activities. The First World War was a particularly seminal event. Many senior officers had served during the first global conflict, and their views were instructed by its outcome and the shaky peace that followed. Officers commissioned after the war were taught and mentored by veterans and steeped in the conflict's lessons learned. George C. Marshall, who served on Pershing's staff in the American Expeditionary Force, ordered the writing of the influential book

Infantry in Battle.[16] Comprising twenty-seven vignettes from the war and corresponding lessons on everything from "rules" to "miracles," the text was meant to impart to junior officers an appreciation of the character of modern military operations. *Infantry in Battle* was the kind of book young warriors read to learn about their profession. In its pages they found nothing about the challenges of the fight for peace.

Military leaders had little reason to critique official writings and doctrinal formulas that ignored the importance of noncombat tasks, since their intellectual efforts did not extend to postconflict missions or their impact on foreign affairs. In fact, officers received virtually no education on the affairs of other states. Although West Point's traditional curriculum had been expanded after World War I to include a modicum of coursework on history, international relations, and comparative government, this instruction had little impact on its graduates. Walter Kerwin, a World War II veteran who eventually rose to the position of army vice chief of staff, recalled: "I suppose if I had come out of there [West Point] and had been asked to discuss the geopolitical strategic parts of the world, I would have been flabbergasted. We just didn't get to that sort of thing."[17] Senior service schools provided little more. The Command and General Staff College focused almost solely on teaching military campaigning, and the Army War College, with a curriculum overwhelmingly devoted to mobilization and military strategy, provided only a shallow grounding in international relations.

Some officers gained experience in foreign affairs through postings at embassies or on the War Department staff, but even these men received little or no training. The army, for example, posted Maj. Truman Smith to Berlin, an international "hot spot," in 1935.[18] The only preparation he received was a brisk two weeks of instruction from the Military Intelligence Division. Once overseas, army representatives generated thousands of reports that the General Staff promptly ignored. The War Department, only narrowly concerned with issues of national defense, was primarily interested in data on military organization, equipment, manpower, mobilization plans, and doctrine. The staff had little use for information on international affairs or the conditions in foreign countries. There were exceptions. A few officers not only had long experience in foreign affairs, but also played a significant role in shaping U.S. policy. These men were the exception rather than the rule, and none of them would play a significant role in the planning or conduct of the Austrian occupation. More typical were those training at Caserta. "The group," one observer recalled, "could not be considered particularly international in outlook."[19]

The army's conception of foreign relations was fairly conventional, reflecting popular notions of an American ideology that colored interpretations of wartime experiences and foreign policy.[20] Soldiers believed in a national mission of promoting liberty abroad and, at the same time, were suspicious of revolutionary movements that broke from the American norm. Thus, World War I represented the welcome death-knell of undemocratic and destructive political elites like the old Habsburg emperors. Equally evil was the threat of virulent nationalism such as the ethnic agitation that precipitated the outbreak of the First World War, or the pan-Germanism that had exploded into Nazi aggression. Regional hegemony and unconstrained nationalism were the principal hazards to a stable international order. Peace could only be maintained by cohesive, independent, democratic nation-states sharing common goals and objectives.

If war returned to Europe again, it would be because the victory had not been sufficiently decisive and postwar efforts had failed to eliminate the remnants of the enemy threat. A history of World War II commissioned for army veterans captured this spirit well. The war was the "unfinished" phase of the First World War, the inevitable result of the failure to crush the military power of the exponents of world conquest.[21] This mistake was not to be repeated.

Dangerous nationalist movements and power-hungry politicians had to be identified and vanquished to ensure the success of postconflict operations. This required the minimum investment necessary to ameliorate social conditions so that the military could turn its full effort to ensuring that the enemy's physical and ideological resources were destroyed and replaced by a more pliant order. It was this line of thinking that led to the disease and unrest formula, a postwar prescription for quickly turning a once resolute enemy into a docile, postwar state.

As for determining how to administer the cure, the army's rhythm of habits played a powerful role here as well. While the armed forces routinely neglected their peacekeeping history, when such tasks could not be avoided there was remarkable consistency in how the services conducted such operations. The reason for this pattern of behavior was that the military always gravitated toward what it did best: fighting wars. American forces, as much as possible, made postconflict duties mirror the organization and routine practices of traditional combat activities. World War I was a case in point. In a contemporary juvenile novel, *The Khaki Boys Along the Rhine* (1920), the intrepid doughboys spent their days quelling riots, chasing spies, and foiling secret military plots. This slice of popular culture was not far off the mark, as most of the energy and resources of the occupation force were dedicated to demobilizing and disarming enemy forces and planning to counter civil unrest or armed uprisings.[22]

When World War II broke out, lacking a fully developed formal doctrine, the official report on the Rhineland occupation was used as a guide in planning and training for postconflict operations.[23] During the war, the army gained additional expertise, conducting civil-military operations in North Africa, Italy, and France.[24] These efforts remained true to the military's conventional approach to unconventional operations.

Experience only reinforced the tendency to organize peacekeeping activities like combat. And it was not just Austria. The army's other major postwar peacekeeping operations—Trieste, Germany, Korea, and Japan—exhibited many common characteristics.[25] American and British operations were also similar. This should not be surprising, given that their military forces shared many traditions and operational practices.[26]

Division of Labor

One important characteristic of the military approach was that the army tried as much as possible to divest itself of peacekeeping tasks. Traditionally, the services preferred establishing a "firewall" between civilian and soldier activities to prevent civilian tasks from becoming an overwhelming drain on military resources.[27] But distancing itself from noncombat missions limited the interaction between the army and other agencies. As a result, cooperation on policy making was generally poor.

Although Washington bureaucrats eschewed interagency cooperation, there admittedly were a few attempts to link military strategy with postconflict planning. The State Department made some efforts to coordinate policy, and a civil affairs committee composed of various federal agencies attempted to develop a coherent occupation program for Austria.[28] The Office of Strategic Services (OSS) and the Foreign Economic Administration, a division of the Executive Office of the President, proposed various civil affairs guides. The committee generated a wealth of material, much of it used by the overseas commands as background and source material.[29]

Although the efforts of civilian agencies within the government did not go entirely to waste, the ad hoc nature of activities created a significant shortfall. Military leaders lacked adequate institutional mechanisms to harmonize operations with other agencies. In particular, the army's links to the State Department for formulating policy guidance and vetting plans were tenuous at best. While the department participated in the civil affairs committee, it was not involved in day-to-day administration. The State Department did not establish an assistant secretary for occupied areas until 1946, when Hilldring, the architect of army civil affairs policies, retired and took the job.

As one analysis concluded, "the Army, in lieu of timely policy guidance, has tended to make its own policy."[30] No government agency was satisfied with this arrangement. The scope of postwar European reconstruction would dwarf any operation that the United States had conducted since the Civil War. The military simply could not do everything, nor was it clear that it was appropriate for the army to undertake all the tasks associated with postwar reconstruction. However, in keeping with traditional practices, the generals assumed they would perform the combat missions and relegate the rest to other agencies. The military expected the newly established United Nations Relief and Rehabilitation Administration (UNRRA) to undertake the most problematic civilian tasks, such as handling refugees and emergency economic aid.

Even though responsibilities might be divided, as one senior State Department official involved in postwar preparations pointed out, strategy could not be divorced from policy and the army had to become "more politically conscious."[31] There was a modest exchange of personnel between the two, an attempt to teach soldiers how to be diplomats. Overall, however, the civilian presence and influence on Army planning, even in theater, was limited. The war was almost over before the State Department's John Erhardt, who would serve as the political adviser for Austrian affairs, and David Sulzberger, the UNRRA liaison, joined Flory's staff.

Despite the lack of coordination during almost a year of planning, Erhardt found very little to complain about at the outset. He worked closely with the army and billeted with Flory and Carey in a comfortable villa overlooking Verona. When they briefed McNarney on the status of operations, Erhardt recalled that he was impressed with how much had been accomplished in so short a time. The political adviser could find little with which to disagree.[32]

While Erhardt fostered a close relationship with Flory, on the whole the army showed minimal interest in integrating civilian and military tasks. In July, 1945, the occupation headquarters had only eighteen civilian employees. This limited integration effort was unfortunate. The implementation of military tasks would no doubt set the conditions for moving on to the civilian challenges of reconstruction. Likewise, civilian agencies would require the military's assistance and support. Simply splitting responsibilities in two would turn out to be wholly unrealistic.

The tendency to bifurcate postwar missions also extended to how the Americans planned to integrate their forces with troops from Allied nations. Again, the rhythm of habits played a powerful role. The army only grudgingly shared command of its forces with other countries. During the First World War, the French and British had sought to integrate U.S. troops into their divisions, rather than letting the doughboys fight in separate formations. The United States, however, insisted on obtaining its own distinct area of responsibility. Coalition operations became, in effect, *parallel* operations.[33] While the overall direction of the war might be coordinated and integrated at the highest levels, in the field, each national army had its own zone of responsibility, lines of communication, and means of logistical support.

During World War II, the United States continued the practice of maintaining distinct areas of responsibility during operations. Major campaigns were designed to ensure the cohesion of national forces. Cross-attaching units between national commands was the exception rather than the rule. Dividing forces geographically ensured that countries never had to sacrifice sovereign control over their armies. There were also practical considerations for keeping national forces separated. Different languages, military terminology, customs, equipment, logistics, and doctrines all complicated the efficient conduct of combined military operations. These obstacles could be overcome, but it was far simpler and more politically expedient for each country to supply and command its own forces. On the other hand, the lack of full integration limited the extent of trust, confidence, and cohesion between the Allies. Nevertheless, cooperation rather than full integration had worked, if imperfectly, at least adequately to secure victory in two world wars.

Ensuring the integrity of forces remained the operative principle for planning postwar occupations as well. After World War I, the Rhineland was divided into areas of national responsibility, a practice also followed in World War II. Throughout Europe, Allied occupation commands were not integrated into a single unit, but instead consulted through liaison teams and coordinated only at the highest level—a similar command arrangement to the one that had been used following World War I. National cohesion was the first imperative. The United States even insisted on positioning its forces in Austria adjacent to the area occupied by troops in Germany in order to simplify operations.

While the U.S. approach insisted on autonomy over the command of troops in the field, it also recognized that strategic decisions had to be a product of negotiation and compromise. In order to maintain unity of effort, there had to be agreement on the overall objectives. During both World War I and World War II, the generals were reluctant to plan or undertake major operations without first consulting and coordinating with Allied forces. Army leaders assumed the principles of cooperation, negotiation, and coordination would carry over into postconflict activities as well. They expected at least a modicum of Soviet cooperation in response to their efforts.

In practice, unity of effort proved difficult to achieve. Although the U.S. and British staffs worked closely together, the teams had absolutely no contact whatsoever with their Soviet counterparts. They had anticipated that the occupation would be administered jointly, but had no idea what the Soviets intended. This lack of knowledge was exacerbated by an AFHQ forecast that the Soviets would be in Vienna by March, 1945, and would conquer all of Austria before American and British troops reached the frontier.[34]

Lacking any guidance, one of Flory's first efforts was to produce a planning paper suggesting six options for Soviet participation. His recommended proposal was for an integrated operation that would include all of the occupying powers. The least-desired option was for each nation to control a separate territory. Such an approach would complicate the country's eventual unification under a single central indigenous government. Since most of Austria's industry and population was located around Vienna, it also would be impossible to divide the country's resources equally or viably among the three powers. Regardless of the option selected, he stressed that coordination with the Soviets must begin as soon as possible. This paper was a provocative and remarkable piece of staff work. Its recommendations contrasted significantly with the typical military approach to coalition and occupation operations. The proposal also represented a substantial departure from plans for the occupation of Germany, which envisioned a tripartite division of the country into U.S., British, and Soviet zones.

Allied Forces Headquarters and the British War Office made a strong case for close cooperation, suggesting that the Soviets send a planning detachment to Italy or Belgrade, Yugoslavia.[35] But nothing came of it. Vyacheslav Mikhailovich Molotov, the Soviet foreign minister, showed little interest for delegating postwar planning below the ambassadorial level. The British Foreign Office, already suspicious of the Soviets' postwar intentions, expected little cooperation. "What will happen," reported B. Henry "Hal" Mack, a British Foreign Service officer, "will depend a lot on who gets there first."[36] He added that he thought it well to omit what a "hideous muddle" they expected to face in Vienna and be unduly discouraging toward the intensive planning efforts being conducted by Flory and his men. The diplomats allowed the planners to assume that the traditional methods of coalition operations would suffice for the peace.

Shadow of the Bear

Cooperation required, if not trust and confidence, at least an appreciation for a coalition partner's interests and objectives. Unfortunately, this was something the Americans lacked. They could only guess. They were not alone. Maxim Maximovich Litvinov, Molotov's deputy and chairman of the ministry's special commission on postwar order and preparation of peace treaties, also pondered the future.

Litvinov's adult life had been driven by revolution, war, and great power politics. At twenty-nine he had joined in the aborted revolution of 1905 and then spent years in exile abroad. He married a prominent British radical and became fluent in English. Back in Moscow under the new Soviet regime, Litvinov rose to prominence as the commissar for foreign affairs. He obtained American recognition of the Soviet Union in 1933 and his country's entry into the League of Nations in 1934. After the Munich Pact of 1938, when Great Britain and France capitulated to Hitler's demands in Czechoslovakia, Litvinov's diplomacy, aimed at collective security and isolating and neutralizing Germany, had all but failed. Premier Joseph Stalin replaced him with Molotov in 1939 and signed a nonaggression pact with Hitler. Rehabilitated after the German invasion of the Soviet Union, Litvinov was named ambassador to the United States, where he served until 1943.

After returning to the Soviet Union, Litvinov produced, over a two-year period, a series of recommendations on postwar strategy. He envisioned the division of Europe by the victorious powers with a recognized "sphere of security" for the Soviet Union. Litvinov also argued for a string of neutral states separating the British and Soviet spheres. Under this arrangement, Austria was to be included in a neutral zone that would serve as a buffer and prevent the resurgence of German power. Both Molotov and Stalin studied Litvinov's proposals, though it is still unclear how representative they were of Soviet policy. [37] Yet, with a regime run by a man like Stalin, Litvinov's thinking could not have strayed too far from the orthodox line.

Western diplomats, through private conversations and study of unattributed Soviet writings, had some notion of the Kremlin's views and held out hope for some kind of postwar détente, but there was no consensus on the influence of those ideas or the intent behind Soviet plans for postwar occupation. For the army, more comfortable with the certainty of knowing who was friend and who was foe, this ambiguity was maddeningly frustrating and no help in planning operations for the day after the battle.

The Sturdy Lifeline of a Guiding Idea

Unclear of Soviet intentions, generals relied on another important, perhaps the most significant, habit to shape the occupation: a penchant for formal and standardized operational planning. The Americans were nothing if not methodical planners. *Infantry in Battle* concluded that it was "axiomatic that in war there will always be a plan . . . in every operation there must run from the highest to the lowest unit the sturdy life-line of a guiding idea; from this will be spun the intricate web that binds an army into an invincible unit embodying a single thought and a single goal."[38]

For a combat leader, planning was the essence of decision. Service procedures for carrying out combat missions were codified during World War I. After the war, the so-called staff estimate became the centerpiece of the Command and General Staff School's curriculum. During World War II, use of the estimate was standard practice in every theater. The process was not just used for preparing for battle. Civil affairs training schools taught an identical planning method for military government operations.[39]

The most important aspect of the army process was that it was mission oriented. The first planning task was to articulate the mission in terms of a clearly identifiable and obtainable objective. For the war in Europe, the armed forces' task was to unconditionally defeat Germany and destroy its capacity to make war. If postwar peace operations were to be considered relevant, they had to be thought of as an extension of this objective and planned accordingly. The habits of military practice required army commanders to map out the occupation like any other campaign.

As for the objective of the occupation of Austria, this proved to be a subject of some debate. Following the Anschluss, the country ceased to exist as an independent nation. Although the Allies agreed Germany and Austria had to be separated, it took a long time to settle on a clear vision for the country's future. During the war, both the United States and Britain considered settlements that looked at solutions other than recreating a separate country. One proposal looked at establishing a Danubian federation of several countries under a single political authority.[40] Nevertheless, on November 1, 1943, at the Moscow Conference of American, British, and Soviet foreign ministers, the Allies issued the Moscow Declaration, which proclaimed the country a victim of Hitler's aggression and vowed to reestablish an independent Austrian nation free of Nazi tyranny. This was the mission bequeathed to the U.S. planners.

Austrian Hopes

Flory and his beleaguered team were not alone in desiring to know what the United States intended to achieve and what the Soviets might permit. The Austrians were in turmoil over what would happen after Germany's inevitable defeat. After World War I, the United States had abrogated responsibility for the leftovers of the Habsburg domains to the great European powers. But with the assurances of the Moscow Declaration, the Austrians assumed that when the foreign armies pressed across their borders, gum-chewing GIs would be among their ranks, walking the streets of Vienna.

No one had greater visions for America's place in Austria than Archduke Otto von Habsburg. Born in 1912, he was the eldest son of Karl I, Austria-Hungary's last emperor. His father abandoned the throne in 1919 and died two years later. Otto then became heir to the crowns of both Austria and Hungary. At forty-six, outside of Sigmund Freud, the energetic archduke was arguably Austria's most famous expatriate. Otto acted very much the royal refugee, counting among his friends the U.S. president, who on occasion invited both the archduke and his mother to visit the Roosevelt estate at Hyde Park, New York.

Otto remained a committed monarchist and an active proponent of reestablishing the family at the head of the proposed postwar confederation of Danubian states centered on Austria. He also advocated forming battalions of Austrian expatriates to fight on the side of the Allies, and offered himself as an expert on the country's affairs to help guide the effort. President Franklin Delano Roosevelt dabbled in promoting Otto's proposals, much to the annoyance of the State Department, which was thoroughly skeptical of any possibility for the monarchy's restoration.[41] Otto, however, remained hopeful that he could still parlay commitment to the Moscow Declaration into a return of monarchical rule.

The Fruits of Victory

It would be simple to dismiss Otto as an anachronism, but in the last year of the war few would hazard to predict the future. In April, 1945, Austria's future was still uncertain, even as Nazi armies were slaughtered across Europe. American and British troops were fighting the battle of the Ruhr Pocket, encircling and annihilating German forces on their own soil. Allied forces stormed the last mountain strongholds in Italy, and Soviet troops fought in the back streets of Vienna. Yet, as the Allied armies pressed for decisive victory, Austria's fate was far from clear.

When the U.S. and British governments approved the Moscow Declaration, they were still not fully committed to restoration. The declaration was meant primarily to inspire the Austrian underground to heighten its activities. But here, the army's disciplined planning process for linking objectives and efforts played an important role. Military-style decision making needed a mission on which to anchor planning, in this case the Moscow Declaration, and the threats to future peace that it clearly articulated was all the generals had to go on. The army therefore assumed that this text would serve as the basis for the occupation. The objectives and assumptions of the declaration, despite any ambiguities and indecision in the minds of the policy makers behind the document, became embedded in the military's plans and thus directed the initial concept for the operation. Reestablishing Austria became part of the army's mission to ensure the total destruction of the Nazi regime.

The principles of the Moscow Declaration can be found infused throughout key army directives, particularly the handbooks prepared for the occupation forces. They described how operations to reestablish Austria would contribute to American security by preventing a repetition of the conditions that had led to World War II. Specifically, this meant not duplicating the imperfect peace implemented after World War I. The peace treaty, the handbooks explained, had left Austria a dysfunctional nation that became "a fertile breeding ground for the development of Nazi pan-Germanism."[42] In the handbooks, a brief history explained how Nazi power grew out of the Paris conference's failure to root out threats to long-term peace. The lesson was clear: Unless postwar operations completed the enemy's destruction, "the fruits of military victory will be lost . . . and all the sacrifices will have been in vain."[43]

The handbooks went on to articulate a series of objectives for creating a new Austria and meliorating the social and political conditions that might foster a resurgence of Nazi ideology. Preparatory training at the military government and civil affairs schools mirrored the occupation handbooks. The goal was to destroy all armed opposition, as well as the economic and political remnants of fascism, leaving behind a docile, but independent state.

Secondary Concerns, Primary Habits

The cumulative affect of the army's rhythm of habits was to ensure that the force looked at its postwar duties from a combat soldier's viewpoint. Planners articulated objectives in military terms and placed the destruction of the enemy at the forefront of operational planning. This limited perspective made all other issues related to the postconflict mission a secondary concern, and important only insofar as they concerned the means of achieving a decisive victory. The focus remained on prevailing in war, not reconstruction and rehabilitation—winning the peace.

Habits also ensured that the army would be generally unprepared for the enormous tasks of postwar operations, applying too few resources too late. Without question, the military faced an intractable problem in equitably sorting out priorities. Inevitably, requirements for peace operations would not be placed at the forefront, and with some justification. It would have done little good to invest heavily in preparing for the day after the battle, if in the process the war was lost.

Still, even with the few resources available, the army's effort could have been greatly improved. The tradition of forgetting, lack of experience, inadequate skills in interagency operations, unimaginative doctrine, poor training, and shallow professional education thoroughly exacerbated the army's limitations in men and equipment. A better-prepared corps of leaders, staff officers, and trainers could have gone a long way toward offsetting these shortfalls, but the service waited too long before seriously turning its attention to the fight for peace.

CHAPTER 2

A FAR COUNTRY

Only days before the surrender, Allied Forces Headquarters was still asking if the Soviets were going to participate in the joint government of Austria. In two years of planning, such elemental but unanswerable questions were a matter of course. Among the many obstacles in preparing for the occupation, anticipating the conditions the troops would face at the conclusion of the war proved to be the most monumental challenge. No one appreciated this more than SHAEF's acting assistant chief of staff (G5), Brig. Gen. Frank J. McSherry. From a small, cluttered office in England, McSherry had the unenviable task of planning civil affairs support for the devastated communities of war-torn France, while at the same time trying to envision military government requirements for Germany and Austria.

Commissioned in the Coast Artillery on August 15, 1917, his preparation for this kind of war was almost nonexistent. He had undergraduate degrees in mineralogy and metallurgy. Before World War II, his only foreign service consisted of participation in the American Expeditionary Force as a lieutenant. After serving on the General Staff in 1942, he deployed overseas to command the U.S. military government contingent in Algeria. From there, McSherry joined Eisenhower's staff in London.

One of McSherry's most perplexing concerns was planning for the Austrian occupation. He was more than happy to pass off the bulk of responsibility for the mission to Flory and AFHQ, though SHAEF could never fully disengage from the Austrian problem. Throughout the year of the ground war, from the fateful June landings in Normandy to the final offensive in the spring of 1945, McSherry always faced the possibility that the course of events could dictate that SHAEF, rather than the command in Italy, would direct the first troops in Austria. From everything he had learned thus far, McSherry knew that occupation was as precarious an activity to predict as the outcome of a battle. It was impossible to anticipate everything. Confusion, debate, controversy, and change were the hallmarks of civil affairs operations. Austria proved true to form.

An Unnatural Task

Uncertainty was the greatest enemy. With few resources to spare, for the most part the forces that fought the war would be the same ones that would conduct the occupation. Knowing what conditions would be like inside the country; the duties to be preformed; how, when, and where the troops would move in; and the extent of their responsibilities was essential for determining how to efficiently balance wartime missions and postconflict requirements.

Of the many unknowns the army faced, the first major issue to be dealt with was the scope of its postwar role. Roosevelt wanted occupations to be civilian-led efforts, but only the military had the resources to conduct these missions, and there seemed to be no practical way to place forces in a combat theater under civilian direction without threatening unity of command. A protracted debate over which department should spearhead occupation duties was not resolved until a year and a half after the attack on Pearl Harbor, when the president acknowledged that there was no serious alternative to military run operations.

The decision to assign the armed forces as the lead agent did not begin to answer all the questions. It would be another year and a half before the government finalized the extent of the mission in Austria. During the November, 1943, meeting at which Allied foreign ministers issued the Moscow Declaration, they confirmed a decision made by Roosevelt, Winston Churchill, and Stalin to create a European Advisory Commission (EAC) to coordinate all postconflict policies. Over the next two months, while the commission was organized in London, the British chiefs pushed to finalize an overall scheme for Austria that included a prominent role for U.S. forces, reflecting Churchill's desire to seize as much of the country as possible before the Soviets arrived. The American generals agreed.

Roosevelt was reluctant to follow through, however. His strategy had been to exert maximum effort to defeat Germany while fighting a holding action against the Japanese in the Pacific. Once the war in Europe was won, the United States planned to shift its focus to the invasion of Japan. While Roosevelt always assumed the nation would play a role in the German occupation, the president did not want forces to participate in the occupation of Austria. He believed that the region held no significant national interest for the United States, and was more than ready to abdicate all responsibility to Britain. He also conceded that the Soviets would probably play a prominent role in postwar Austrian affairs.[1]

Domestic pressures also argued against U.S. participation in the occupation. As soon as the war was over, the government wanted to demobilize troops and return to peacetime conditions. That was certainly what Americans wanted. One survey on attitudes toward postwar policy found that 66 percent favored keeping out of foreign affairs. Fifty-eight percent of respondents thought setting up small, independent countries like Austria was a bad idea. Only 33 percent wanted to maintain a large force to "keep the peace."[2] Roosevelt shared their predilection for a modest postwar effort. Estimates for a presence in Europe ranged from as little as six months to at most two years. In February, 1944, four months after the Moscow Declaration, Roosevelt ruled that the occupation of southern Europe was not a "natural task for the United States. . . . Our principal object is not to take part in the internal problems of Southern Europe, but is rather in eliminating Germany as a possible or even probable cause of a third world war."[3] Austria was not a priority.

The president formally rejected the combined chiefs' plan calling for an American contingent, and directed the U.S. chiefs to push for an occupation zone including only Germany and northern Europe. Roosevelt's turnabout caused major problems for Ambassador John Winant, who served as the point man for coordinating the particulars of postwar policies. Replacing Joseph Kennedy at the Court of Saint James, he became an early advocate for establishing the EAC, and became deeply involved when the commission formally began operations.

The U.S. representative at the EAC certainly did not lack for advice on what should be done. His staff found that in Britain there were already "more than forty committees, organizations, political parties, and groups of individuals who have issued reports on some phases of post-war reconstruction . . . in addition to official committees."[4] Winant also received private letters from Britain and the United States with comments like "we should electrocute every German and Japanese officer above the rank of lieutenant," and "German territory should be divided among the adjoining nations or turned over to Russia."[5] Winant had no shortage of advisers.

Unfortunately, the president was not among those sharing his thoughts. Winant's tenure on the EAC was difficult. The administration failed to keep him properly informed on developments, and senior officials rarely sought his counsel. This made resolving the EAC's most contentious issues especially thorny. How to deal with Austria proved a particularly annoying question. Winant had little interest in or knowledge of the relevant issues. His primary concern was finalizing policies for postwar Germany. The ambassador thought the Austrian dilemma needlessly complicated his work. Although he was ambivalent, both Britain and the Soviet Union actively sought U.S. participation in the occupation, hoping to use its presence to limit the other's influence.

Winant held that if accepting British and Soviet demands for an American role would ease negotiations over Germany, it would be a small price.[6]

The president also began to take measure of the problem. Roosevelt envisioned a postwar system of "open spheres," with each of the great powers maintaining order in areas that were strategically important to their security. The president's notion of postwar zones differed in a significant respect from the proposals offered to Stalin by Litvinov and Molotov. In Roosevelt's conception, commerce, people, and ideas would flow freely across the divisions of responsibility. Such a vision required a strong degree of continued cooperation between the Allied powers. Ending the war with a standoff on the Danube was the last thing Roosevelt wanted.

In May, 1944, Winant flew to Washington to consult with the president. He returned with astonishing news. The ambassador announced to the EAC on May 31 that Roosevelt had given permission for American participation in the occupation of Austria. Winant promptly cabled the State Department. This message perplexed the military chiefs, who had already reversed themselves once and formally declared, in line with the president's previously stated wishes, that U.S. troops would not occupy the country. Confusion reigned. Roosevelt had not shared the guidance with anyone other than Winant. Many remained skeptical.

A month later, General Hilldring, was still trying to figure it all out. Anxious to clarify the president's desires, he drafted a position paper for the chiefs matching the ambassador's version of Roosevelt's guidance. Meanwhile, the combined chiefs told anxious field commanders that the composition of the military government was still a "matter of study for the EAC."[7] As late as November, 1944, the British understanding was that the United States would provide only a token garrison for Vienna. Finally, in December, the president formally accepted responsibility for an occupation zone, having delayed a firm American commitment for more than a year.

Even after the Unites States accepted a role, major questions remained. Roosevelt, Churchill, and Stalin met at Yalta in early February, 1945. Success in the field had placed renewed pressure on the Allied leaders to reach an agreement on postwar plans. Yalta, in turn, stimulated progress in the EAC, and the commission finally began to substantively address the task of occupying Austria. These developments proved a mixed blessing. When planners reviewed the proposals being floated by the Soviets, they saw significant problems. For one, the proposed American zone in Vienna did not possess adequate administrative and transport facilities, and it lacked an airfield. In addition, the Soviet plans contained no provisions for the automatic right of transit through the zones of other occupying forces. These arrangements troubled Flory. Without reliable lines of communications, supplying forces under the difficult and chaotic conditions they expected to encounter in Austria would be tough.[8] This concern was well founded. Debates over zones, transportation facilities, and transit rights would become the most contentious issues of the early occupation.

Red Star Rising

The EAC's work offered cold comfort to both Flory and McSherry, and as time wore on, it became apparent that most coordination would have to be worked out on the ground. Unfortunately, the man with whom the Allies would have to make their arrangements was otherwise preoccupied: Marshal Fyodor Ivanovich Tolbukhin, the future commander of Soviet occupation forces, was spearheading the invasion of Austria.

Born to a peasant family in 1894, Tolbukhin had trained to be a bookkeeper. Drafted in 1914, he rose to command a battalion in the czarist army. He joined the communist forces after the revolution, fought in the civil war, and in 1931 joined the Communist Party. In 1934 he graduated from the Frunze Military Academy. During the war he commanded an army at the battle of Stalingrad, directed more than forty-five divisions in the counteroffensive in the Crimea, and led the Soviet invasion through southern Europe. He was considered a skilled and determined commander. While Flory and McSherry fretted over plans for occupying Austria, Tolbukhin's troops pressed ahead, relentlessly slaughtering anyone in their path as they pressed toward the Danube—and Vienna.

Tolbukhin's instructions from Stalin were a mystery to the Anglo-American Allies. The behavior of his troops when they reached the Austrian frontier and the general's first actions as occupation commander served only to deepen their incomprehension. To further complicate planning, the U.S. staff learned that the Allies planned to accede to the newly established French government's request for an occupation zone. Making matters worse, the French had yet to organize a planning team. The staff thus had to prepare for a four-power occupation without knowing the plans of half of the occupying force. Moreover, while the American generals knew little of the Soviets' intentions, Stalin knew a good deal about American and British postwar planning efforts through remarkably effective agents such as Harold Glasser of the U.S. Treasury Department.[9]

A Foreign Land

The scope of Allied occupation duties was not the only unknown factor hampering preparations. Planners also had to guess at conditions inside the country and how their forces might be received. Areas of particular concern were the potential for active resistance to Hitler's regime and, on the other hand, possible support for a nazi guerilla movement, particularly for an Alamo-like defense in the Austrian Alps, the so-called National Redoubt (Alpenfestung).

Ever since the Anschluss, most British and American understanding of conditions in the country had come from expatriates.[10] Sources ranged from dreamy monarchists like Otto to ethnic separatist, socialist, and communist groups, each with its own particular agenda. This information was fragmentary and not always accurate. One British analyst complained: "there are indications that things are beginning to move inside Austria—but vast clandestine (Socialist) organizations exist only in the wishful thinking of Revolutionary Socialist émigrés. . . . I deprecate the use of official memoranda for circulating through the medium of A/DX the bogus claims made by a section only of the Austrian political émigrés in this country, and I wish most emphatically to disassociate myself and my section from such pronouncements."[11] Exiles could hardly satisfy the information requirements of planners who needed detailed, unbiased, current intelligence.

The resources available to reduce uncertainties were woefully inadequate. The Allies' most highly prized intelligence came from signal intercepts. At Bletchley Park outside London, in the gracefully aging mansion that concealed the Government Code and Cipher School, cryptologists decoded thousands of top-secret German radio messages. In the meantime, U.S. intelligence broke the Imperial Japanese Foreign Ministry's cipher, making the Japanese ambassador to Berlin the best spy the Allies had in occupied Europe. Through these sources, code-named Ultra and Magic, senior commanders had ready access to summaries from decoded enemy military cables. With regard to Austria, however, signal intelligence was maddeningly inconclusive. In February, 1945, for example, SHAEF's estimate concluded that although information on the Alpine Defense Zone had increased steadily in bulk, it "still furnishes no specific details."[12]

The National Redoubt was not the only target on which the generals lacked conclusive intelligence. Allied Forces Headquarters intelligence summaries were mostly based on aerial photos. The reports also contained bits and pieces garnered from a handful of covert sources, radio intercepts, and newspapers. The summaries had their uses, providing the location and composition of industrial areas, police and government facilities, fortifications, and some political intelligence.[13] But photographs and rumors could not answer the critical question: What would people do when GIs marched down the streets of Salzburg?

The British attempted to fill out this picture with covert operations.

After the fall of France, they set up the Special Operations Executive (SOE) under the minister of economic warfare to conduct clandestine missions and gather strategic intelligence. The British contemplated conducting full-scale operations in Austria as early as June, 1941. During the early years of the war, however, the SOE's primary focus was making contact with Chetnik and partisan forces in Yugoslavia. Active operations in Austria did not begin until 1943. Supported by a handful of operatives, SOE conducted a series of covert missions code-named "Clowder." The hallmark of these operations was extreme risk and constant peril. One agent disappeared and another was lost and presumed killed during these operations. When another team parachuted into the midst of a German patrol, one agent was shot and two were captured.[14]

Despite all the hardships, dangers, and privations endured by SOE operatives, they did produce some useful results. The SOE correctly concluded, "It is most unlikely that any widespread resistance movement will develop in Austria before Germany herself suffers total defeat."[15] The agency turned its main effort to "Trigger," an operation promoting anti-Nazi resistance among the Slovene minority in Austrian Carinthia. In 1945, it shifted the focus of operations to supporting the occupation. The SOE's activities were largely confined to areas the British planned to control and did not penetrate deep into the country. They also failed to turn up much information on the National Redoubt.

The Office of Strategic Services, the SOE's American counterpart, conducted operations in Austria as well.[16] This organization, created during the war to provide strategic intelligence and organize covert missions under the direction of the War Department, also obtained some useful intelligence, concluding that prospects for an uprising in Austria were bleak. Sources for this analysis included deserters, prisoners of war, and, more importantly, a few remarkably effective Austrian agents such as Fritz Molden.

While growing up between the two world wars, Molden witnessed the endless, rough and tumble political battles among the First Republic's left- and right-wing parties; the eventual domination by the fascists under Engelbert Dollfuss and then Kurt von Schuschnigg; and, finally, the Anschluss. Molden's anti-Hitler sympathies earned him a stint in prison and service on the Russian front. Wounded, he was posted to Italy to recover, and soon became involved with a local resistance cell. Then he deserted. The fledgling freedom fighter joined a coalition of small groups representing a broad cross-section of the mainstream socialist and conservative factions linked together in a loose resistance framework.

In the summer of 1944, Molden made his way to Switzerland. His task was to make contact with the Western powers. In Bern he was introduced to a forty-nine-year-old former New York lawyer named Allen Dulles, the local OSS agent. The fresh-faced Austrian became his trusted link to the underground, ferrying out bits of information and carrying news to resistance leaders on the plans for the occupation.

Perhaps more important than the intelligence he provided, Molden came to represent the kind of leaders the U.S. commanders would come to rely on during the occupation. Expatriate activists like Otto carried little weight with the military. Those who resisted or were persecuted by the Nazis had more credibility. They also seemed to share the Yankee passion for the disease and unrest formula, demonstrating a willingness to share power and influence with disparate political groups for the sake of national stability, in marked contrast to the internecine politics of the First Republic.

Even after establishing solid contacts with the underground tremendous gaps in the military's knowledge of Austrian affairs remained. OSS also conducted at least eleven covert missions. The undertakings were remarkably dangerous and frequently fatal ventures, the best known of which was Operation Greenup, an incredible tale of hardship, peril, and daring.[17] That the OSS was willing to mount such desperate ventures reflected its great frustration over the lack of accurate information. The worth of these heroic efforts is highly debatable. For example, shortly before the end of the war, an OSS intelligence estimate provided to the president anticipated that the Allies might face a guerrilla army of as many as forty thousand men—a prediction that proved to be absurdly inaccurate.[18]

Uncertainty is Certain

The extent of uncertainty, from the veracity of opposition to the scope of responsibilities for the occupation, while frustrating, did not completely paralyze the army. Not all the military's rhythm of habits worked against it. The service's penchant for planning had its constructive side. Officer education and training taught leaders to expect a high degree of ambiguity in any operation. *Infantry in Battle* cautioned that "obscurity and confusion are normal. Late, exaggerated, or misleading information, surprise situations, and counterorders are to be expected. . . . uncertainty is certain."[19] The primary tool for dealing with unknowns was constant and continuous preparation.

Commanders could not afford to simply stand still while Roosevelt mulled over Austria's future. A month before Winant announced the change in U.S. policy, General McSherry had already begun to prepare for the operation, helping set up what would eventually become General Flory's planning team.[20] The initiative came about because the combined chiefs anticipated that Germany might collapse long before the EAC was organized and agreed on postwar policies. They had directed preparation of Operation Rankin for the immediate occupation of Germany and Austria in the event of a sudden surrender. The first Rankin directive had been issued in 1943, but failure to reach an agreed upon inter-Allied position delayed serious planning. After the Normandy invasion, interest in Rankin received renewed attention.

Since SHAEF had primary responsibility for Rankin, and frustrated by the lack of progress on planning thus far, on July 4, 1944, McSherry made a strong case for speeding up preparations. For a period, the chiefs transferred planning authority from AFHQ to SHAEF anticipating that Germany's collapse might be imminent and that Allied troops could race across France and Germany into Austria. Although Rankin conditions never materialized, the contingency planning helped energize staff effort, generating a host of plans that could later be modified and adapted.[21]

Planners were still hamstrung by the fact that throughout the summer and autumn campaigns there was no final decision on the scope of operations. Eisenhower wrote to Marshall in July, pleading that instructions be published without delay, but the basic directive for the occupation was not released until almost a year later. Eisenhower did receive some preliminary direction, but the order was equivocal, suggesting only a symbolic role for the United States, although acknowledging that the Allies had not yet formally agreed on an arrangement. This ambiguity was too much to bear. Over the next month, the field headquarters and the combined chiefs engaged in a frenzied exchange of messages debating and clarifying guidance.[22]

By September, when it was apparent that Germany was not on the verge of collapse, the chiefs shifted responsibility back to AFHQ, at the same time insisting that the planning team remain in London until official policy was hammered out. Nevertheless, once the preliminary guidance was given and responsibility assigned, efforts began in earnest. Allied Forces Headquarters soon drafted a proposal for the employment of U.S. and British forces. In October, a new plan, Freeborn, replaced Rankin. Lieutenant General Mark W. Clark's 15th Army Group was designated to command the U.S. occupation troops, with Clark also serving as the high commissioner for the American zone and representative to the Allied council that would manage the country.[23]

Operation Freeborn envisioned employing two forces. Tactical units would defeat, disarm, and demobilize enemy troops, as well as provide security and intelligence for the occupation. Meanwhile, civil affairs personnel would lay down a military government carpet, administering local communities and implementing occupation policies such as denazification and separating the German and Austrian institutions and economies. Military government units were organized under the deputy chief of staff for civil affairs (G5), initially under Flory's operational control. There was a military staff for each *gau* (province). Under each *gau* there were subordinate staffs for *kreis* (local) or *bezirke* (county). In general, the organization of the military government paralleled a traditional military chain of command. The *kreis* would report to the *gau* and the *gau* to the G5, just as divisions reported to a corps headquarters and the corps to a field army. Both the military government troops and the tactical forces would be under Clark.

Freeborn was never fully implemented.[24] Progress in the European and Mediterranean theaters proved far slower than expected, while Tolbukhin pushed relentlessly toward the Nazi empire's heart, racing through Hungary and crossing the Austrian border. On April 13, 1945, the Soviets captured Vienna, but few Americans celebrated. The nation was stunned by the news that President Roosevelt had died the day before. Vice President Harry S. Truman, largely ignorant of Roosevelt's grand scheme for postwar Europe, assumed the mantle of leadership as Soviet troops took control of the rubble-strewn streets of Austria's once and future capital. Meanwhile, it appeared that U.S. forces in the European theater would reach the frontier before troops from Italy. To account for the changing conditions, SHAEF was ordered to occupy Austria. McSherry would have some extra work after all.

Crossing the Line

Even the most dedicated staff work could not eliminate the great unknowns. To fill in the gaps, particularly the concerns about postconflict threats, commanders fell back on the habits and practices that had sustained them in war. On May 1, 1945, as the military newspaper *Stars and Stripes* made Hitler's death public, SHAEF troops from the 12th and 6th Army Groups and soldiers from the First French Army reached the frontier. Yanks from parts of twelve divisions under four different corps poured into Austrian territory. Contrary to the well-laid plans, units were, as Clark wrote, "dispersed by the fortunes of war, without regard to political boundaries or the areas designated for occupation by the respective Allied commands."[25] Men charged ahead with only one thought: decisive victory.

Among the forces spearheading the drive across the Austrian countryside was Maj. Gen. Stanley Reinhart's 65th Infantry Division. For Reinhart's infantrymen, veterans of the invasion of Germany, the final week of the war dawned with less than forty-five miles separating U.S. and Soviet troops. The division's last mission was to drive southeast through a narrow zone between Regensburg, Germany, and Linz, Austria, from the Isar River to the Enns River, and make contact with approaching Soviet forces.

Soldiers from the 103d Infantry Division outside Schnaritz, Austria, May 1, 1945.
Courtesy National Archives.

Bitter street fighting slowed the advance. On May 2, in Passau, Germany, soldiers fought a pitched battle with three hundred SS troops in the cratered streets of the once picturesque town. On May 5, following the banks of the Danube River across the former border with Austria, the division reached Linz where their progress was slowed by masses of surrendering Germans. In one week 61,602 prisoners of war turned themselves over to the division. Truman proclaimed VE-Day on May 8. The linkup operation quickly devolved into a spontaneous carnival. One veteran remembered that it appeared as though every Russian soldier sported a gallon of vodka and every GI produced a carton of cigarettes. Soldiers embraced, cheered, cried. Reinhart met his counterpart outside the village of Erlauf, Austria, and the two smiling commanders posed for the cameras. It was over.

Continuous combat operations until almost the last moment and a jubilant rendezvous with the Soviets were not the only impressions imprinted on U.S. soldiers' minds. Southern Germany and northern Austria were dotted with concentration camps—putrid, filled with the ragged, disease-ridden starving, dying, and dead—a stern reminder of the occupation's military purpose: the destruction of Nazi evil. The men's combat experiences

The last battle, May 1, 1945. Courtesy National Archives.

and the horror of the camps served as reinforcement for higher headquarters' directives emphasizing physical security and denazification as the first priorities.

The War for Order

There were, in fact, very real security challenges in the opening days of the occupation, but not from Nazis. Instead, the first great danger to peace came from Yugoslav incursions into Carinthia. The Allies had expected some irredentist claims. The areas bordering Italy, Yugoslavia, Hungary, and Austria had long been in dispute, with ethnic groups from all sides scattered across the region without regard to formal borders. Relations between Austria and Yugoslavia had the potential to be particularly tense. In addition to territorial disputes and partisan activity, the largest group of displaced persons in Austria was from Yugoslavia.

The British, who were destined to occupy the area bordering the two countries, prepared a paper for the Yalta Conference suggesting that the Yugoslavs might press their claim for Carinthia. There was a significant Slovene minority in the territory whom the Yugoslavs considered part of greater Yugoslavia. The British paper warned that force might be required to settle the issue. The paper advocated a strong statement reaffirming support for Austria's pre-Anschluss borders. On February 1, 1945 the British delegation shared its analysis with U.S. representatives, but the issue never came up. Instead, the British elected to quietly submit a note to Molotov.[26]

An additional warning came from Lt. Col. Franklin Lindsey, an OSS agent stationed in Yugoslavia. Lindsey's assessment proved remarkably accurate. While a pro-Soviet Communist Party controlled the state, its leader, Marshal Josip Broz Tito, put his country's interests first—and he was seriously interested in territorial expansion. Special Operations Executive teams issued similar predictions, and AFHQ's intelligence staff reported that "Tito's partisans will probably make a strong bid" for Carinthia.[27]

General Alexander knew Yugoslav incursions would be a threat. First, a move into Trieste would block his line of communications, making it difficult to move troops and supplies quickly and securely from Italy into Austria. Second, the Austrian area claimed by Tito overlapped with territory assigned for Allied occupation.

The supreme Allied commander in the Mediterranean sought to forestall confrontation. In July, 1944, Alexander invited Tito to visit his headquarters outside Rome. Talks continued in Belgrade in March, 1945, and Tito agreed that Trieste and the area between Italy and Austria should be controlled by the Allies. Nevertheless, Tito announced on May 1 that he planned to continue his advance. When Alexander protested that the maneuvers were a clear violation of the Belgrade agreements, the Yugoslav leader replied a few days later that the situation had changed and repudiated the March accords. Tito now had to think about these territories as both prime minister and supreme military commander. From a political viewpoint, he was justified in moving into these areas since they were legitimate parts of Yugoslavia.

Alexander resigned himself that, at least "for the present we must accept the fact that the two armies will both be in the same area and that our road movement is bound to be interfered with by their columns."[28] The Allies hoped negotiations might settle the issue, while at the same time fearing that an inadvertent clash might precipitate a crisis. On May 8, Maj. Gen. C. F. Keightley's British V Corps, part of Lt. Gen. Sir Richard McCreery's British Eighth Army, entered Austria and barely beat advancing Yugoslav forces into Klagenfurt. The next day, V Corps moving into Styria found German and Croatian troops being shot and shelled by Yugoslavs while the hapless enemy was trying to surrender to the British.

On May 12, Alexander informed Tito that he had been ordered to occupy Carinthia and Styria. At the same time, he tried to appear sympathetic to Yugoslav claims. The British would administer the area impartially, Alexander promised, "with no prejudice to your claims for territory."[29] Meanwhile, field commanders were told to stand by. McCreery warned Keightley to put no military pressure on Tito. "You should take steps and make arrangements so that hostilities involving your forces and those of Jugoslavs can only occur through result of attack on your forces by the Jugoslavs."[30]

Tito ordered the U.S. and British missions and OSS contingent out of Belgrade on May 14, and Alexander warned Eisenhower that "at any moment hostilities may break out."[31] By May 20 there were 160,000 Yugoslav troops in southern Carinthia, with no end to the military buildup in sight. Four days later, McCreery called the situation "unmanageable." He not only had to contend with the presence of Yugoslav forces, but also with a mass of surrendered enemy, displaced persons, and refugees totaling more than four hundred thousand.

Reports from the theater triggered a flurry of transatlantic cables. General Marshall proposed a show of force. His suggestion coincided with Alexander's request for U.S. battle units from the European theater, not only to expel the Yugoslavs, but also to help out with a wave of more than five hundred thousand displaced persons and enemy forces fleeing from both the Yugoslavs and Tolbukhin's troops. When the Russians reached Austria, Tolbukhin issued a proclamation declaring that Soviet forces had arrived as liberators and that "the peaceable population" had nothing to fear. Nevertheless, disturbing reports of rape, looting, and mayhem made the prospects for resolving occupation issues even more worrisome.

In response to Alexander's request for assistance and at Washington's direction, SHAEF drafted Operation Coldstream, a plan calling for an overt threat of attack on Tito. While the Allied leaders worked out the details of the military response, political leaders finally moved on the diplomatic front. Truman proposed a joint U.S.-British statement. Land-grabbing tactics, the president warned, might be appropriate for the Nazis, but they had no place in the postwar world. At the same time, to further intimidate Tito, the United States made known that Gen. George S. Patton Jr., who had earned a reputation for being America's most aggressive combat commander, would be leading the troops into Austria.

The U.S. committed substantial forces to Coldstream. The troops under Patton's command would include two corps with a total of five divisions—four infantry and one armored. It is clear from the message traffic racing back and forth during these critical weeks that some military leaders assumed Coldstream was more than just a show of force. Clark informed Mc-

Creery that he envisioned limited "offensive action" to eject Yugoslav forces.[32]

Commanders not only threatened action, they actually began to implement Coldstream. Patton was in London preparing for a brief leave when he was suddenly recalled to SHAEF headquarters in Reims, France, because Tito had been "raising hell." He reviewed Coldstream with Bradley and Eisenhower that same evening, then flew to Regensburg the next day to meet with the staffs of the Third and Seventh Armies and 12th Army Group. "The idea," Patton told them, "is to make a strong bluff along the Enns River and if offensive action becomes necessary to cross it."[33]

By May 21, Coldstream was under way. Patton planned to move into an area from Tamsweg to Spittal, freeing the British V Corps to take up positions in strength along the border. American commanders had already begun coordination and launched reconnaissance elements. Two reinforced cavalry groups from the U.S. Third Army made contact with the British V Corps. The U.S. Ninth Air Force provided air support.

When political negotiations resumed, Coldstream was put in abeyance. Nevertheless, conditions in the area remained incredibly tense—as illustrated by the advance from Italy of Maj. Gen. Geoffrey Keyes's U.S. II Corps. American forces had extended their occupation to the town of Tarnovo, and as soon as the U.S. 91st Infantry Division moved into the area it received a stiff protest from the commander of the Yugoslav 13th Division. The assertive Keyes, moving quickly to intervene, demanded a parlay. When the Yugoslav commander refused to meet with him, Keyes responded with a terse letter warning that U.S. forces would not withdraw. He had been ordered to hold his ground and be prepared to reinforce with a regimental combat team and subsequent regiments every twenty-four hours. After two anxious days, the Yugoslavs relented.

Backed by the threat of force, Alexander took a stern line and refused to renegotiate. On June 7, Lt. Gen. W. D. "Monkey" Morgan, Alexander's chief of staff reported, "all our information from Belgrade is very optimistic and it looks as if Tito will swallow the whole agreement."[34] The Yugoslavs signed the accord in Belgrade on June 9, and Trieste the next day.

Many military leaders believed the Soviets had instigated Tito's aggression and that the Yugoslavs backed down in the face of Operation Coldstream.[35] There is, however, evidence to suggest that Tito withdrew under pressure from Stalin, who had no desire for a confrontation over Austria.[36] For the Yanks, the standoff arguably represented their first postwar experience in the use of force as a political weapon, and although the evidence was ambiguous, they drew the firm conclusion that military power was a necessary and adequate deterrent to aggressive powers. The politics and diplo-

A column of U.S. troops moving through Innsbruck, May 23, 1945. Courtesy National Archives.

macy involved in resolving the dispute were largely forgotten. This incident also did much to reinforce the tendency to view postconflict operations in traditional operational terms, relying on the threat of force as a hedge against the unknowns of occupation.

Mission to Vienna

The standoff with Yugoslav troops and the movement of SHAEF's forces into Yugoslavia further postponed AFHQ's plans. Despite the delay, General Flory and his team were far from idle. Flory had received a memorandum from McNarney directing him to proceed to Vienna and begin negotiations with the British, French, and Soviet representatives on the joint occupation of the capital.[37] He did not, however, have Tolbukhin's approval to enter the city, and with no clue as to the Russian general's future plans, Flory could do little more than assemble his team of experts and wait.

The great-power debates over the Allies' entry into Vienna have been well documented based on a blitz of diplomatic cables, many of which have been reprinted in the Department of State's *Foreign Relations of the United*

States. However, the most intimate and revealing account of Flory's historic mission is a chapter from his own unpublished account written in the 1960s. When he penned his memoirs, the State Department volume had been recently published and the general could see for the first time how great-power politics shaped the initial conduct of the occupation.

In preparing for the mission to Vienna, one of Alexander's most significant decisions was to exclude the participation of diplomatic officials. Initially, Erhardt, Mack, and their French counterpart, Phillippe Baudet, all planned to accompany the teams. Alexander, however, thought it would be better to leave them behind. Without foreign policy representatives, the mission could avoid being drawn into sensitive political issues and might appear less threatening. By including only uniformed members, the delegations would maintain a more strictly military character—that of a reconnaissance by cooperating Allied forces. Flory, Brig. Gen. Paul Cherrière of France, and Britain's Brig. Gen. Thomas John "Jack" Winterton would lead the team.

The U.S. mission consisted of seventy-eight officers and men. While exclusively composed of military personnel, it was not completely devoid of foreign policy expertise. Two American officers, Edgar Allen and Charles Thayer, had both served in the State Department before the war. They were added to the mission at the request of Erhardt who, though barred from the team, wanted to ensure continued close cooperation between the army and the foreign service.[38]

Thayer had served in the embassy in Moscow and spoke Russian fluently. He had also worked for the OSS, but he was officially listed as Flory's interpreter. The initial roster also included a representative from the OSS's R&A Branch, but he was later dropped from the roster. Flory also forbade Thayer from engaging in any covert operations.

While the team prepared for its mission, U.S. and British officials entered a running debate on the wisdom of the operation. From the embassy in Moscow, the State Department's George Kennan argued against the project. He worried the mission might affect final negotiations for occupation sectors in Vienna, and Kennan did not trust the military to safeguard U.S. interests. Despite these reservations, the team received permission to proceed just as the Carinthian crisis was being resolved. On June 2, Flory flew from Florence, Italy, to Klagenfurt, Austria, which was in the zone occupied by the British V Corps. From there the American, British, and French teams convoyed to Vienna. When they reached the Soviet lines the next morning they were met by a major general, a band, and an honor guard. At 5 P.M. the convoy arrived in Vienna with the Stars and Stripes, Union Jack, and French Tricolor whipping from poles on the lead vehicles.

The U.S. mission consisted of air, engineer, health, signal, and civil affairs personnel who, over the next eight days, fanned out across the old imperial capital, checking on electrical power, hospitals, telephones, and the water supply, as well as housing, food, fuel, and physical security. The Americans also scouted for buildings to be used as headquarters, billets, training areas, and recreation and logistical facilities. They found Vienna in ruins, filled with a dissolute and demoralized people.

Reports covered a wide variety of subjects ranging from the state of Soviet military government and occupation troops to the status of health, legal, finance, traffic, education, economics, labor, prisoners of war, displaced persons, and public safety. While his men scouted the city, Flory and his team held ten official meetings with the other Allied contingents. The mission also participated in a number of social events, including a banquet at which Flory received a standing ovation for kissing a singer from the Ukrainian First Army choir that the Americans had nicknamed "the Russian Bombshell."

Cooperation and confrontation characterized the mission to Vienna. One of the most contentious issues was the disagreement over which airfields would be available for Allied use. Soviet intransigence on this and other points of contention would later assume ominous proportions, particularly when the U.S. military began to consider the possibility of a Soviet blockade of Vienna. In contrast to Berlin, the American zone in Vienna did not include airfields that could be used to fly in supplies for the civilian population.

The disagreements of the summer of 1945 were not precursors to the Cold War. Soviet attitudes seemed far more influenced by a desire to make the burden on their forces as light as possible. Their occupation troops were clearly expected, Flory's team reported, to "live off the land." The Soviets wanted airfields, industry, agricultural areas, transportation networks, and other infrastructure to support their own operations and, where possible, contribute to the economic rehabilitation of the Soviet Union. There was no evidence of the machinery required for an extended occupation. "The Russians," Flory's report noted, "have nothing in Vienna even vaguely comparable to our G-5. They make no attempt to control or supervise local government and administration." Nor were the Soviets intentionally obstructing the occupation of Vienna by the other Allies. In fact, they wanted the other powers to move into the city as quickly as possible to help feed the local population. If anything, the Soviets' preparations seemed far more haphazard and improvised than did the U.S. and British efforts.[39]

That the Soviets had made very few preparations for the occupation should have been expected. When General McNarney cabled Maj. Gen. John Deane, the military representative in Moscow, to enlist his aid in coordinating planning with the Soviets, he got a discouraging reply. Deane responded that the Soviets "do not bother very much about planning in advance . . . [they] leave it to the troops of occupation to solve problems as they arise."[40]

Another factor that probably influenced the Soviets was the dramatic change in the course of the war over the last year. As it became apparent that their troops would reach Austria first, Stalin and Molotov undoubtedly recognized that they would be in a stronger negotiating position after their forces occupied the country. Giving further cause for caution was, perhaps, a belief that they had been unfairly treated during the negotiations over the surrender of German forces in Italy. The Soviets had the upper hand in Austria, and the favorable tactical situation further encouraged a wait-and-see attitude. In fact, the Soviets had already taken advantage of their position. Without consulting the other Allies, Tolbukhin had installed a provisional government.

The British seemed suspicious of Soviet motives from the outset. On June 9, Churchill cabled Truman, complaining about the lack of Soviet cooperation: "Here is the capital of Austria which by agreement is to be divided, like the country itself into four zones: but no one has any powers there except the Russians and not even ordinary diplomatic rights are allowed. If we give way in this matter, we must regard Austria as in the Sovietized half of Europe."[41]

In contrast to Churchill's rhetoric, the British team was far less pessimistic. Winterton reported satisfactory cooperation with the Russians. When a Soviet officer failed to show up at a scheduled meeting, his superiors had the man confined to his quarters on bread and water. Obviously, they were serious about relations with the Anglo-American Allies.[42]

The U.S. assessment also cast Soviet behavior in a positive light. Erhardt reported that he had been informed that the "utmost cooperation was shown by local red army commanders . . . the Soviet authorities proved to be most hospitable and friendly."[43] Even the worst aspects of the Soviet occupation were given a positive spin. While the Americans found extreme apprehension on the part of Austrians over the conduct of Soviet soldiers, including numerous horrifying stories of rape and mistreatment, Flory stated: "the fact that many unescorted females of all ages are on the streets as late as 2200 hours would indicate that the dangers are not as great as they have been reported. It is also significant that civilians freely express their opinion and their criticism of Russian activities."[44]

If the American reports seemed a bit rose colored with regard to the Soviets, it was understandable. The teams had been ordered not to provoke a confrontation. The Russians were, after all, their allies, and U.S. commanders had hoped for the best. At the same time, there was a natural caution in dealing with the Austrians, who, while technically liberated, had continued fighting for the enemy until May 8, 1945. Trust would not come easy. Still, Flory could have been critical in his secret report. He had been sent to make a frank assessment. There was nothing preventing him from being more harsh if he thought such comments were warranted.

The missions left Vienna on June 13. Flory went ahead and met with Erhardt and Clark's chief of staff, Maj. Gen. Alfred Gruenther, to finalize his official report. On June 16, he flew to Caserta, where he conferred with Gruenther and McNarney. The mission commanders met later that day and, after a lengthy discussion, agreed on a common position on the division of Vienna.

Erhardt recommended that Flory brief Winant, and the general flew to London on June 20. The ambassador rarely attended any of the meetings, leaving such matters to the EAC staff. After he was debriefed, Flory remained in London to observe negotiations, noting how heavily representatives relied on his mission reports. The four powers eventually reached accord on the most contentious issues, including the division of occupation zones in Vienna, and concluded the basic form of the Control Agreement for Austria. Other points, such as when the other Allied forces would move into the city and how the great powers would divide responsibility for feeding the population, continued to be debated over the weeks ahead.

While Flory's report did not lead to the resolution of every issue or satisfy all the tremendous information requirements, it was deemed extremely important. It was so highly classified that he was not allowed to keep a copy, and he did not see it again until it was published in *Foreign Relations of the United States*. Flory wrote in his memoirs that, "No event in my military career has afforded me with more satisfaction of a job well done than my mission to Vienna." It might not have been war, but it was enough like it—and a victory to boot, as far as he was concerned.

The Fog of Peace

One Clausewitzian concept with which Flory and other army leaders became very familiar during their years of military schooling was the "fog of war," the unpredictable and unknown factors hidden from a commander that could upset his plans and make the outcome of battle impossible to predict. At the close of World War II they discovered the notion applied to winning the peace as well.

In Austria's case, the fog of peace wreaked havoc on U.S. preparations. There were, however, identifiable root causes behind the apparent chaos.

The inability to predict conditions at the end of the conflict resulted from a lack of consensus by Allied governments on the purpose, organization, and scope of the occupation; the course of tactical operations; inadequate knowledge of the area; and unclear requirements for force protection. In addition, not knowing who, when, where, or how operations would be conducted posed serious difficulties, delaying recruiting and training, hampering Allied coordination, and placing additional burdens on scarce civil affairs resources. Finally, the diversion of the Yugoslav incursion and the delay in coordinating deployment of the mission to Vienna postponed full implementation of the occupation machinery for more than a month.

All of these shortfalls resulted in part from a lack of adequate preparation. Senior leaders had invested only a modicum of effort in laying the groundwork for the postwar period. In part, this limited investment was understandable. Strategic intelligence assets, military forces, and diplomatic efforts could only be spread so far. With the occupation of Germany a given, and a war still to be won in the Pacific, capital spent on Austria could only be paid out at the expense of dealing with other more pressing issues. Even if the United States had committed itself to the occupation early on, and pressed harder to gain strategic intelligence, resolve territorial disputes, and settle occupation issues, there could be no guarantees. Nevertheless, American efforts clearly failed to set the right conditions for the occupation and the United States found itself reacting to events as they unfolded, rather than establishing the agenda for the postwar period.

One important result of being ill prepared was an intensification of the influence of the army's traditional practices and behaviors. Even the mission to Vienna encouraged old habits. The Allies left the city concluding they could forge, as they had during the European campaign, a workable, if occasionally contentious, partnership. Flory's success suggested that the military's routine method for conducting coalition operations would prove adequate. Others may have had fears of an impending Cold War, but the liberators of Austria were concerned only with forging a functional partnership. Their resolve would be tested in the days ahead.

CHAPTER 3

SHEPHERDING MIDNIGHT'S CHILDREN

On February 12, 1944, a legion of newspapermen gathered in the Italian hills to watch one of the most publicized attacks of the war. In order to break through the German lines, the Allies planned to bomb the abbey at Monte Cassino. The reporters gaped as the ancient buildings disappeared with a thunderous crash, gushing flames, and billowing clouds of smoke. Bombing the abbey, a symbol of vast political, cultural, and religious significance, had been a heart-wrenching decision. One of the key participants in the deliberations was Maj. Gen. Alfred Maximilian Gruenther, a forty-five-year-old officer who was short in stature but large in presence. Gruenther served as Lt. Gen. Mark Clark's deputy and chief of staff throughout the grueling campaign and the first tense months of the occupation. Intense, tireless, and demanding, Gruenther was reputedly one of the army's finest thinkers. Clark had tremendous confidence in him.

Born in Platte Center, Nebraska, Al Gruenther graduated near the top of his West Point class in November, 1919. Throughout his career he earned high marks as a top-flight professional. Gruenther's reputation as a brilliant and dependable staff officer proved well earned. In 1942, Eisenhower brought him to London to serve as deputy chief of staff. The following year, he became Clark's number-two man. Gruenther flourished under both commanders and the pressures of helping them confront monumental decisions. The difficult decision to bomb the abbey on Monte Cassino was but one example. In the summer of 1945, he faced a new challenge: transforming U.S. forces from a weapon of battle into an instrument of peace.

Gruenther's most immediate trial was dealing with an unsteady trinity: the attitude of the civil population, the conduct of a defeated enemy, and the behavior of American troops. Determining how to cope with this triumvirate would constitute the first important decisions of the occupation.

Here, the shortfalls of preparation and the great unknowns facing the troops took their toll—and the burden was Gruenther's. Until Clark arrived in Austria on August 12, 1945, the chief of staff supervised the command.

Army Bound

Although Brig. Gen. Lester Flory's mission to Vienna had been a success, the methodical establishment of military government and the immediate separation of Austria and Germany envisioned by his planners never occurred. Troops under SHAEF control, not Allied Forces Headquarters, blanketed the countryside, establishing a haphazard, improvised framework. The XV Corps, commanded by Lt. Gen. Wade H. Haislip and headquartered in Salzburg, had overall responsibility. Haislip divided the U.S. zone into three operational areas, rather than along the lines of responsibility assigned to the military government detachments. Major General Maxwell D. Taylor of 101st Airborne Division became military governor for Salzburg. Reinhart's division occupied Oberdonau, while Maj. Gen. Anthony C. McAuliffe's 103d Infantry Division governed Tirol.

Flory and his team did not participate in this operation, though he did send a small liaison detachment including Lt. Cols. George McCaffery and Charles Howard (the latter representing the State Department) to SHAEF headquarters. McCaffery and Howard could contribute little. Pressed for time and resources, SHAEF opted to issue directives that proved virtually carbon copies of their policies for Germany.

Rather than planning assistance, SHAEF was desperate to obtain additional civil affairs personnel. Flory dispatched his teams to supplement its ranks. They were almost comically ineffective. A group bound for Linz flew from Italy to Paris in April, 1945, assembling at a camp outside the city. Following a circuitous route behind the advancing armies, they arrived to find the situation completely daunting. There had been no time for detailed coordination during the rapid advance, so combat units largely ignored the civil affairs teams. When a division headquarters staff arrived, it would promptly evict the local team from the offices it had occupied and take over the building. Most teams were content to hole up in local residences and simply wait for the 15th Army Group to arrive.[1]

Nor did the State Department legation affect policies. State's John Erhardt had few people, little equipment, and no authority. All the State Department provided him was six typewriters, three filing cabinets, and two staff cars. The success of his operation depended on whatever he was able to cajole from the military. "We are operating mostly with Army gear," Erhardt

Brigadier General Lester Delong Flory, June 2, 1946. Courtesy National Archives.

reported.[2] When Clark's headquarters headed toward Austria by way of Verona, Erhardt followed with his "gypsy caravan," the appearance of the contingent reflecting its poverty.

Erhardt made considerable effort to get his people into the country to put "over the point of view that Austria should not be governed according to the German directives."[3] The army allowed him to attach one team to a convoy headed for Salzburg on June 1. A 15th Army Group military survey

team led by Col. John Colonna also visited the XV Corps area from June
10–13. Its reports were not encouraging. "Conditions were utterly confused
and 'army bound.'"[4] American troops in Austria were acting like the occupiers in Germany. In response, Erhardt penned a critical, albeit diplomatic,
memorandum.

Directives from SHAEF sometimes arrived late due to the speed of the
occupation, and combat forces were faced with restoring order without previous civil affairs training geared for Austria. Policies varied from one place
to another. Sometimes regulations and practices, through the fault of no
one, proved ill-advised. Such was the case in Salzburg, where troops were
billeted without considering the politics of the Austrians to be evicted. As a
result, many of the occupiers were quartered in property belonging to anti-
Nazis while the dwellings of Nazis went untouched.[5]

These examples led to an undeniable fact: SHAEF's policies were
counterproductive. All of the excellent preparatory work by Flory and his
men was virtually ignored. To make matters worse, units repositioned frequently, leaving no opportunity to establish consistent policies. Six divisions, over a hundred thousand men, moved in and out of the country
within weeks.

After a month of near chaos, Clark's 15th Army Group took over. On
July 5, the headquarters was reorganized as U.S. Forces Austria (USFA), a
semi-independent command, responsible to Eisenhower's headquarters—
formerly SHAEF, but recently reestablished as U.S. Forces European Theater (USFET)—for administration and logistical matters. Clark reported
directly to Washington on issues of strategy, policy, and military government. He also served as the high commissioner, making him both the civil
and military head, as well as the American representative to the Allied
Council, which was to administer the country until the signing of a formal
state treaty. Supporting his role on the commission was an additional staff,
the U.S. element of the Allied Council for Austria, which set up shop in Vienna. Clark later moved part of USFA's headquarters from Salzburg to the
capital as well.

Brothers in Arms

While the United States took control of Upper Austria south of the Danube
River, French troops under Gen. Marie Antoine Emile Béthouart occupied
Vorarlberg and Tirol. General McCreery's British forces controlled
Carinthia and Styria. The Soviets governed Lower Austria, Burgenland, and
Upper Austria north of the Danube. The commander of these forces was
Marshal Ivan Stepanovich Konev.

Rivaled only by Marshal Georgi Zhukov, Konev was considered one of the Soviet Union's premier field commanders. Born in 1897, he left school at the age of twelve to work as a woodchopper. Conscripted in 1916, Konev became a junior officer before being demobilized. He joined the Communist Party and the Red Army in 1918. A graduate of the Frunz Military Academy, Konev vied with Zhukov for Stalin's favor and command of the forces in Western Europe during the Second World War. In 1944, he led one wing of the counteroffensive that swept through the Ukraine, Poland, and deep into Germany. A man of austere habits who did not drink, which was highly unusual for a Russian general, Konev also carried a deep respect for Stalin and a reputation as a staunch party loyalist.

The Americans were mystified when Konev replaced Tolbulkhin as commander of Soviet occupation forces. They were skeptical of the official explanation: that Tolbukhin's Ukrainian Third Army was being demobilized. An OSS report speculated that the real reason was that Stalin was displeased with the lack of discipline demonstrated by the Soviet troops who sacked Vienna. In the West, some had argued that acts of intimidation and oppression in the Soviet zone were precursors to forcibly pulling Austria into Stalin's orbit. If the OSS report was accurate, then perhaps such rumors were not true. The change boded well for the future of U.S.-Soviet relations. With Zhukov in charge of the occupation troops in Germany, the fact that Stalin had placed his second most prestigious commander in Austria suggested that he was taking matters seriously.

Shortly after the start of the Potsdam Conference, when Truman met Churchill and Stalin for the first time, the prime minister complained that Soviet forces were still delaying the entrance of other Allied troops into their assigned zones in Austria. Shortly afterward, Konev wrote to the other occupation commanders and offered his complete cooperation. Two days later, on July 22, Stalin announced that Soviet troops had begun to withdraw from the other Allied zones. Churchill and Truman took this as a positive sign, and Gruenther reported that his first meetings with Konev's deputy had gone well. This was all for the best. Each Allied power had more than enough trouble organizing operations and caring for the populace in its own zone. The United States was no exception.

Soldiers Become Governors

In the American sector, the transition from tactical commands to military government was a near disaster, although Gruenther, running the headquarters in Salzburg, ameliorated the situation a good bit. Rather than simply imitating SHAEF, USFA began to implement the policies drafted by

Flory's team, and the military government detachments gradually assumed control of local administration from tactical units. Still, putting aside conflicting policies and responsibilities, the detachments' work proved overwhelming. Thirty officers and fifty enlisted soldiers supervised thirteen subordinate detachments responsible for an area covering four thousand square miles that contained 1,300,000 civilians, legions of boisterous GIs, and thousands of defeated enemy troops.

Complicating the task was the delay in recognizing Austria's new political structure. After the liberation of Vienna, the Soviets selected elderly Karl Renner, a former chancellor in the First Republic, to set up a provisional government. The prewar socialists joined under Renner to form the *Sozialistische Partei Österreichs (SPÖ)*. The conservatives, purged of hard line fascists, were reorganized as *Österreichische Volkspartei (ÖVP)*. Although the communist movement had been suppressed under Dollfuss's prewar regime (a tradition carried on well by the Nazis), the *Kommunistische Partei Österreichs (KPÖ)* also emerged as a political force thanks to Soviet support. Archduke Otto and other royalists were not invited to join the administration. The government opened its doors on April 27, 1945, and from the outset Renner encouraged a corporatist approach with the major political parties sharing power. The portfolios of the state secretaries were distributed among the three, with each secretary assisted by two undersecretaries from the other parties. The Soviets immediately recognized Renner's government, but the other Allies did not follow suit. This decision left Austria little better off than Germany, which had also been divided into four occupation zones and, with the abolition of the Nazi regime, had no recognized federal government.

America's reluctance to accept Renner frustrated the Austrians. On July 7, the OSS passed a memorandum to Truman that included a message from Adolf Schärf, a member of Renner's cabinet.[6] Schärf argued that the provisional government was legitimate, not simply a tool of the Soviets, and sincere in its intent to discard the destructive ideological battles waged by the parties of the First Republic.

Born in Moravia in 1890, Schärf was raised in Vienna, where he studied law. Wounded on the Italian front during World War I, Schärf became active in socialist politics after the armistice. Imprisonment by the Nazis cut short his public political career, although he was later allowed to return to his law practice, where he maintained covert ties with Renner and the resistance movement. Schärf had great faith in Renner's policies and doubted that the communists would remain part of the power-sharing model. He believed they feared early elections because the results would demonstrate that the communists' assurances to Moscow of their party's ability to command

Karl Renner opens the Austrian assembly, September 25, 1945. Courtesy National Archives.

significant electoral support would not be borne out. Schärf suggested that frustrated communists might attempt a putsch. He wanted the Americans and the British to move quickly to establish their authority. By holding back, the United States might strengthen rather than weaken the Soviet position.

Although men like Schärf and Renner were the kind of leaders with whom the United States would have liked to work, Washington withheld recognition and Truman asked for an assessment of the situation. "We have no great complaint against Renner or his government," his advisers cautioned, "but we and the British have protested vigorously against the manner in which the Soviet authorities have permitted the formation of this government in the part of Austria under Russian occupation and influence without consulting us."[7]

Truman had left Potsdam believing he could deal with Stalin even though he did not trust the Soviet leader. Thus, until there were signs that the Soviets would fully respect the postwar agreements, the president was not inclined to show any deference.

Without a recognized regime, the challenge of imposing order on the chaotic conditions in Upper Austria fell on Col. Russell Snook, the senior military government official.[8] Snook appointed provisional committees at each level of government, with a chairman serving as *Landeshauptmann*, *Bezirkshauptmann*, or *Bürgermeister*. His scheme had one fatal flaw: all politics are local. On June 6, Adolf Eigl was appointed *Landeshauptmann*. He took his office quite seriously, providing Snook scrupulous, detailed reports. He quickly gained the colonel's confidence, but in August, Eigl was arrested as a collaborator. Joseph Zehetner, an *ÖVP* activist, applauded his detention. Eigl had joined the National Socialists and enjoyed close associations with party leaders. Another *ÖVP* principal, Heinrich Gleissner, claimed Eigl was no Nazi and had been kept on only because of his administrative skill. Local *SPÖ* and *KPÖ* factions approved of Eigl's removal, but they had been vehement critics of his brief administration.

The combination of small-town politics and army efforts to purge from public life every tainted official wreaked havoc on Snook's capacity to govern. Gleissner warned "it might prove difficult to find another man willing to take the *Landeshauptmann's* position because of a fear of arrest for unknown reasons after a month or two in office." Meanwhile, Snook had to deal with a surge of civil affairs crises. People lacked for everything. There was no gas and little coal. Furniture was chopped up for firewood. Most lived on a starvation diet of a few loaves of bread. No vegetables. No meat. Nor were clothing, shoes, or other "luxuries" available—except in a burgeoning black market where people who had something to trade could acquire things. Unfortunately, most had nothing. One report said that the only thing many Austrians had left of value was their wedding rings, and they would not part with those. The housing shortage swelled as authorities struggled to find quarters for troops, returning enemy personnel, and refugees. In Vienna, citizens rebuilt their homes with their bare hands and makeshift wheelbarrows. The electrical system functioned occasionally. Crime and plundering increased as the ranks of displaced persons ballooned. During the first week of September, the command reported 321,629 displaced persons in the area. Authorities managed to evacuate only two thousand.

By September 10, three weeks after Eigl's arrest, Snook still had no replacement. Instead he governed through a committee that included Gleissner and another ÖVP representative, Franz Lorenzoni. Then Lorenzoni was arrested. Although anti-Hitler since the Anschluss, he had served in the finance ministry, thus falling under denazification directives. Snook railed that removing his only responsible and effective administrators made the task of governing impossible. Few were sympathetic. One Austrian official chalked up Snook's willingness to back ex-Nazis who had victimized their country to being either "poorly informed or ill-meaning." Snook was undeterred. On October 7, the colonel met with the SPÖ's Ernst Koref, Joseph Stampfl of the ÖVP, and KPÖ leader Franz Haider to resolve the impasse. Snook ended the turmoil once and for all by insisting that all parties support Gleissner since he had proven to be the most successful administrator.

The flap over who should serve as *Landeshauptmann* was instructive. Although USFA had not formally recognized Renner's administration, the command strongly supported his corporatist approach and fostered, and occasionally forced, cooperation. Order gradually returned. Despite the problem of having his administrators arrested, Snook found coordination with local officials quite good and his men handed over more and more responsibility to civilian authorities. The political situation seemed to be stabilizing. On October 20, the other Allied powers recognized Renner's government, and national elections were held on November 25. The vote represented a watershed in military government, the culmination of a successful effort to reestablish competent civilian authority. The new government took office in December. Just as Schärf had predicted, the communists garnered few votes and were dropped from the coalition—except for the token appointment of the minister of power and electrification, a position the KPÖ retained until withdrawing from the government in 1947.

Despite the Communist Party's rejection at the polls, the Soviet Union also accepted Renner's new administration. This represented an important step in shaping the future course of the occupation. Unlike Germany, which was never permitted to elect a single federal government, Austria had legitimate sovereign power—a singular advantage in reestablishing political stability and providing a unified voice for determining the nation's future. Austria was also far better off than Poland, an unquestioned victim of Nazi aggression that had been wholly occupied by Soviet forces. The Polish problem was high on the agenda of U.S. postwar diplomatic efforts and a major topic of discussion at Potsdam. The United States recognized the country's communist government when it was assured there would be free and fair elections. When the communists reneged on their promise, the Americans remained passive, accepting Poland's assimilation into the Soviet sphere, unwilling to risk a

Rebuilding Vienna, September 13, 1945. Courtesy National Archives.

Clearing rubble to make way for a new building, September 13, 1945.
Courtesy National Archives.

An Austrian man with a ration of bread, Vienna, September, 1945.
Courtesy National Archives.

total breech with their wartime ally, even though the affair soured Truman's hopes for striking a fair deal with Stalin over the contested zone of Europe.

While the stake in Austria was not great, unlike Poland, the country had the advantage of having the Americans at hand to serve as a counterbalance for Soviet influence. With the United States engaged and a legitimate central government established, the nation was in perhaps the best possible position for an occupied country. Despite the problems and inefficiencies caused by the initial turmoil of conflicting policies; the lack of coordination between tactical and civil affairs units; and balancing governing with local party politics and denazification, when the new Austrian regime took office the most critical tasks of the mission appeared largely complete. All this seemed to bode well for the future. Even so, there was more to shepherding midnight's children.

Swords into Plowshares

Establishing civil government went on concurrently with the other critical measures for implementing the disease and unrest formula. One of the most pressing was demobilizing enemy soldiers, a task nothing less than monumental. During the European campaign, U.S. forces had custody of more than 7 million enemy troops. United States Forces Austria was responsible for 260,000, originating from thirty-four nations, and another 179,221 enemy troops transferred to the command from others parts of Europe.[9]

While USFET handled overall logistical support, USFA developed its own demobilization plans, coordinating them directly with the Pentagon and the other occupying powers.[10] The plans established three requirements. Primary disarmament included processing personnel and destroying their weapons, ammunition, and equipment. At the same time, USFA began secondary disarmament, removing stocks from supply dumps, depots, and warehouses. Final disarmament, which called for demilitarizing of factories and demolishing fortifications and other military infrastructure, would follow.

The army never published formal doctrine or trained on disarming procedures, but of all its postwar tasks it was best prepared for this job. Military leaders recognized these activities as a legitimate extension of combat and tackled them enthusiastically, drawing on lessons learned from World War I and the Mediterranean and European campaigns to perfect their methods. Troops immediately began the first step, rounding up enemy forces and separating them from their weapons. Most surrendered in large formations. German commands were ordered to retain unit integrity, transporting and sustaining themselves in designated areas. At least that was the idea.

The Americans quickly discovered that the defeated troops did not have adequate resources to care for themselves. In addition to supply and transport assistance, substantial administrative support was needed to register and process enemy personnel and equipment.

The initial priority was confiscating weapons, essential in the event of riots or other disturbances. It was also important to eliminate weapons as rapidly as possible to prevent theft, black market sale, or pilfering war trophies by sticky-fingered GIs. Arms, equipment, and ammunition were demilitarized by the most expedient means at hand: burning, crushing, burying, or blowing up. United States Forces Austria destroyed its fair share of the more than 1 million tons of German equipment seized by U.S. forces.

In the meantime, enemy soldiers were prepared for release. This function was the responsibility of locally appointed military zone commanders. A typical center run by a combat regiment could handle up to eighty-five hundred soldiers a day. Marched to the reception camp in lots of one thousand, the Germans were sent through a series of substations for registration, classification, security checks, fingerprinting, delousing, physical exams, briefings, and receiving discharge certificates and clothes to replace Wehrmacht uniforms. Finally, each group was transported to the men's country of origin.

One of the most innocuous of these tasks offered unexpected problems. Disarmed enemy forces, civilian laborers, displaced persons, and repatriated Allied personnel had all been issued surplus American uniforms. A rash of crimes reportedly committed by U.S. forces led officials to suspect the culprits were really civilians or former enemy soldiers in American military garb. In September, USFET ordered all issued clothing dyed distinctive colors. By December, the command reported the task had been largely accomplished. This was far from true. One problem was a theaterwide shortage of dyes. There was also a howl of protest from displaced persons ordered to don blue uniforms. "They were being forced to wear an identifying badge of a 'lower order,' just as Nazis had required all Jews to wear the Star of David," a UNRRA camp commander recalled, an act that was "bitterly resented." As a result, the UNRAA simply ignored the army, and the rule, which "was never repealed," was never enforced.[11]

Fretting over uniforms reflected the many challenges of trying to minimize security threats while processing thousands of men every day. Counter Intelligence Corps (CIC) agents scrutinized internees and impounded and examined diaries, papers, and identification documents. The screening segregated suspected war criminals and gathered information on underground operations and illegal activities. Meanwhile, combat troops established checkpoints and ran periodic sweeps searching for arms caches, contraband, and stragglers. Sometimes troops even found themselves deep in the Austrian woods chasing high-ranking German officers and shooting it out with fanatical SS men, though these incidents were the exception rather than the rule. By the end of the year, the command discharged over 391,000 prisoners and transferred another 99,343. In July, 1946, USFA reported custody of only 242 enemy soldiers. By March, 1947, secondary and final demobilization were also largely complete.

Disarmament directives also banned all signs of paramilitary activities, including veterans' associations, uniforms, flags, military gestures, salutes, insignia banners, military parades, anthems, and martial music. The command noted that the Austrians had "a disturbing tendency" to form organizations.[12] The Allies took these prohibitions seriously, eliminating everything from youth groups to ski clubs. This was believed to be particularly important as the history of Austria's First Republic was littered with examples where parties had used private armies to wage political warfare. Thus, over the next two years, the occupiers identified and broke up 220 different organizations.

Plans also called for cleansing law enforcement agencies. This practice complicated reestablishing public safety since disarming the police and purging their ranks of Nazis made them essentially ineffective. Austrian leaders complained bitterly because such measures compromised rather than enhanced prospects for establishing a stable state.[13] Some Americans agreed that this step was intrusive and wrongheaded. One military government officer wrote: "I was always disturbed and sometimes shocked when I witnessed a total disregard of the very rights for which I thought this war was fought. As I used to say frequently in Austria, we can never have a world at peace as long as we ourselves resort to practices which give the appearance of Out-Nazi [sic] the Nazis."[14] To military commanders, however, these concerns were less important than establishing a safe and secure environment for their forces and destroying all Nazi influences.

Heightening the concerns over physical security were persistent reports of "Werwolfe," covert teams of Nazi agents trained to conduct espionage and guerrilla warfare. The Werwolf threat played a significant role in shaping perceptions during the initial occupation. According to one report, 150 candidates were recruited shortly before the end of the war. Of these, seventy–eighty—composed of a mix of Wehrmacht soldiers, SS troopers, civilian Nazi Party members, and Hitler Jugend—completed training and were dispatched into the countryside. There were also rumors of twenty-four Werwolfe near Schleedorf.[15]

Intelligence on suspected Werwolf operations persisted through July, 1945. There were also numerous reports of minor acts of sabotage, unexplained fires, explosions, ambushes, and cut communication wires. Although an underground movement never materialized, U.S. fears were not wholly unwarranted. Werwolf organizations did exist, but their operations were ineptly administered, enjoyed little popular support, and withered in the face of massive Allied military force. In the end, the demobilization of Austria was a complete victory for the disease and unrest formula.

Friends and Enemies

While pacifying Austria was an immediate success in terms of reestablishing a pliant political order, U.S. measures had unintended—and not always constructive—consequences on rebuilding civil society. Civil society represented the community's public associations, acquired and nurtured through means other than the mechanisms of government. These were the areas of private sociability and discourse, such as unofficial groups, meeting places, and informal relationships. In terms of rehabilitating society, they would play an equally important role in fostering democracy, toleration, trust, and respect for the rule of law. United States Forces Austria's initial efforts primarily focused on the country's formal institutions. Concern with civil society was primarily limited to supporting the disease and unrest formula through the denazification program.

Dictating how soldiers would treat the Austrian people was an important and sensitive aspect of the effort to rebuild civil society, but commanders gave it little forethought. Neither a liberated country like France nor a defeated nation like Germany, the issue was whether to recognize Austrians as equals and permit a free interchange between civilians and occupation troops or to remain distant. Complicating the decision was the fact that many Austrians had actively supported the Nazi regime.[16] Supreme Headquarters Allied Expeditionary Force opted for strict limits, declaring, "In the initial stages of the occupation all social contacts between the Army and the civil population will be prohibited until such time as the situation warrants the lifting of the prohibition."[17] This directive barred all informal contact, as well as setting a curfew prohibiting civilian movement after dark. These restrictions mirrored the policy for Germany.

Nonfraternization rules were intended to minimize contact between soldiers and the populace. Here the generals had a number of concerns. Physical security was foremost. They were worried about terrorism, sabotage, and inadvertently compromising military secrets. There were unstated issues as well. One was crime. Civilians or German soldiers wearing American uniforms aside, criminal offenses by U.S. soldiers were not infrequent. In particular, the gains from exchanging goods and services on the black

U.S. military police and Austrian officials coordinating a raid on the black market, October 6, 1946. Courtesy National Archives.

market were extraordinary and a great temptation. Limiting contact with civilians was one technique for discouraging profiteering.[18]

Discipline and health issues were also concerns. Restrictions, it was hoped, would, "avoid the lax morals and numerous temptations present in a country whose social codes had been overturned by Nazism and the influx of refugees from many lands."[19] Prospects for contagious diseases, especially venereal infection and typhus ran high. Not surprisingly, the rate for social disease among soldiers skyrocketed.[20] In addition to health concerns, minimizing contact would preclude confrontations that might explode into civil disturbances. Finally, there were constant worries that any sensational publicity over fraternization might portray the occupation in an unfavorable light. Troops that seemed too generous or familiar might prompt further resentment from a people who preferred to have their men returned home as soon as possible.

While the generals wanted to be cautious and prudent, many GIs were desperate to meet women. Often-told stories of how high-ranking USFA officers socialized with Austrians and unsubstantiated rumors that German

Military and Austrian police arresting black marketers in the Karlsplatz, Vienna, October 2, 1945. Courtesy National Archives.

prisoners of war were roaming freely in the United States heightened resentment. Enforcing the ban on fraternization became a serious discipline challenge. "If ever there was an order that had to be explained," one general lamented, "the non-fraternization order is it."[21]

The predicament faced by commanders was not new. The United States had adopted a nonfraternization rule after World War I for the same reasons. That policy was an abject failure.[22] In fact, commanders found that total nonfraternization hindered rather than improved conditions. Fraternization policies after World War II proved no more successful. Commanders used lectures, pamphlets, films, newspapers, and magazine articles to justify policies. Some units employed special patrols or conducted bed checks. Others relied on the military police. These efforts had little effect. There were no standardized rules, penalties, or enforcement procedures.

In general, nonfraternization proved to be highly unpopular and, according to an official army report, was never seriously imposed in Austria.[23] Americans were not the only ones who disapproved. The French ignored all attempts to restrict fraternization. Soviet commanders had a policy, but issued no specific regulations to implement it. The British pursued a course similar to the Americans but found their soldiers equally reluctant to accept prohibitions.[24] The Austrians also deeply resented such rules. Treating the country in the same manner as Germany seemed contrary to the promise of a free and independent state.

In the absence of an overt threat and faced with widespread dissatisfaction, commanders felt pressured to reconsider. Pentagon officials authorized backtracking on nonfraternization rules, but Generals Clark and Eisenhower were wary, wanting to judge the reaction both in the United States and Europe before loosening prohibitions. In July, while discontent mounted, Clark left for a whirlwind trip to Rio de Janeiro to welcome home the Brazilian expeditionary force that had fought under his command in Italy. In his absence, General McCreery decided to relax the rules for British troops. General Gruenther called an emergency meeting of USFA's staff and penned a statement for the press concluding that the improving security conditions meant restrictions could be relaxed soon. He intended to release the statement on Clark's return. Then Field Marshal Bernard Law Montgomery announced the immediate lifting of all restrictions in the British zone of Germany. Eisenhower felt compelled to issue a parallel decree. When the draft was forwarded to USFA, Gruenther protested when he discovered that it applied to both Germany and Austria. Fraternization, he contended, was a political issue for which Clark was responsible directly to Washington. The flurry of finger-pointing prompted Erhardt to remark that he was reminded of a tag line from Jimmy Durante's radio skits: "Everybody is trying to get into da act." On July 14, Eisenhower lifted the theaterwide ban on conversations with civilians in public. To avoid embarrassment and confusion, Gruenther hastily released a statement proclaiming that Clark had "stated today that the modification of the non-fraternization order issued by General Eisenhower would apply to United States Forces in Austria."[25] It was a neat trick given that the USFA commander was still in South America.

The declaration met with little public enthusiasm—in part due to confusion surrounding the announcement and in part because many thought it did not go far enough. One State Department official called the policy a "tragi-comedy."[26] Soldiers were being ordered to ignore the Austrians, even those who had opposed the Nazis and been sent to concentration camps. "It looks like," his report continued, "A deliberate effort—and an effective one—to perpetuate and to stimulate hatred. You can't square it very well with the Moscow Declaration and the high plane of most of our declarations. Our boys are supposed to, and to a considerable extent do, walk through the streets not seeing anyone but each other; if they have to do business with Austrians they should not smile, there should be no courtesies and of course they shouldn't shake hands."[27] Regardless of any contributions nonfraternization rules might have made to physical security, everyone agreed they inhibited establishing bonds of trust and confidence between soldiers and civilians.

After General Clark returned from Brazil and consulted with the other high commissioners, he decided to end the policy once and for all. On August 24, 1945, all restrictions except for consorting with Nazis or marrying Austrian nationals were removed. War brides were also a contentious issue, and this prohibition proved equally unsuccessful. It was discontinued on November 29, 1945.[28] Without question, the army's attempt to manage contact between soldiers and civilians was an abject failure.

GIs and *Haus Fraus*

Rather than attempting to prevent contact, the military would have been better served by focusing its efforts on ensuring that interactions between the occupiers and the occupied were positive and productive.[29] For most Austrians, the troops were a remote and imposing presence, and widespread negative perceptions emerged over time. Gaunt, unshaven liberators were gradually transformed into a privileged, well-fed, tanned ruling class. Local communities found themselves overwhelmed by the Yanks. Vehicles jammed town squares and crammed narrow, winding country roads with endless lines of olive-drab convoys. Muddy-booted GIs occupied their homes. They ate the best food, dated the most attractive women, and always had a cigarette.

Interactions remained strained even after the nonfraternization order was rescinded. One official report concluded: "the attitude of Austrians toward the American occupation troops was and is generally friendly. The people are cooperative, docile and generally submissive to military government rule."[30] This was true, but the *official* view glossed over the tensions building up between occupiers and occupied. Thomas Brush, a young soldier stationed in Austria, wrote:

"it seems to me that the Austrians are undergoing a subtle change of attitude towards us. They jostle us in passing on the streets, and our greedy fraternization has done little to help our appearance in their eyes. 'We came as conquerors,' proclaimed the posters signed by Eisenhower that bedecked all the walls when we arrived . . . actually it appears that Americans have no ability to act as conquerors, and now our position seems to be more that of a pitiful poor relation at a family dinner, whose poverty swallows their pride. Nothing angers me more."[31] The Yanks had worn out their welcome—and it was not just that the soldiers and civilians spoke different languages. Brush, who spoke fluent German, had almost no interaction with the local populace, rarely speaking with anyone other than his barber.

Austrian attitudes did little to improve the situation. After an initial wave of euphoria, people appeared morose and resentful. In August, 1945, intelligence officers reported that the people viewed the occupation as a heavy and grossly unfair burden. The Yanks were not seen as liberators or protectors, but as a dead weight on the economy. The GIs were little more than competitors for food, fuel, and housing.[32] This was the Austria of Graham Greene's *The Third Man*. The grainy, shadow-draped images of Carol Reed's film version of the novel fittingly captured the grimness of everyday life.

Many were particularly distressed over the conditions of public safety. There were bitter complaints. Interior Minister Oskar Helmer frequently vented his concerns to the Allied Council.[33] United States Forces Austria was generally pleased with the security situation and found such complaints exaggerated.[34] These official assessments hardly squared with Helmer's protests. In fact, local officials and even some American representatives shared his sentiments.[35]

The Gold Train

One area of particular concern was the fate of personal property. Planners had assumed there would be difficulties in recovering possessions, authenticating ownership, and reimbursing individuals. They had prepared a manual and assigned property control officers to the military government detachments. Commands made a serious effort to implement control procedures. When troops identified caches of gold and art, each was assigned a guard force until the material could be inventoried and turned over for storage.

Nevertheless, in the turmoil of occupation, there still were lapses. Often only a handful of guards were available to protect sites, and there was confusion over responsibilities and procedures. There was also the persistent bugbear of individuals masquerading in U.S. uniforms. On June 23, 1945, a disarmed enemy soldier claimed that he had seen an SS officer in the custody of two Americans recover a hoard of several million dollars—the private trove of Reichsminister Heinrich Himmler. The loot, he claimed, had been hidden in a pig stable. Officials had no idea who the men might have been, or even if they were really Americans. They turned the matter over to USFA's criminal investigation division. Such stories of pilfered treasure were legion.[36]

Most people were more concerned about bits and pieces of their own lives than they were about caches of loot. In a country ravaged by war, every serviceable home and unbroken piece of furniture was invaluable. Austrians were less than pleased when U.S. forces commandeered housing, requisitioned furniture, and procured domestic implements. Much of this material went to outfit senior officer quarters, messes, and housing for military families joining the troops. Requisitions were legal under the terms of occupation, though this was an admittedly questionable practice if the Americans hoped to build up goodwill. Nevertheless, provisions for taking property were to be strictly controlled. Commanders warned their personnel to "take steps to provide adequate security on all properties under requisition which contain furniture in order that no pilfering take place."[37] Friction with civilians was to be minimized, and art, heirlooms, and items of value and cultural significance were to be left alone. Finally, the baggage of all redeploying troops was inspected. Some undoubtedly smuggled out contraband and war trophies, but on the whole the army made a good-faith effort.

More problematic was accounting for captured goods seized from Jews and other Nazi victims. The infamous "Werfen train"—fifty-two freight cars on the rail siding at Werfen filled to the top with artwork, gold, furs, rugs, jewelry, dresses, museum pieces, and silverware—proved to be one of the most famous and controversial cases.[38] Much of the property had been seized from Hungarian Jews, although it was reported some belonged to non-Jews trying to keep their valuables from the Russians. When the army assumed custody it posted a twenty-four-hour guard. The cars were then taken to Salzburg, where they were unloaded, inventoried, and their contents warehoused. The paintings were stored in the *Karabinersaal Residenz*.

There were reports of looting even before USFA took control of the train. During the ensuing period, controversy, lapses in property control, and no small amount of confusion followed. General Clark ruled that establishing the ownership of individual possessions was impractical. Many of the items had been intermingled in transit, this was often because when property was inventoried it was segregated by type and removed from all identifying suitcases and containers. Clark reasoned that the military had procedures for individuals to reclaim missing items or receive restitution and that the army could meet its legal obligations by properly storing and safeguarding material.

Like other material in the property-control warehouse, items from the train were requisitioned for use by the occupation forces. In June, 1946, USFA discovered that it could not account for much of the property. The command ordered an end to requisitioning and began to retrieve issued items. The loss of control reflected a sad state of affairs. All of the officers in the Salzburg property control section had been redeployed. Sergeants replaced officers, and later the positions were civilianized. Whether soldier or civilian, there were few personnel available to secure, inventory, maintain, manage, and protect property. Worse, the only preparation these men had for handling the massive collection—which contained everything from priceless masterpieces to table linen—was their on-the-job training. In addition to few numbers, limited experience, and rapid turnover, the section had vast responsibilities, including eighty factories, four hundred properties, and all of the items requisitioned by U.S. forces, a substantial amount of which had signed for by various high-ranking officials scattered throughout Salzburg and Vienna. Officers who had signed for property were constantly being moved, reassigned, or redeployed. Some items turned up missing during inventories, although it proved difficult to determine if the accounting was correct or that the items had been misinventoried, lost, stolen, broken, misplaced, or simply discarded. An investigation of the warehouse in July, 1947, showed that records were still incomplete and poorly organized, while the art stored in the *Karabinersaal Residenz* lay forgotten.

As property losses swelled, so did the controversy. The United States repeatedly rejected demands by the Central Bureau of Hungarian Jews for the return of the Werfen train—and with good reason. There were competing claims, and Jewish refugee groups doubted the Hungarians could rightfully provide fair restitution. Some also suspected that the Hungarians and Soviets only supported the bureau's demands because it embarrassed the United States. United States Forces Austria turned all valuable items over to the International Refugee Organization, which included them in a New York benefit auction. On April 13, 1948, the Austrian government took custody of the remaining property and assumed responsibility for restitution claims.

Without question, the accounting for properties was deeply flawed. However, given postwar conditions and the monumental tasks the army had to accomplish in such a short time to forestall disease and unrest, it appears the occupation forces made a credible attempt. Some individuals may have profited, but there is no evidence of systemic corruption, and USFA made repeated efforts to correct its deficiencies. Nevertheless, the problems of accounting for property, compounded by crime, food shortages, lack of coal for heating, and economic dislocation left many Austrians uneasy about their future, despite frequent U.S. pronouncements that the disease and unrest formula had taken hold and that the country was making sure and steady progress.

USFA's Dilemma

Austrian attitudes were not the only concerns facing Gruenther and other senior officers. The Americans had trials of their own. Absent a visible threat, there was little for the combat troops to do. An initial report found that "the soldiers are wonderfully well behaved although it's evident they aren't to be fooled with. They are not arrogant or domineering—you'd be proud of them."[39] Nevertheless, there were a number of incidents that gave both the Austrians and U.S. officials pause. To combat indiscipline and low morale, USFA directed a combination of recreation, education, and training programs to fill the soldiers' empty hours. Of the three initiatives, recreation proved the most effective. The GIs particularly enjoyed trips to the Austrian Alps or taking leave in Paris. Yearbooks, duffel bags, and letters home were filled with black-and-white snapshots of those halcyon days. Young soldiers skiing, swimming, playing baseball, and sightseeing rather than ruined cities and their gaunt, haunted survivors were the images soldiers chose as their last memories of the European campaign.

Commanders were equally vigorous in pursuing information and education programs. Thomas Brush wrote home that he and his comrades were required to attend lectures twice weekly. United States Forces Austria developed a six-hour program of mandatory instruction titled, "Soldier You Are Helping in Austria." The briefings provided a detailed explanation of the occupation's purpose, organization, and conduct.[40] Meanwhile, improvised unit schools offered everything from music to language classes, although it is difficult to measure whether these initiatives had any influence on reducing indiscipline.

Training also was totally ineffective. The United States, which had planned to send the bulk of the forces in Austria to the Pacific after Germany's defeat, included continuous training as part of the postwar scheme. However, following the atomic attacks on Hiroshima and Nagasaki and Japan's capitulation in August, 1945, all thought of maintaining readiness vanished. Commanders still hoped to use training as a disciplinary tool. United States Forces Austria intended to keep its troops on a "war footing," but turbulence and personnel and equipment shortages made the goal unrealistic. As a result, the command focused instead on ensuring proficiency in basic military duties.[41] Yet even this modest goal was unpopular. "[T]here is a rumor they'll have us start training again!" wrote Thomas Brush. "Jesus don't these bastards know the war is over!"[42]

With Japan's collapse, the emphasis shifted to demobilizing forces rapidly, a process that further strained morale and discipline. From June to December, 1945, redeployment occurred at a frenzied pace. The exodus was managed by a numerical system. Rather than transferring entire units, individuals received points for overseas service, combat time, awards received in battle, marriage and children, and length of enlistment. Soldiers with the most points went home first. Troops found little equity in the plan, and the point system had a detrimental effect on morale. Brush wrote that he had heard a poll of soldiers had been used to develop the rule, but he "could never find a GI that got polled."[43] In January, 1946, troops conducted public protests that nearly became riots. The military newspaper *Stars and Stripes* carried frequent articles on the issue, as well as reports of demobilization demonstrations in the Pacific, and the many calls in the United States to "bring the boys home." Congressional pressure to speed up demobilization was unrelenting. All the attention given to the subject seemed only to fuel discontent.[44]

The demobilization process also destroyed unit integrity and competency. Troops were sent home regardless of duty or location. Soldiers with critical skills required for occupation duties, such as trained intelligence personnel supporting denazification, were redeployed as quickly as less-essential troops. Units that prided themselves on their wartime effectiveness now became little more than holding companies. According to Tom Brush, "the Army is falling apart." The wartime veterans were shipping out, he lamented, and "behind them they leave a small and wretchedly trained group of men."[45] By January 1, 1946, the command had a tactical strength of only 12,306—two divisions at less than half their authorized strength. United States Forces Austria initiated a hopscotch reassignment policy, transferring the remnants of some units depleted by redeployment to fill out others. This policy further exacerbated the lack of unit cohesion. Individual replacements from the United States were generally less mature and proved poorly disciplined. Many were new enlistees under twenty years of age who had not graduated from high school or attended basic training. One officer complained these soldiers were little more than callow youths acting like "swaggering conquerors."[46] When the provost marshal, Col. William Yarborough, complained about the quality of troops he was getting to represent the United States in Vienna, he was told, "you take your share of the people just like everybody else."[47]

Organizing the Occupiers

Senior commanders soon found that the forces they had on hand were inadequate to meet the requirements of postwar duty and the twin dangers of disease and unrest. Although there was no serious conventional threat to justify the presence of combat troops, there were significant concerns over public safety—particularly with regard to violent crime, black-market trafficking, and border and population control, as well as rising troop indiscipline. These problems had been exacerbated by disarmament and denazification operations that had rendered Austria's police force useless.

Although the Americans had shown they were fearsome warriors, their wartime organizations and training proved inappropriate and inadequate for occupation duty. Fighting forces were organized to act as *combined arms teams,* blending all kinds of weapons and combat support into a single integrated effort—a capability that far exceeded the needs for postwar duty. They were also ill equipped for the tasks at hand. Troops lacked nonlethal weapons for crowd control. Poor mobility was another problem. Infantry units had few vehicles, and armored units had a large number of heavy tracked vehicles unsuited to patrolling civilian areas, especially along the narrow, fragile roads in Austrian towns and villages. Retaining battle organization with postwar downsizing and depleted, understrength units only exacerbated the problem, making units even more ineffective.

The type of training conducted was also a problem. Tactical training focused on coordinated combat action, which had little utility for occupation duties consisting of many diverse activities conducted by small units rather than large-scale organized campaigns involving regiments and divisions. Still, some skills—such as patrolling, guard duty, and manning checkpoints—were useful for occupation duties. Also, the initiative, discipline, and ability to plan and execute small-unit actions that U.S. troops had honed in months of combat served them well in postwar duties requiring initiative and dependable small-unit leadership. Unfortunately, most of the best-qualified men were heading home. Yet even well-trained soldiers were deficient in many of the critical tasks that more closely paralleled police activities, including investigation, arrest, detention, search and seizure, interrogation, negotiation, and riot control. Some of these skills were resident in the force. Intelligence commands, for example, contained trained interrogators. But no organization possessed all the capabilities needed.

Another shortcoming was that the mere presence of tactical troops impeded a return to normalcy. Battalions, regiments, and divisions were a constant reminder to the Austrians that they lived in an occupied country. At the same time, regular military units could represent a potential threat to the other occupation powers. An overreliance on tactical forces impeded building trust and confidence among occupiers and occupied and delayed the return to normal civic life.

At the end of the war, some army commands experimented with employing specially organized occupation forces, but the idea of establishing a constabulary command never received serious consideration.[48] The priority of winning the war and the expectation of a short occupation made the issue of special troops a low priority. The success of units toying with reorganization, the speed of redeployment, and the limited utility of tactical forces caused the army to rethink the idea.

In September, 1945, USFET unveiled its plan for a constabulary force. General Clark endorsed the concept, but commanders in Germany voted down the proposal, arguing that a constabulary would be inefficient, uneconomical, and impractical. These reservations were overcome when Generals Eisenhower and Marshall became personally involved, a factor that undoubtedly was instrumental in dampening the service's dogmatic opposition to fielding specialized occupation troops. In December, 1945, as redeployments peaked and the Allies braced for a winter of hardship and deprivation in the occupied territories, Marshall authorized reorganizing part of the occupation troops into a constabulary force.

The constabulary was to be a mobile reserve that could respond quickly to public disorders and also conduct patrolling and search-and-seizure missions, apprehend wanted persons, recover contraband goods, and assist counterintelligence units. Thus empowered, the constabulary could largely relieve military forces from dealing with the civilian population. Organized into three brigades, each with three regiments, each regiment contained three squadrons. A squadron had five troops, each with 135 men. The troops consisted of teams of twelve- or thirteen-man sections with three jeeps and an armored car that served as a command and control vehicle. Regiments had a mobile reserve of light tanks for riot control, as well as horses for scouting mountainous terrain and motorcycles for highway patrol. Except for the tanks, the constabulary had no heavy weapons. Rather, they relied on small-caliber rifles and handguns more suitable for police work.

Constabulary soldiers wore a unique uniform consisting of a bright yellow scarf, polished combat boots, and distinct patches, making them easily distinguishable from combat troops. Rather than a combat helmet, soldiers wore a painted helmet liner that prominently displayed the constabulary insignia: a gold disk with a blue border cut by a red lightning bolt. The uniforms were so distinctive that the troops became known as "Circle C Cowboys" and "Potato Bugs."[49] The nicknames were significant, suggesting that civilians could readily identify constabulary troopers from regular soldiers.

The constabulary also received special training. A school was established at Sonthonfen, Germany, where soldiers underwent a special four-week course. Instruction covered geopolitics, police procedures, military tactics, communications, and general military skills such as first aid and map reading. Constabulary troopers were expected to be better trained and disciplined than the average postwar combat soldier.

United States Forces Austria, which commanded its own constabulary troops, implemented the concept even before the War Department had given final approval. On November 28, the 4th Cavalry Group, consisting of the

4th and 24th Cavalry Squadrons, was directed to act as a constabulary force. Later, one troop moved to Vienna. On March 26, 1946, the group was re-designated the 4th Constabulary Regiment and its headquarters was established in Linz. Since the size of the force was limited—about sixteen hundred troopers for all of Austria—operations were focused on specific areas, special missions, and major thoroughfares.

That the constabulary came into being at all was a considerable achievement considering the obstacles the commands faced. There was absolutely no doctrine for its duties. The curriculum in the training school and guidance for the conduct of field operations were developed by trial and error. As force levels plummeted, the constabulary had to recruit and retain the high-quality soldiers needed for the decentralized and often sensitive nature of constabulary duties. The force also had to obtain and maintain its vehicles—no easy task considering the theater's many other logistical priorities. In practice, the constabulary never achieved the hoped-for level of manning, proficiency, or discipline. Nevertheless, it was successfully employed until February 1, 1949, when the regiment was reorganized and its civil policing functions turned over to the Austrians. During its brief history the force proved an effective asset for helping bridge the gap during the difficult months of the occupation after the bulk of the army had redeployed and the police were reestablished. It also proved to be a more appropriate instrument for ensuring public safety while civil conditions returned to a semblance of normalcy.

Taking Stock

From the army's perspective, the occupation had been a clear success, implementing the disease and unrest formula before the first winter set in. Helped in large part by the docile nature of the Austrian people and the passivity of the defeated forces, the army quickly and effectively performed what it believed to be its only appropriate postconflict tasks: demobilizing the enemy and eliminating the physical remnants of Nazi influence.

Other duties, such as military government, were looked on as little more than unavoidable postwar burdens. Initially, the tension between winning the war and occupation duty caused serious problems as combat forces disregarded the comprehensive scheme laid out in Operation Freeborn. As a consequence, their efforts actually worked against the stated objectives of quickly separating Austria and Germany and winning the full cooperation and confidence of the Austrian people. Yet despite initial setbacks, the military responded and adapted. The army's achievement was laudable given the tremendous tasks it faced in disarming enemy forces, caring for displaced persons, establishing order and security, and preventing starvation and the spread of disease. Even more remarkable was that USFA accomplished this feat while redeploying the bulk of its forces.

The command was particularly pleased with its performance and sounded an optimistic note in its first year-end report: "The year 1946 signifies the beginning of many new things—to the Austrians it meant a new birth or renascence [sic] of freedom under the guidance of the four allied powers (France, Great Britain, Russia and the United States). These four nations acting together as an Allied Commission were the teachers and leaders in establishing a new Austria, an Austria independent, economically, politically and socially."[50]

This optimism was short lived, however. Over the next two years, U.S. concerns over the shadow of disease and unrest would be overtaken by even darker fears.

CHAPTER 4

THE LARGEST SINGLE INDUSTRY

Allied commanders often feuded over how to fight World War II. It was a tradition they carried into the peace. No one appreciated the war within the war more than Maj. Gen. Lyman L. "Lem" Lemnitzer. Lemnitzer, who served as General Alexander's deputy chief of staff, had an excellent vantage point from which to observe the situation from all sides. During the course of the Italian campaign he had heard General Clark complain that the British were always trying to steal credit for his battlefield victories. The British, on the other hand, grumbled that Clark was a first-class publicity hound. There were always troublesome issues to be negotiated or angry feelings to be smoothed over.

Postwar operations proved equally contentious. Lemnitzer helped draft plans to deal with Tito's intransigence over Carinthia and Venezia Giulia. He also helped negotiate the resolution of a similar standoff between the American and French armies. When the U.S. Fifth Army encountered French forces moving into a disputed border area near Nice, the French threatened to hold at all cost, and the Americans "wanted to go in and kick hell out of the French."[1] Alexander was able to convince the French to withdraw before hostilities broke out. To Lemnitzer, this was another lesson in how alliances operated. Forging and maintaining coalitions was tough work that required a modicum of trust, willingness to compromise, and an occasional show of stiff determination—that was the army way.

Lem Lemnitzer's preparation for coalition warfare was typical of the military leaders of his generation. After graduating with West Point's class of 1920, he began a twenty-year career of solid, if unremarkable, service. In 1939–40, Lemnitzer attended the Army War College. Among the subjects he studied were alliance operations in World War I, which led to the rise of a popular saying, "if we have to go to war, let's do it without the allies."[2] After graduation, Lemnitzer saw duty in Washington, London, and the Mediterranean, undertaking a series of increasingly important staff positions and earning a quick graduate education in alliance warfare. Throughout those years he found that the U.S. approach to coalition operations, though troubled at times, proved adequate to win the war and establish successful occupations in Italy, Trieste, and Austria. Whether it would prove sufficient to keep the peace over the long term was another question.

Change of Mission

Lemnitzer and his colleagues rarely discussed Clausewitz or his ideas during the debates over the conduct of the occupation. This was hardly surprising since the Prussian thinker had virtually nothing to say about an army's role, let alone the relationship of coalition states, after the battle. Clausewitz's thoughts on the value of intelligence are perhaps an exception because they are as relevant to peace operations as they are to war. He concluded that most reports from the field were contradictory, false, or uncertain. Nevertheless, he lamented, few commanders are sufficiently skeptical. "As a rule," Clausewitz wrote, "most men would rather believe bad news than good, and rather tend to exaggerate the bad."[3] This was a caution in Clausewitz's writings that the army ignored—and with significant consequences, since one tool on which the United States relied heavily to help determine the future course of relations among the Allies was strategic intelligence.

After the war, USFA gathered data on the other occupation forces, Austria, and the surrounding countries. Austria's proximity to Eastern Europe; the constant flow of Soviet deserters, political refugees, former Nazis, and displaced persons; and a vast network of Austrian sources offered a steady stream of information. One State Department official, recalling that there were at least thirty separate ongoing operations, concluded that intelligence collection was the "largest single industry" of Vienna.[4]

At the outset, few anticipated the country would become an invaluable listening post for strategic intelligence. Having prevailed against uncertainties over the conditions inside the country and vague arrangements for the four-power occupation, as well as accomplishing their initial objectives for implementing the disease and unrest formula, U.S. forces expected the mission in Austria to come to a rapid conclusion. The United States had anticipated that its troops could be withdrawn once a treaty formalizing relations between Austria and the occupying powers was signed. The details of the treaty were to be hammered out in a series of postwar conferences between the foreign ministers of the four powers.

Great-power diplomacy proved sorely lacking, however. It was readily apparent after the war that Germany was the key to all of the Allies' plans for the security and political regimes that would govern postwar Europe. Few were surprised when negotiations on a German settlement proved protracted and difficult. In contrast, Austria was of peripheral importance. Nevertheless, the disagreements over the Austrian treaty proved as intractable as the situation in Germany. Years of negotiation failed to yield an agreement.

As relations between Washington and Moscow worsened, USFA played a significant role in initiating an extraordinary transformation. As a result, the occupation force underwent a gradual transition from liberators and occupiers to cold warriors. Standing fast against their former Soviet allies became the military's new mission. The dramatic change in the character of the occupation was propelled in large part by the influence of the military intelligence effort. An endless stream of classified reports reshaped perceptions, providing the evidence to compel jettisoning constabulary duties in favor of more traditional warrior tasks.

The role intelligence traditionally played in the military's planning process made its influence during the occupation thoroughly pervasive. Once a mission had been assigned, the staff's first task was to evaluate the threat. Threat analysis then drove the remaining steps of planning and execution as all effort was directed to the enemy's decisive defeat. Since the wartime planning process remained central to military practices during the occupation, intelligence proved to be another powerful rhythm of habit.

Hunting the Nazi Terror

Intelligence planning for postwar operations began in November, 1944, with the drafting of Operation Freeborn, which called for a wide range of activities including monitoring and censorship of telephones, radio, mail, and newspapers; monitoring border and travel control; the detention, arrest, and interrogation of Nazis; and collecting and analyzing documents. The purpose of these operations dovetailed with the occupation mission to provide for the security of U.S. troops, assist in the dissolution of the Anschluss, and support denazification. Each task, in its way, was designed to support the overall objective: the complete and utter obliteration of Hitlerism. Freeborn's planners even had hopes, which proved fruitless, of coordinating intelligence operations directly with the Soviet occupation forces and went so far as to propose a joint Allied intelligence operations coordination center.[5]

Intelligence collection began immediately after the cessation of hostilities. The small planning staff that developed the security components of Freeborn became the nucleus of the U.S. effort. Advance elements entered Austria shortly after V-E Day with the 6th Army Group. The bulk of the team followed by truck through a snow-covered Brenner Pass in June, 1945.

They began to issue periodic summaries almost immediately after their arrival. When USFA was established, the command issued a series of directives essentially implementing all the intelligence components of Freeborn.[6]

United States Forces Austria had two primary means for collecting information on the Nazi threat. The first was through tactical units. From battalion to field army level, each headquarters had its own separate intelligence staff. Up to regimental level, the staffs were referred to as the S2. At division and higher they were designated G2. Much as in wartime, the S2/G2 staff collected information from combat units and integrated it with data from other sources to provide commanders an assessment of the enemy's strengths, weaknesses, dispositions, and capabilities.

The second intelligence-gathering means employed was field agencies. These units contained interrogators, document analysts, order of battle specialists, and counterintelligence agents. These technical personnel were combined under the Military Intelligence Service (MIS) for administrative and operational control. The MIS formed the backbone of the postwar intelligence network.[7]

In addition to the standard means of intelligence collection, other elements of the occupation force provided information and analysis on political, social, economic, and military activities. The army's Information Services Branch was responsible for managing all media outlets—including radio, newspapers, magazines, and films—and provided occasional analysis of the Austrian civilian and Soviet military press.[8] John Erhardt's office prepared assessments on the domestic scene. Although the political adviser reported independently to Washington, the work of his office and the G2 was coordinated, and State Department intelligence was integrated into USFA summaries. The OSS also maintained a section attached to USFA headquarters.[9] Even General Flory's Civil Affairs Division provided intelligence indicators.[10] The intelligence section also maintained liaison with its Army Air Forces and navy detachments, ministers of the Austrian provisional government, and representative leaders of the major political parties. Staff responsibility for harmonizing collection and analysis fell to the USFA G2, who integrated all the incoming information and incorporated it into command summaries.

During the first few months of the occupation, reports were preoccupied with the Nazi threat. The army had expected some resistance, and the official military government handbook warned that the most likely problems to be encountered were "those arising from the Allies' determination to eliminate Nazism."[11] Although the threats of a National Redoubt and Werwolf attacks proved unfounded, there were tense moments. All of the activities reported by the postwar collection effort, tracking down every hint of

subversive intent and scrupulously reporting each outrageous rumor, reinforced the seriousness of the search. Throughout the summer of 1945, occasional acts of defiance reinvigorated army intelligence's fixation on the
National Socialist danger.

By autumn, overt acts had diminished considerably and there was
clearly an absence of a credible security concern. The remnants of the German Intelligence Service had been thoroughly neutralized, although USFA
concluded that operatives still at large represented "a certain danger as a nucleus of potential recruits for a future [covert intelligence] service."[12] Nevertheless, German espionage did not constitute an active threat. In another
sign of diminished anxiety, USFA also relaxed monitoring of the Austrian-
German border. While the army continued to report any rumors or acts of
Nazi activity, accounts of overt resistance decreased continually through the
remainder of the year.[13]

By 1946, intelligence support focused primarily on supporting the denazification program by conducting background checks and interrogations.
In February, the Allies turned control of the program over to the Austrian
government. A year later, army intelligence specialists concluded that their
participation in denazification was all but complete. Their role became
mostly passive, conducting monitoring programs, preparing special reports,
and compiling statistical analysis.[14]

The Rosy Glow of Russian Hospitality

During the period in which intelligence analysts chronicled the rapid decline
of the Nazi threat, there was no corresponding rise of concern over the activities of the Red Army or the Austrian Communist Party. In fact, initial
reports on conditions in Vienna claimed that the occupation was "shot
through with the rosy glow of Russian hospitality."[15] Intelligence officers
concluded that any accounts of Soviet oppression or lawlessness "should be
treated with caution."[16] On July 31, 1945, analysts described relations with
the Soviets as "very friendly."[17] The U.S. element on the Allied Council,
which began to produce periodic intelligence summaries, included virtually
no information on Soviet forces or indicators of subversive communist activity.[18] The tactical units reported much the same story. One unit noted that
a *KPÖ* group was forming in Salzburg, but that it was "not a security threat
to law and order."[19] In the spring of 1946, intelligence logs and reports from
divisional units identified only one adverse incident with Soviet forces: Russian border troops complained that the Americans did not arrest a woman
who was cursing hysterically at Soviet soldiers from the U.S. side.[20]

However, some army intelligence assets did collect and submit adverse reports on the Soviets and *KPÖ* from the onset of the occupation. Counter-intelligence officer Maj. James Milano revealed that his unit, one of the first to be deployed in the country, began "within a few weeks after their arrival to turn their attention to the potential threat of the Soviet Union" and produced sensitive material highly critical of the Soviet forces.[21] These reports included information from deserters, telephone and radio intercepts, and reports from secret agents. Reports on the Soviet forces and *KPÖ* were also collected by the OSS's successor organization, the Strategic Services Unit (SSU). Despite the fact that these organizations reported to the USFA G2, adverse findings on Soviet occupation troops were not included in official periodic updates. Much of the information on contrary Soviet behavior produced in 1945 was, in fact, dismissed as anti-Soviet propaganda, the acts of individual undisciplined soldiers, or an understandable tendency to treat Austrians more as a defeated enemy than a liberated people.[22] The Soviets might be difficult to get along with, but that often proved the case in alliance relations.

United States Forces Austria's view paralleled the position taken in the Pentagon. In one of its first postwar assessments, the Joint Strategic Survey Committee, a high-level group of officers advising the military chiefs of staff, reported that the United States needed to review its military position "in the light of Russian policy as it has developed in the past year and as it can be forecast on the basis of the recent uncompromising attitude of the Soviet Union."[23] This assessment reflected concern and caution, but it was not the start of the Cold War. When General Lemnitzer joined the committee in November, 1945, he spent more time working on postwar occupation policies for Japan than he did worrying about Soviet intentions in Europe.[24]

Dangers Lurking

By mid-1946, intelligence priorities and USFA's interests in the Soviets began to change. In June, the War Department Military Intelligence Division revised the basic directive that provided guidance for the format and requirements of army intelligence worldwide. The cover letter, signed by Eisenhower, concluded: "The transition from war to peace has necessitated changes in the War Department intelligence requirements. During the war the emphasis was placed, necessarily, on obtaining *military* intelligence concerning our enemies. Intelligence needs have now become all-inclusive, covering every nation in the world with equal emphasis on military, political, economic, sociological, Who's Who and scientific intelligence."[25]

This document foreshadowed a new priority. While the Nazi threat itself had apparently waned, threats to security remained in the form of potential social and economic dislocation that might return Europe to the post–World War I chaotic conditions that had preceded Hitler's rise to power. The task of military intelligence became to search out all forms of these potentially destabilizing dangers.

The shift mirrored conditions in Austria, where reconstruction of a fully functioning civil society was barely under way. Bits of normal life had begun to return. On October 6, 1946, Vienna held its first postwar fair. Weeks later, a touring exhibition of Austrian art opened in Zurich. But these cultural achievements were overshadowed by the persistence of harsh postwar conditions. The Austrians also held a secret national council in October, 1946, to discuss the deteriorating economic conditions, the strains of occupation, and the troublesome burden of transients and refugees. By the following winter, the government was issuing public appeals to bolster morale as shortages of fuel and food left much of the population suffering deprivation and depression.

Austrian fears reflected the larger trend toward instability throughout Europe and growing uncertainty over future threats. On February 22, 1946, George Kennan sent his famous eight-thousand-word "Long Telegram" arguing that Soviet behavior proceeded from an assumption of permanent hostility against capitalist powers. A week later, Churchill delivered his renowned "Iron Curtain" speech in Fulton, Missouri. In May, a communist-led civil uprising broke out in Greece. Warnings of an emerging Soviet threat and concerns over how much the unsettled conditions in Europe were driven by Soviet designs became subjects of great debate. The only conclusion the Washington defense establishment could agree upon was that circumstances in Europe were troubling and bore watching.

Detailing these and other potentially volatile conditions and warning signs, army intelligence responded with a mass of information on all aspects of life in occupied Austria. United States Forces Austria prepared extensive reports on social, religious, and economic affairs, including the problems of displaced persons, youth groups, education, management-labor relations, coal production, food supplies, and black market activities.[26]

Accounts of Soviet activities were mixed into this collage of reports. The army detailed Soviet efforts to help rebuild their economy by exploiting Austrian industry, oil reserves, and agriculture. United States Forces Austria also looked beyond Austria's borders. The MIS reported that "during 1946 another primary mission was added to provide positive intelligence of the Soviet Union, Soviet-occupied countries, Soviet satellites, and other information as required by the War Department."[27] To help manage these tasks, the MIS was reorganized into internal and external security sections. The internal unit focused on conditions in Austria, while the external unit gathered information on neighboring countries and the Soviet Union.

Although demands were increasing, the resources for analyzing intelligence information declined. As a result of demobilization, within six months after operations began, all units were chronically understrength. The army, anticipating that occupation duties would be terminated by 1947, further accelerated the drawdown. Meanwhile, the OSS, which had two hundred personnel in 1945, was replaced by the SSU with a severely reduced cadre. The SSU section in Austria was later reorganized under the Central Intelligence Group (CIG), which had only thirty-seven personnel by April, 1946.

Manpower shortfalls threatened the quality of intelligence gathering. Personnel were initially trained at the Military Intelligence Center at Camp Ritchie, Maryland. During the war, however, training was found to be "inadequate to prepare intelligence specialists to enter upon their work in the European Theater of Operations."[28] Another study complained about the shortage of trained and experienced intelligence officers and also concluded that the army needed "better personnel, better training, and better coordination on all levels."[29] In the course of the war, intelligence support improved with in-theater training and practical experience, but postwar demobilization sent many skilled analysts home and replacements lacked the veteran's expertise and seasoning.

Austrians and Intelligence

Taking stock of Renner's government proved an especially unique challenge. Collecting political intelligence was a process with which the Army had scant experience. Here, USFA came to rely heavily on a few gifted and energetic men. One of the most noteworthy was Martin Herz. Herz was no stranger to the country. As a young boy, he and his family left the United States in 1922 to live in Austria. After receiving his primary and secondary school education in Vienna, Herz returned to America in 1936. Drafted in 1941, he served in SHAEF's psychological warfare section, where he authored many of the propaganda leaflets dropped over Germany. Herz also became adept at interviewing Austrian deserters and prisoners of war, trying to gauge the depth of support for Hilter.

In May, 1945, Herz was posted to what would become USFA's political division. During the Flory mission, he was one of the first Americans to meet with the Soviet liberators of Vienna and officials from the fledgling Austrian government. Demobilized in 1945, he joined the diplomatic service, returning as a civilian employee at the Legation in 1946. He remained there until 1948.

Working closely with army intelligence, Herz became a specialist in political analysis and an expert on both the Austrian government and Soviet occupation policies. Having no formal background or training in collecting political intelligence, he developed his skills on the job. Nevertheless, Herz's reports were widely sought. Although it is impossible to measure the full extent of their influence, it is known that they were widely circulated in Vienna and Washington. Some became required reading at USFA headquarters.

Herz's primary sources of information were his contacts within Austrian political circles. Local officials proved all too eager to share their views on current affairs. Molden and Shärf retained their close ties with the Americans, as did many others including *SPÖ* leader Alfred Migsch. Born in 1901, Migsch quickly rose to prominence in postwar politics. A member of the Second Republic's parliament since its inception, he was considered an *SPÖ* intellectual, among the party's top ten leaders, and, Herz reported, a "coming man" among the country's fledgling political leadership. His energetic support of denazification during the first years of the occupation made him a particularly attractive contact.

In 1947, Migsch replaced Karl Altmann, the only remaining *KPÖ* minister, who had resigned when the communists formally withdrew from the coalition government. In his new position, Migsch proved to be a strong advocate for continuing good bipartite relations between the *SPÖ* and *ÖVP*, a view that also pleased USFA officials. As an influential political insider, Migsch was more than willing to share his assessments with USFA. In May, 1947, for example, Herz reported on an evening's conversation at his quarters in Vienna with Migsch and two other prominent socialists. Herz asked them about the views of some *ÖVP* leaders who had argued for a treaty at any price that would get the troops out and leave the Austrians free to work on undercutting the Soviets' political and economic influence.

Migsch agreed. He believed the Soviets were only in Austria for economic gain. Within their zone the Soviets had assumed control of several industrial enterprises and organized them under the *Sowjetische Mineralölverwaltung* (Soviet Mineral Oil Administration, *SMA*) and *Uprawlenije Sowjetskowo Imushtschestwa w Awstrii* (Administration of Soviet Property in Austria, *USIA*). Migsch maintained that the government could make Soviet-controlled enterprises unprofitable and they would then quit the country in disgust. Herz doubted Migsch's idea would work, but he dutifully reported it in a memorandum to Erhardt, who tossed the information into a sea of other indicators.

An Insatiable Appetite

Herz, who coordinated his reporting with army personnel, admitted in retrospect that overreliance on the Austrians probably undercut the balance and objectivity of what was being sent back to Washington. It did, however, help satisfy an insatiable appetite.[30] Meeting the government's tremendous demands for relevant insights placed additional stress on an overworked and underresourced intelligence network. Requirements saddled the system with the Herculean task of accumulating vast amounts of information at a time when there were fewer and fewer qualified people to process the data. The Intelligence Branch of the Office of the Director of Intelligence concluded: "With present personnel strength it is a physical impossibility to attempt to thoroughly examine, analyze and report all information of intelligence value coming into the Branch, and due to present and probable future personnel shortages, much material will die in the files for lack of time to exploit and report this information properly."[31] The workload was truly daunting. An information report produced in October, 1947, claimed to have in seven days summarized 858,887 letters, 27,365 telephone calls, and ten thousand censorship intercept reports collected over a two-week period.[32]

Analysts often failed to use or only superficially analyzed the data collected. Information was passed along as raw anecdotal and unfiltered intelligence that could be selectively employed or taken out of context. Analysts realized that misleading and incorrect information could easily be confused with positive, verifiable intelligence. One report admitted "just how fertile a breeding ground for rumors is present day Austria."[33] It was not unusual for intelligence reports to contain a mélange of rumor, opinion, and unsubstantiated stories along with verified sources and statistical data. With the limited number of personnel available, there was little USFA could do other than gather, interpret, and pass along information as best it could.

While information on the diverse global threats to stability and security poured in, the Truman administration, reflecting on the shortcomings of fighting World War II, proposed legislation to strengthen the mechanisms for managing national defense. The National Security Act of 1947 created a number of new organizations. Among them were the Joint Chiefs of Staff (JCS), the Department of Defense (DOD), the Central Intelligence Agency (CIA, which replaced the CIG), and the National Security Council (NSC). As the Cold War between the United States and the Soviet Union crystallized, however, these institutions were being debated, developed, and organized. As a result, critical strategic assessments made during these crucial years still relied heavily on clumsy instruments such as the intelligence network in Austria.

Red Alert

While Washington was still gearing up its new national security apparatus, priorities again shifted from a concern over many threats to focusing almost exclusively on Soviet intentions. The newly established Department of the Army (formerly the War Department) began to issue worldwide alerts on the international communist threat. The preface of one such announcement stated that these reports were "intended to aid commanders by providing this type of information on a broad scope so that incidents occurring within your command may be viewed from their standpoint of greater significance."[34] The imperative became increasing watchfulness of the growing Soviet menace.

Stalin fueled the Americans' concerns by promoting policies that were far from transparent. During the difficult period 1946–49, the enigmatic and often hostile mask of Soviet Austrian policy was Gen. Vladimir V. Kurasov, Stalin's representative to the Allied Council. At forty-nine, Kurasov did not have the heroic reputation of Tolbukhin or Konev. During the Great Patriotic War he earned an excellent reputation as a chief of staff. In 1945, he was appointed chief of administration in the Soviet Group of Forces, East Germany, then deputy commander in chief of the Central Group of Forces, and, finally, commander in chief of the Central Group of Forces.

Kurasov's task was not to make foreign policy but rather to carry out directives from Moscow. Many leaders were unclear whether their purpose was to simply protect Soviet interests or intentionally provoke the West. Not Kurasov. In 1947, he relieved three federal police chiefs in the Soviet zone because they reportedly had not done enough to purge fascist influences. Austrian ministers complained to Kurasov. Getting no satisfactory reply they protested to the other representatives on the Allied Council that the Soviet action presaged an attempt to completely take over. Other actions proved equally antagonistic. Kurasov refused to account for the continuing rash of unexplained kidnappings in the Soviet zone. At the same time, he was adamant over demands for reparations claims against German assets in Austria, a contentious issue that had persistently stymied state treaty negotiations. Kurasov's complaints of slights against the Soviet occupation forces by Austrians and the other Allied powers were frequent and invective. When the feisty Migsch delivered a speech critical of the communists and administration in the Soviet zone, Kurasov protested to Chancellor Leopold Figl about the "inadmissible and aggressive slander of the Soviet people" and warned he might have to prevent such things in the future.[35] These encounters served only to fuel the West's growing uneasiness over Stalin's interests in Austria.

In response, efforts to collect Soviet-related intelligence accelerated. In 1947, USFA established an intelligence section whose primary function was "to collate, evaluate and interpret all information received pertaining to the Soviet Army."[36] The MIS was tasked not only with providing data on issues related to Austria, but also on matters of strategic interest, including information about Soviet atomic programs and potential industrial targets inside the Soviet Union.

That autumn, responding to the joint chiefs' apprehensions over Western Europe's stability and State Department concerns about European economic conditions, the intelligence section prepared a report on activities in the country. The analysis concluded that the Soviet occupation forces' influence was "sufficient to deliver Austria into Soviet hands within six months."[37] This estimate was one of USFA's first overt warnings, moving the Soviets to the front of the pantheon of social, political, and economic obstacles to postwar reconstruction.

In February, 1948, the high commissioner's monthly report for the first time singled out Soviet behavior as the root cause for the failure to successfully conclude the state treaty. In addition, reports began to focus on the KPÖ, the Soviet Union, and other Iron Curtain countries as potential military threats. In March, 1948, USFA intelligence estimates concluded that although Soviet occupation forces admittedly were understrength, they were "battle worthy and are capable of and psychologically prepared for offensive military action."[38] Other reports highlighted armed confrontations between U.S. and Soviet military personnel, the kidnapping and coercion of Austrian civilians, reports by Russian deserters of impending attacks, and subversive activities by the Austrian Communist Party.[39] The preponderance of intelligence suggested that the Soviets had emerged as dangerous and aggressive agitators determined to extend their hegemony over Austria and threatening Italy and Germany as well.

In turn, USFA's findings generated further caution in determining the future of the occupation. Charles Ginsburg, a member of the U.S. delegation at the 1947 Council of Foreign Ministers, concluded—based in part on intelligence reports of activities in Austria—that the Soviet Union's presence represented a serious threat and made negotiating the state treaty problematic.[40] Future dealings over Austrian affairs had to be tempered with greater vigilance.

Hitler Revisited

During this period, army intelligence reports also showed an upswing in reporting on potential Nazi activity, in particular reflecting concerns about a rise in anti-Semitic incidents and the impending formation of a right-wing political party. The renewed interest in denazification had very little to do with what had once been the army's core mission. Extremist activity was now a matter of concern because of its potential impact on the nature of the

Soviet threat. Despite Kurasov's frequent antifascist rhetoric, USFA feared communists might be secretly recruiting former National Socialists. Military intelligence officers launched a full investigation into the matter.[41] Alternatively, USFA believed the Soviets were using any signs of right-wing activism as an excuse to criticize Western occupation forces and the Austrian government for encouraging anticommunist sympathies. Soviet harangues were launched with an eye toward destabilizing the country and creating conditions for a coup or perhaps direct intervention. Finally, USFA was also concerned that the right-wing movement might threaten the current corporatist arrangement in the Austrian government, making the country even more vulnerable to Soviet penetration.

The command adjusted policies accordingly. Scaling back on denazification programs in the judiciary and transferring legal authority for most cases from the military courts to the Austrians was seen as one way to enhance the status of the Austrian government and draw it closer to the United States.[42] United States Forces Austria wanted to appear firmly anti-Nazi on the surface, while actually placing as little pressure as possible on the Austrian government. At the same time, intelligence specialists and agents were fervently collecting information on right-wing activity to prevent exploitation of the situation by the Soviet menace.

Concerns over the threat of domination from the Kremlin dovetailed with thinking in Washington. Lemnitzer observed the changing perceptions of America's former ally from Washington, first as a member of the Joint Strategic Survey Committee at the Pentagon, then as deputy commandant of the National War College at Fort McNair. In addition to the newspaper headlines on confrontations with the Soviets in Austria and other countries, he was privy to the flow of increasingly concerned intelligence reports, all of which suggested that the Soviet Union had crossed over from being a recalcitrant partner to a dangerous opponent.

In the summer of 1948, Lemnitzer was dispatched to London on a top-secret mission that drew heavily on his now considerable experience in coalition operations and European affairs. He participated in a series of clandestine meetings with the military committee of the signatories to the Brussels Treaty which, signed on March 17, established the West European Union. His mission was to determine what assistance its members would require to defend against a Soviet invasion. Although the United States was not a member of the treaty group, Lemnitzer was there to demonstrate U.S. concern and revive the wartime spirit of coalition partnership. These efforts and the changing perception of the Soviet role in Austria would have a dramatic impact on how USFA viewed its mission in the years ahead.

Fallacy and Fear

Over the course of four years, the Soviets went from representing no threat, to being *a* threat, to being *the* threat. What is most remarkable is that while USFA's assessments changed radically from 1945–48, this transformation had very little to do with the intelligence on hand. A detailed review of the command's reports demonstrates conclusively that the United States did not have the evidence to accurately gauge changes in Soviet behavior. Rather, USFA reinterpreted available evidence to meet current requirements.

Indeed, the character of raw intelligence information collected during these years changed little. Throughout this period, the command received reports on border incidents, KPÖ activity, the kidnapping of Austrian citizens, military training and maneuvers, and economic penetration of the economy. However, reports that were ignored or explained away in 1945, were mentioned in 1946, and highlighted as the root of all troubles by 1948.

From the outset, there is little doubt that senior commanders knew full well about the scope of Soviet misconduct. General Clark described Soviet behavior during this period as "Russians running around killing, looting, stealing, raping."[43] At the time, however, these incidents were interpreted as unfortunate shortcomings, misunderstandings, or minor irritants. The difficulties were part of the challenge of working with multinational forces; they were no more ominous than the problems frequently experienced in working with the French. Soviet activities were not portrayed as symptomatic of any real security threat to the United States.

By mid-1947, U.S. forces began to highlight the kinds of Soviet and communist behavior that had been all but ignored in the previous years of the occupation. In addition, not only were similar kinds of activities being cited as indicators of a growing danger, but previous acts were resurrected and reinterpreted as threats as well. One military report cited disputes over food distribution, disagreements over denazification, Tito's postwar invasion of Carinthia, disruption of transit to Vienna, and disagreements over reparations, to portray a pattern of Soviet action consistent with attempting to exert hegemony over the country. Past intelligence was used to confirm a deliberate, aggressive strategy in Austria dating back to the earliest days of the occupation.[44] In the end, it was the identification of the Soviet Union as a threat that provided mission focus and clarified for USFA's analysts the ambiguities in Soviet behavior.

Increasing tensions between East and West, fueled by several dramatic regional developments, provided further impetus to view events in Austria as part of an orchestrated campaign of Soviet hostility. On Europe's periphery, Soviet and U.S. interests clashed in Greece, Turkey, and Iran. In 1947,

communist agitation rocked France and Italy. The following year, communists overthrew the government of Czechoslovakia and Stalin ordered a par-
tial and then total blockade of Germany's capital, Berlin. In every direction,
USFA saw visible signs of Soviet aggression and assumed it was all part of a
concerted plan that included expanding the Soviet sphere of influence over
both Germany and Austria.

The Search for Secrets

The utility of USFA's effort in determining the intent behind Kurasov's rail-
ings and the activities of his troops is questionable. The most recently revealed high-level Soviet policy documents contradict USFA's intelligence
analysis and suggest that while Stalin sought to consolidate Soviet hegemony
over the European heartland and intended to bargain hard with the Western powers, he did not contemplate overt aggression against his wartime Allies.[45] This handful of documents will certainly not be the last word in un-
covering the history of Soviet intentions. It may be some time before a
sufficiently full accounting of Soviet activities is available to match up side-
by-side with USFA's intelligence analyses, and thus be able to fully gauge the
accuracy of the command's assessments. Nevertheless, while historians
await a fuller understanding of the Soviet position, definitive conclusions
can be drawn on the character of the U.S. military effort. United States
Forces Austria did not provide unbiased and critical analysis. Following the
rhythm of habits, the command generated intelligence based on the *identified* threat. In turn, USFA's reporting method justified concerns over Soviet
intentions with a tendency to reinforce existing preconceptions.

Meanwhile, the rapid postwar decline in the quality of military intelligence capabilities at the same time the demands for information and the volume of reports collected were dramatically increasing seriously exacerbated
the problem. True, much intelligence, particularly information about Austrian domestic politics, was helpful and put to good use. However, in the
larger context of U.S.-Soviet relations at the outbreak of the Cold War, the
worth of USFA's effort is debatable.

A further difficulty was that this questionable intelligence also under-
mined the military's traditional approach to coalition operations. American
military leaders knew that the Allies could be difficult, but they always extended a modicum of trust that served as a basis for negotiation and cooperation. In this case, however, adverse intelligence assessments destroyed
any confidence that they had in working with their Soviet counterparts.

Making matters worse, both sides maintained the fiction of cooperation
through occupation machinery that was designed for allies who possessed a

American, British, French, and Soviet military police patrol, Vienna, October 2, 1945.
Courtesy National Archives.

degree of trust and confidence in one another. The Allied Council had few institutional mechanisms to ensure transparency, such as the joint police patrols in Vienna. Once suspicions grew to unmanageable proportions there was no means to rebuild a productive relationship or resolve ambiguities and uncertainties, nothing to break the accelerating cycle of mistrust and confrontation.

In the period following this breakdown of Allied relations, army intelligence played a significantly less important role in shaping perceptions. As the Cold War intensified, the United States shifted to other means that could penetrate behind the Iron Curtain. Initially, signal intelligence assumed greater importance in collecting information. By 1948, U.S. intelligence operatives were intercepting and reading classified communications from no less than thirty-nine countries.[46] Meanwhile, with the establishment of the CIA, that agency gradually assumed primary responsibility for collecting human intelligence, providing national strategic assessments, and conducting covert operations. The United States also began to rely more heavily on aerial reconnaissance and overflights of the Soviet Union. Increasingly national

Guarding USFA Headquarters, 1945. Courtesy National Archives.

means of strategic and technical intelligence were more valued than the observations, rumors, and interrogations collected in Vienna.

While Austria's value as a strategic listening post declined, the impact of intelligence operations on the future course of the occupation would prove long lasting. Commanders armed with a fully documented and acknowledged Soviet threat, and foreseeing the prospect of a new European military alliance supported by the United States, could now make an argument for rethinking USFA's purpose, turning the occupation into a real military mission.

CHAPTER 5

ON-THE-JOB TRAINING

Brigadier General Thomas F. Hickey had a warrior's heart. Born in Massachusetts in 1898, he enlisted in the army in 1916, and later received a lieutenant's commission. Hickey fought in savage battles during the Saint-Mihiel and Meuse-Argonne campaigns for which he received a Purple Heart after being wounded in action. During World War II, Hickey headed to the Pacific in command of the X Corps Artillery. He later served as corps chief of staff in the Leyte campaign, and then commanded the 31st Infantry Division Artillery.

Following V-J Day, General Hickey was briefly reassigned to a stateside post before being sent overseas in 1946 to replace Alfred Gruenther as USFA's chief of staff. It was a position he would hold for almost four years. Before Austria, his career was a long list of schools, conventional military assignments, and combat. The one thing missing from his résumé, aside from two years of occupation duty in the Rhineland as a lieutenant after World War I, was any background in foreign affairs or military government.

Hickey's limited experience with occupation matters actually made him a comfortable match for Mark Clark's replacement, Lt. Gen. Geoffrey Keyes. Hickey and Keyes represented a generation of leaders least experienced in civil-military affairs. In quieter times this lack of experience might have mattered little. As the Cold War intensified, however, these men found themselves at the point of the spear.

Strange Friends

A rapidly deteriorating postwar coalition was not the army's only obstacle to providing effective administration. Occupation duties also required commanders to cooperate with a wide range of federal, international, and nongovernmental agencies in addressing the complex tasks of reconstruction. As American concerns rose, the pressure to harness all the instruments available to speed European recovery increased commensurately. This was no small challenge in Austria's case because the United States had not yet developed a long-term strategy. Lacking an overarching strategic framework to guide their actions, and with no practices, doctrine, or educational institutions to develop their cooperative skills, occupation officials were forced to learn how to integrate the military and civilian efforts on the job.

Since the army had little practice in operating with other agencies, this particular rhythm of habit did not bode well for the future. Working with the UNRRA was an unqualified disaster. The newly established civilian agency was neither properly organized nor equipped for the mission of caring for 1.5 million refugees and displaced persons. Even UNRRA officials admitted there were serious problems and that a "thorough house cleaning" was required.[1] United States Forces Austria personnel had little patience for the civilian organization's ineffectual first efforts. One official complained that the UNRRA set back the country's recovery by six months. Nor was the UNRRA the only agency that had difficulty working with the army. "The military authorities," an investigative report concluded, "have shown considerable resistance to the entrance of voluntary agency representatives, no matter how qualified they might be."[2]

On the other hand, the two most important players, the army and the State Department, initially appeared to function together quite well, following wartime precedents with the army in the lead and State supporting. Much of the credit belonged to the tireless efforts of John Erhardt. Erhardt had far more experience in the issues surrounding the occupation than the senior military leaders for whom he worked. A career foreign service officer with much experience in European affairs, he had served as consul general in Hamburg from 1933–37. Erhardt had also worked extensively with the State Department's Postwar Programs Committee.

By all accounts, Erhardt, Clark, and their people functioned well together. In fact, Clark, who was merciless in his treatment of USFA's military staff, readily accepted his political adviser's suggestions and opinions. Eleanor Lansing Dulles, an economic analyst in the legation, recalled that for the most part Erhardt "handled Mark Clark quite well. Once in while he would say 'Mark Clark you are kind of an idiot you know, you shouldn't do that,' but by and large he went along with Mark Clark."[3] Another official called Austria a "model of military and civilian cooperation."[4]

Despite the reputation for close collaboration and the fact that the State Department had no objection to Clark being followed by another military commissioner, his departure in May, 1947, revealed symptoms of a rift. Clark's farewell speech included a strong and unambiguous statement of

American military government officials receiving a complaint, 1945. Courtesy National Archives.

support for Austria. The State Department complained that the pronouncement had not been properly cleared with Washington. Moreover, the general's remarks suggested an unrestricted, unending commitment to the country, while in fact, the United States had not settled on its future course in the treaty negotiations.[5]

Responsibility for implementing whatever long-term strategy did evolve fell to Clark's successor. If any figure comes to mind in association with the occupation it is the tall, flamboyant Mark Clark. Time would prove, however, that Keyes, not Clark, was without question the single most influential individual shaping U.S. policy toward Austria.

In many respects, Keyes was typical of the senior leaders the army produced during this period: unlikely candidates to assume key political-military roles in postwar Europe. Born in Fort Bayard, New Mexico, and educated at West Point, Keyes had been posted outside the United States only three times. He participated in the punitive expedition into Mexico in 1916, served in the Panama Canal Zone from 1927–30, and attended the École Supérieur de Guerre in Paris in 1933.

Like Hickey, Keyes was a fighter. He attended the Army War College in

The first meeting of the Allied Council, September 11, 1945. Pictured *(left to right)* are Maj. Gen. Alfred Gruenther, Gen. Mark Clark, and John Erhardt. Courtesy National Archives.

1937, then, after a Washington assignment, reported to the newly formed 2d Armored division at Fort Benning, Georgia, where he served under George Patton. An early pioneer in the Armored Force, Keyes briefly commanded the 9th Armored Division from June–September, 1942. Promoted to major general, he again served under Patton in North Africa and Sicily as deputy I Armored Corps commander. Keyes later led the U.S. II Corps in Italy. After breaking through the Gothic Line, his corps was attached to the British Eighth Army and remained astride the Yugoslav border until the end of the war. In July, 1945, the headquarters moved to Salzburg where it was inactivated. Keyes remained in Europe, however, and commanded the U.S. Seventh, and later Third, Armies.

The general's expertise in political-military affairs was largely confined to his wartime service: negotiating an armistice with French commanders in North Africa, facing off against Tito's troops, and dealing with the initial occupation of Germany. Keyes's greatest asset was that he gained the complete trust and confidence of senior military leaders under whom he served, including Marshall, Patton, Bradley, Eisenhower, and Clark. With the exception of Marshall, these men were all Keyes's contemporaries, and each considered him an intelligent, competent, courageous, and dependable man.

Lieutenant General Sir Richard McCreery *(center)* at the Allied Council, December 7, 1945.
Courtesy National Archives.

Before being assigned to Austria, Eisenhower briefly considered appointing
him to head the Military Advisory Group in China.

Keyes was part of the second generation of occupation commanders.
The first—Clark, Eisenhower, and MacArthur—had been chosen for the
prestige and authority they brought to the task. In contrast, Keyes represented a new cohort: deserving fellow officers who, though they would
probably never be elevated to four-star rank, deserved to be retained, promoted, and rewarded with a high-profile caretaker job. Thus, while many
of his contemporaries were being shunted off into retirement, Keyes pinned
on a third star.

As for the trials of occupation duty, Keyes's minimal on-the-job training in political-military affairs would have to suffice. Austria was not meant
to be a difficult assignment. Although relations with the Soviets had been
contentious, at the time Keyes assumed command many officials believed
the approval of a state treaty was imminent, despite Moscow's intransigence.
The gathering of foreign ministers in Moscow in March, 1947, had failed to
produce an agreement, but there was still hope that progress might be made
at the next conference scheduled for November. In the end, Keyes might

Lieutenant Generals Geoffrey Keyes *(left)* and Albert Wedemeyer reviewing troops from 350th Infantry Regiment, July 4, 1948. Courtesy National Archives.

prove to be nothing more than a temporary commander responsible for the final withdrawal of U.S. troops.

At the Crossroads

Absent a treaty, however, there still were significant issues at hand. Occupation policy was at a crossroads. The Austrian government wanted the United States to begin troop withdrawals even in the absence of an approved settlement, arguing that withdrawal would give them greater flexibility in dealing with the Soviets over the contentious issues delaying final treaty negotiations. The legation wanted to consider the proposal, but Keyes rejected the idea outright. He especially resented the fact that State Department representatives had contradicted him. Their approach, Hickey reported, is "to support the political advisor's theory that the High Commissioner is just a figurehead." The political adviser, he complained, had fallen for the Austrian line that the whole idea was "get the Army out and things will be easy in Austria."[6]

Keyes was convinced that the Soviets intended to use Austria as a springboard for further incursions into Western Europe. His mistrust of the

Russians was well known. Suspecting a communist-inspired attempt to embarrass him the first day on the job, he had ordered extra security measures. Keyes soon found himself in the midst of a general strike that led to an unprecedented fourteen days of riots in his first month of command, leaving the general believing that the communists had planned a putsch and deeply suspicious that the Soviets were behind it all.[7]

The general's frustration was heightened by Washington's failure to provide overarching guidance for the occupation. Military planning, so fundamental in the army's approach to fulfilling its responsibilities, required clear, decisive, and obtainable objectives, and objectives were derived from the ends, ways, and means prescribed by strategy and national policy. However, other than the Moscow Declaration, whose main objective, the destruction of Hitler's regime, had, in fact, already been achieved, the United States lacked a coherent, comprehensive statement of how it intended to deal with Austria. Lieutenant General Albert C. Wedemeyer, the army's deputy chief of staff for operations, summed up the military's dissatisfaction in a meeting of the Committee on National Security Organization on September 10, 1948: "Our position of world leadership today makes the necessity for firm policy on our part even more pronounced than in the past. There is a serious dearth of national policy now, although the military services and the State Department are getting much closer together than they have been. The military services are not asking to determine national policy but only to be told what it is so that they may more effectively support it."[8] With respect to Austria, Keyes's assessment was even more critical. He considered army–State Department cooperation a complete failure and the lack of strategic guidance crippling.

Austria, Keyes believed with all his heart, was a key piece in an emerging geostrategic confrontation between East and West. Although the country had never figured prominently in strategic planning either during or after the war, Keyes believed it would be the linchpin for holding back communism. For this, he could draw liberally on the voluminous intelligence reports being generated by the USFA staff. Completing the state treaty was a secondary concern. Austria should not be free until it could resist Soviet influence. Hickey summed up his commander's position this way: "It must not be overlooked from the political standpoint that anti-Communist forces are not necessarily strengthened by the sovereign state of Austria."[9] Keyes concluded that U.S. forces should remain until four conditions were met: a plan to ensure economic independence was in place; an Austrian security force had been created to insure the country's territorial and political integrity; the state treaty was completed; and it was agreed all occupation forces would be simultaneously and expeditiously withdrawn. He proposed a two-tracked approach involving a combination of economic assistance and military aid to accomplish these goals.[10]

Keyes envisioned an economic scheme that would piggyback off the newly announced Marshall Plan. Shortly after his appointment as secretary of state, on June 5, 1947, Marshall announced in a speech at Harvard University the creation of what would become the European Recovery Program. Keyes argued that the initiative could be used to ensure Austrian independence and fight off Soviet influence.[11] In October, he formally proposed a neutralization plan for Austria, an economic assistance package that would neutralize Soviet economic and political penetration of the Austrian economy. His plan, first proposed by Eleanor Lansing Dulles, a member of Erhardt's staff, included specific objectives far over and above the provisions of the European Recovery Program. Keyes wanted funds for industrialization and other investments to jump-start the Austrian economy. Rather than simply being used to strengthen the Western democracies, the general envisioned the program as a weapon for rolling back Soviet power. The neutralization plan called for undermining the viability of Soviet-controlled industries, strangling them by reducing their access to rolling stock, energy, and raw materials, and boycotting products. Keyes warned that without this virtual declaration of economic warfare, the country would easily succumb to Soviet economic domination after the withdrawal of American troops.

The general also believed that physical protection was equally important. Thanks to demobilization and denazification Austria had no military capability. The presence of U.S., British, and French forces was the only obstacle blocking more aggressive Soviet action. Keyes feared what the British called the "gap period," the time after the approval of the state treaty between when the occupation forces withdrew and the country set up its own defense forces. As the 1947 riots demonstrated, a government without the benefit of armed troops would be at Moscow's mercy. However, in arguing for maintaining troops in Austria, Keyes had to balance his desires with the stark realities of U.S. demobilization and the apprehensions of the Austrian government. After the rapid drawdown following World War II, occupation duties strained the army's few resources and manpower. Keyes had only one combat regiment at his disposal. Still, while even these limited forces were becoming tiresome to the Austrians, the general rejected the notion that any troops could be safely withdrawn.

As confrontations with the Soviets exacerbated poor relations between the superpowers, Keyes's confrontational approach seemed to dovetail well with America's emerging policy of containment, a gradually growing commitment to block any expansion of communist power. In addition to clashes

over Greece, Iran, Turkey, and Germany, the United States and the Soviet
Union became engaged in quasi-economic combat. The Soviets refused to
participate in the Economic Recovery Program, and Stalin tightened his control over the Eastern bloc, preventing local governments in the Soviet occupation zones in Germany and other East European countries from considering the American offer of economic aid. Meanwhile, Keyes continued to
pepper Washington with assessments demonstrating how conditions in Austria fit clearly into the overall Soviet threat to Europe and required a determined a response. United States Forces Austria had identified four thousand
agents in the Western zones working to expand Soviet influence. There was
a legal, well-organized, and disciplined Communist Party, 150,000 strong
and responsible, Keyes believed, directly to the Kremlin.[12] Not only did the
USFA commander paint a troubled future for Austria, he also passionately
held that the country represented an important strategic asset that should
not be readily given up. Keyes stressed the benefits of continued occupation
in the event of hostilities, not only as an extension of the defense of Germany, but also for its own positional advantages.

Advocacy for more aggressive measures received a considerable boost
in February, 1948, on a damp, cold Saturday morning in Prague as snow
dusted the statue of Jan Huss in the old town square. Despite the inhos-
pitable weather, people gathered around the statue—first a few, then a rush,
a mob screaming for the government ministers to step down. By Monday,
February 23, rough men wearing blue workers' jackets and red armbands
had surrounded the U.S. embassy, and it was clear by midweek that Pres.
Edvard Benes's government was in trouble. Forced to accept the resignation
of his ministers and their replacement by members of the Communist Party,
Benes effectively ceded all control of the government. The communists
called it *Vitezny unor* (Victorious February). In the West, they called it a
coup.

To Keyes, the putsch in Czechoslovakia and the establishment of a Soviet client regime demonstrated that Stalin could not be trusted. Molotov's
wrangling over the state treaty was only buying time until the communists
figured out how to take over completely.[13] When the Allies prepared to resume negotiations later that year, Keyes was a forceful voice. Even Erhardt,
in the wake of the Czechoslovakian affair, supported him. Parroting Keyes,
he concluded that there seemed little to recommend giving up the position
the United States held without a firm guarantee for Austria's security.[14]
Keyes's ideas gained additional support when the State Department asked
the Joint Chiefs of Staff to review the situation. The JCS, in a report released
only a month after the Czech coup, did little more than rubberstamp Keyes's
position.[15]

Troopers of the 4th Constabulary Regiment near Linz, November 23, 1948. Courtesy National Archives.

From the Kremlin's Window

What is remarkable is that Keyes's views held such authority when he had no special knowledge of what was happening on the other side of what Churchill had dubbed the Iron Curtain in his Fulton, Missouri, speech. Behind this dividing line between East and West was not a unified block, but a seething political landscape held in check largely by the presence of a handful of strong-arm regimes, Soviet forces, and Stalin's direction—a volatile mix that would be difficult to predict under the best of circumstances. One man who knew this well was a figure as close to Stalin as anyone: Georgi Maximilanovch Malenkov. Born in 1902, he was too young to take part in the Revolution, but he served in the Red Army during the civil war—as a political commissar, not a line officer. He joined Stalin's entourage in the 1920s. Malenkov was tough, intelligent, and ambitious. He played a prominent role during World War II, though not in uniform. Malenkov slipped into obscurity immediately after the war, but in 1948—following the suspicious death of his chief rival, Andrei Zhdanov—he became Stalin's heir apparent. At forty-six, he was twelve years Molotov's junior and relatively young among the senior leadership.

American intelligence agencies viewed Malenkov as largely a man of mystery. He never traveled to Europe or America, and he had few official contacts with Western leaders. He was known to have two habits: sleeping and working. The CIA studied his speeches and writings with a passion, searching for any insights into the Soviet decision-making process. Malenkov, by many accounts, advocated ameliorating the Cold War confrontation by withdrawing some troops from Eastern Europe and diverting more economic energy from defense to domestic production. It was even suspected that he was interested in improving quadripartite relations in Austria. Western intelligence largely dismissed his calls for peaceful coexistence as merely repeating "standard formulas." But they could only guess.

There was little opportunity to test the veracity of Malenkov's views. Although he was the second most powerful man in the Soviet Union, Stalin kept a close watch over issues regarding the country's socialist neighbors and the occupied zones, and ministers who poked their noses in these affairs without Stalin's blessing risked his wrath. It was the premier who ultimately guided Kurasov's hand. But the intent behind that policy, Stalin's personal views of the role the country was to play in his scheme for a Soviet European security zone, is still not fully understood. The Soviet leader was far less transparent to Keyes, who saw events only through the imperfect lens of U.S. intelligence and his contentious association with Kurasov on the Allied Council.

Stalin and other Soviet leaders did share one core belief: a conviction that the inherent contradictions of Western capitalism would lead to its own downfall. The alliance between the United States and the Europeans, with Great Britain in particular, would not last. Petty squabbling over their self-interests would doom any common effort. Yet the cohesion in the West, although shaken by postwar hardships and East-West confrontation, appeared persistent. Meanwhile, Stalin was having problems consolidating the support of the socialist states within in his own ranks, which was dramatically revealed by the situation in Czechoslovakia, and, as Malenkov's return to power demonstrated, within the leadership of the Kremlin as well. Such concerns did not bode well for a quick resolution of the Austrian question. On the other hand, there was little evidence that these troubles suggested a determined wave of Soviet expansionism, although Keyes passionately believed this to be so.

Friendly Fire

Despite his apparent policy successes, Keyes continued to be frustrated. Disappointed by the Americans' lack of knowledge and interest in Austrian affairs, he wrote to the army staff, pleading for government officials to make more favorable references to the country in their public speeches. In response, Wedemeyer wrote the State Department and asked for help in bringing attention to the Austrian government's "gallant fight against Communism."[16] Keyes in turn complained to Erhardt: "Congressional committees stay here two or three days, and from the 'Stars and Stripes,' anyhow, sometimes give the impression that they are permanently domiciled in Berlin."[17] When Keyes demanded that the State Department stress Austria's importance to Congress, Erhardt responded that State was fully aware of the country's importance. Keyes doubted it.

The general also grumbled that his command was being treated as the poor stepchild of the German occupation. General Lucius D. Clay, the high commissioner for Germany, denied any serious disagreements with Keyes, although documentation reveals they had differences on trade issues, command relationships, and even the need for occupation forces in Austria.[18] In truth, Clay gave the country scant attention. He was far more concerned by his rapidly deteriorating relations with Soviet occupation authorities in Berlin. In 1947, the United States, Great Britain, and later France agreed to merge their occupation areas in Germany into a single western zone—a move Stalin bitterly opposed. As tensions escalated, Clay committed his main effort to ensuring the viability of an independent West German state.[19]

Keyes could not abide that his concerns merited so little attention. Clay failed to appreciate the uniqueness of the Austrian situation and had fixated on the German question to the detriment of USFA's operations. Keyes pushed to elevate his command's status. He tried to persuade army leaders in Washington to lobby the Joint Chiefs of Staff for permission to sever all the ties that subordinated him to Clay. "A clean break is the sole solution," he wrote Wedemeyer, "No one in Germany is responsible for the success or failure of my mission here so why should they be given any authority over the means at my disposal to carry out that mission?" Wedemeyer responded that no one questioned Austria's strategic importance, but that the principle of unity of effort dictated that U.S. operations in Europe not be fragmented into separate commands. Keyes wrote back that he would play the good soldier and not "buck" the decision, but the USFA commander clearly chafed under his lack of independence.[20] He refused to let this be the last word and raised the issue at every opportunity. The Pentagon eventually yielded.

In addition to his running battle with the military government in Germany, Keyes had continuing clashes over the administration of European Recovery Program. In addition to arguing that the Marshall Plan did not provide economic aid for his neutralization scheme, he also disapproved of its management. The general wanted the Economic Cooperation Authority (ECA) mission in Paris that administered aid to work through his office. Keyes's proposal was ignored, and not long after the ECA began operations, trouble started. The army became obstructionist, Erhardt reported, creating a "tempest in a teapot" with the ECA management team. On October 20, 1948, he added conclusively, "the honeymoon is over."[21] Flabbergasted, Erhardt proposed that if Keyes would not cooperate with the ECA, the State Department should take over the high commissioner's post. The Marshall Plan, he believed, should not be under the army anyway. The program needed to be set up so that authority could be progressively turned over to the Austrian government. "As I have explained to Keyes," he declared, "our policy is, if I understand it rightly, to let the Austrian Government have more and more authority and to progressively diminish the authority of the Army. Under that formula, whether the Army likes it or not, the authority of the Legation would also progressively increase."[22]

Erhardt was pleased to see Keyes shut out of decision making on the implementation of the Marshall Plan. Not only was the general's request that the ECA be made subordinate to the high commissioner rejected, support for his economic plan also floundered in Washington. The JCS referred the plan to the State-Army-Navy–Air Force Coordinating Committee as a priority project. A subcommittee convened a working group from the newly created Department of the Army and the State Department to study the proposal. The State Department, however, worried that any additional investment in Austria might complicate the challenge of getting the Soviets to agree on a state treaty. In addition, State wanted to focus resources on where it thought they would do the most good, preferring to keep the priority of the U.S. effort on the key Allies and economic powerhouses: Germany, France, and Britain. On April 30, 1948, State succeeded in having the neutralization plan removed from the committee's agenda, effectively killing the proposal.[23] As long as the State Department held preeminence in setting the agenda for foreign aid, there was little prospect that Keyes's proposal would ever be implemented. Events subsequently proved that U.S. investments made under the Marshall Plan proved sufficient to help create a viable Austrian economy.[24]

Although Keyes's economic initiatives went nowhere, his plans for an Austrian security force made some progress. He had the Pentagon's full backing on this matter. "General agreement exists," the JCS informed the president, " that the most urgent problem involved in the conclusion of the treaty is the creation of an Austrian army capable of maintaining internal order during the period immediately following the withdrawal of the occupation forces and pending the expansion of the army to the full strength authorized by the treaty."[25] Unlike economic aid, the Pentagon had preeminent influence on traditional military issues. With the full support of the military brass, Keyes could count on security matters remaining center stage.

Among Giants

For their part, the Austrians continued to push vigorously for an end to the occupation. They too were often at odds with Keyes, who insisted that USFA's utility had to be measured in terms of Western political and strategic gains. He told the JCS that U.S. troops were essential and there was "no obligation or need to make excuses for or further justify an occupation which is the mildest in history." Keyes feared some might be swayed by Austrian public opinion. "Having strongly rejected a policy of appeasement toward the Russians," he warned, "we are now tending to adopt a policy of appeasement toward the Austrians at the expense of our national aims in the struggle for world peace when no appeasement is called for."[26]

Keyes dreaded manipulation by Austrian politicians as much as penetration by the Soviets. In particular, he complained that Foreign Minister Karl Gruber was pushing too hard for troop withdrawals. Keyes had little use for the minister's activist foreign policy. Gruber was the quintessential young man in a hurry. Appointed to a major cabinet post at thirty-six, he lacked both the age and experience of the rest of Renner's cabinet. Born to an Innsbruck working family in 1909, Gruber was raised in the social democrat tradition, though when he moved to Vienna to finish his law studies the future ÖVP statesman took a decided turn toward conservative politics. Near the end of the war, he emerged as an underground leader. Gruber's pedigree as a resistance fighter assisted in his appointment as *Landeshauptsmann* for Tirol during the opening days of the occupation. Through his sound administration and command of English he developed excellent relations with U.S. and British commanders.

Gruber's tenure in the Foreign Office proved remarkable. He maintained a strong anticommunist orientation from the outset, and quickly built close ties with the Americans. Like many Austrian public figures, he was happy to confidentially share his views with USFA. Gruber's secret memorandums were laced with warnings about the growing Soviet danger to Austria. At the same time, the minister worked tirelessly to create an Austrian identity and presence in the international community. All of these efforts were part of a concerted plan to give the nation a role in determining its own destiny, and they exploited the advantages of a small country whose future was of material interest to the great powers. One way or another, Gruber's goal was to get the occupation powers out, while keeping the country free, democratic, and unified. The Germans had opted for Western integration at the expense of national unity. It was a trade Gruber was unwilling to consider.

In the end, the minister helped create a momentum he could not control. As far as Keyes was concerned, Austria's Western orientation, rather than giving cause to move boldly forward in negotiating the removal of occupation forces, suggested that the country could be a valuable foothold that should not readily be abandoned. Gruber, Keyes concluded, was "playing both ends against the middle . . . a dangerous approach in dealing with the welfare of a country."[27] Austria could not be a friend of the West and at the same time ignore its responsibilities for the defense of Europe.

Keyes fully recognized that there were limits in his dealings with Gruber and other Austrian officials. Too much pressure might undermine the governing coalition, which had to balance pulls from the right and the left. While Gruber's conservative *ÖVP* fretted over the impending formation of a far-right-wing political party, the liberal *SPÖ* had its share of troubles. Erwin Scharf, a prominent spokesman for the party's extreme left wing, continually railed against *ÖVP* and Gruber's blatantly pro-American politics. Scharf's tirades against the country's bipartisan foreign policy were a constant source of irritation. He also complained about the party's failure to support increasing workers' rights and wages, as well as its reluctance to show a more cooperative attitude toward the Soviet authorities.[28] Scharf's politics were a subject of concern at USFA headquarters, but Keyes could at

Army Secretary Kenneth Royall meets with Austrian officials *(front to rear)* Oskar Helmer, Leopold Figl, and Georg Zimmermann, December 23, 1948. Courtesy National Archives.

least be thankful that the party leadership was staunchly anticommunist. He was not displeased when Scharf was expelled from *SPÖ* in 1948. Still, the sharp anti-American rhetoric was a reminder that the government's pro-Western stance came at some political cost.

While Keyes continued his battles with Austrian officials, the military government in Germany, and the ECA, his relations with the State Department worsened considerably. The fact that the defense establishment, as a result of the passage of the National Security Act, was in a period of transition did not help. The old interdepartmental committees that had been used to coordinate policies were being abolished. Field commands like USFA now referred their concerns to the military service assigned oversight responsibility. The army was the executive agent for the occupation forces in Austria. In turn, the army chief of staff carried relevant issues to the JCS, where, as long as the army's point of view did not infringe on another service's prerogatives, it normally carried the day. Under this system, the secretary of defense and the JCS chairman had little authority in influencing corporate decisions. Even if the secretary and chairman had the authority to influence strategy, they had little staff or administrative support to conduct policy analysis. For high-level issues, serious coordination with the State Department did not begin until an agenda item reached the newly established National Security Council—where State faced a formidable task when its opinions diverged from a consensus viewpoint offered by the JCS on matters related to national security.

Dean Acheson's reflections on the process were damning: "The Secretary of Defense is so weak that he cannot expose himself to a really equal debate with his colleagues, because he is not on a basis of equality with them . . . he has no control over his department. . . . no independent staff or capability."[29] Working with the JCS was no better, he complained: "The Joint Chiefs can't discuss anything till they have coordinated a staff paper and once they have a coordinated a staff paper, they deliberate, and when the Joint Chiefs sign a paper, at that point you have reached a situation where discussion is almost impossible because the Joint Chiefs have spoken, and it is like the Pope. The Pope has spoken, and they are infallible and you can't go back on this thing. You can't discuss this matter with the Pope before he has spoken, because the Pope isn't a person: it is a colloquium, and no member of the colloquium can speak for any member at all, so you have infinite discussions with all their representatives."[30] In the end, he argued, issues went into the National Security Council and were presented to the president before the departments had thoroughly hashed out a problem.

Marshall's appointment as secretary of state, Acheson felt, improved matters somewhat. The former army chief of staff insisted on thorough coordination, and he commanded enormous respect in the Pentagon. Still, it was a constant struggle. Acheson's own tenure as secretary of state was marked by not a few controversies with the senior military leadership.

Austria offered a case in point. Acheson could never convince the chiefs that Keyes was wrong and that negotiating the state treaty should come first. The general understood this well and used the system to his advantage. Unlike his neutralization plan and economic policy, in matters of military concern, once he won the backing of senior army leaders they carried his case to the JCS. In turn, the JCS position usually won out in the NSC. Following this process, Keyes's policy recommendations were codified in NSC-38/1 on June 16, 1949. The chiefs intended the document to replace NSC-38 (the council's previous decision paper on Austrian policy), which they believed had not given adequate weight to defense issues. The new proposal tightly linked progress on security issues to approval of the state treaty, calling for guarantees that Austrian defense forces would be ready when the occupation troops withdrew.[31] It was a clear victory for Keyes.

An Unbearably Bright Light

Keyes's apparent triumph over the striped-pants types in Washington was punctuated by events in a remote corner of Kazakhstan that added a new sense of immediacy to his arguments. In the early morning hours of August 29, 1949, Levrentii Pavlovich Beria rose for what he hoped would be one of the most eventful days in the history of the Soviet Empire. Beria had spent a cold, windy night in a small cabin near the command post where he planned to supervise a momentous scientific experiment. Ten kilometers away, the Soviet's first atomic weapon sat on a small tower. After the Americans bombed Hiroshima in August, 1945, Stalin had appointed Beria as head of the Special Committee on the Atomic Bomb. These new weapons, Stalin believed, had the potential to upset the balance of power, giving the Americans an undue advantage that they would surely exploit in shaping the postwar settlement. This could not be permitted. Stalin wanted the bomb.

Ruthless and driven, Beria created a Soviet version of the Manhattan Project. Having held powerful positions in both the state and the party, few men were more feared or grudgingly respected for their ability to organize and galvanize the Soviet system. Even though Klaus Fuchs, a physicist who worked for the British and the Americans, had provided a description of one of the bomb designs, Soviet scientists still faced immense technical challenges. In addition, Beria had to create an entire atomic industry to produce the necessary materials and manufacture the bomb. This effort came to fruition on a dull, windy August morning as an unbearably bright light blossomed from the top of the test tower.

The Soviet achievement stunned American intelligence analysts. A CIA report issued on September 20, more than two weeks after a white fireball and mushroom cloud had engulfed the Kazakhstan steppes, concluded that the most likely date for the first Soviet test would be mid-1953. Suddenly, America's atomic monopoly had vanished. For Keyes and many other army generals, the Soviet achievement had changed the calculus of war. They interpreted the atomic test not as an attempt to balance American power, but as a new and troubling threat. If the Soviets held an equalizer for U.S. atomic weapons, both sides might hold back on using the bomb. That made the prospects of a conventional war even more likely and the importance of a strong forward position in Europe more critical than ever.

Despite the growing concerns over Soviet power, the State Department refused to accept the Pentagon's endorsement of NSC-38/1 and its effort to hijack America's Austrian policy. Acheson counterattacked. He penned a letter calling for the withdrawal of NSC-38/1. The military's approach, he argued, was the old case of putting the cart before the horse. Once the treaty was negotiated, the JCS would be consulted about security provisions before the treaty went into effect. Until then, the State Department should not be constrained by preconditions for negotiation. Acheson's letter failed to persuade the council to remove NSC-38/1 from the agenda. Instead, his response was simply labeled NSC-38/2 and added for the president's consideration.

In October, Acheson confronted Defense Secretary Louis Johnson. Although Acheson considered Johnson a "terrible character" and the two often disagreed, on this occasion the defense secretary conceded that the treaty should be concluded. Nevertheless, he felt compelled to offer the president the *military view* as expressed by the JCS. That same day, the two met with Truman to resolve the issue. Making his case without the joint chiefs present, Acheson swayed Truman in his favor and State received the go-ahead to enter into serious negotiations.[32] This victory mattered little. In November, the Soviets again refused to conclude a treaty. In the absence of a settlement, Keyes's approach achieved a de facto triumph and set the tone for U.S. policies through the remainder of the occupation.

Meanwhile, relations between the State Department and the military were as contentious on the Danube as they were on the Potomac. Erhardt and his staff had constant run-ins with Keyes and his single-minded chief of staff, Hickey. The only general Erhardt respected was USFA's Brig. Gen. Jesmond Balmer. He was the one officer effective at maintaining quadripartite relations in the Allied Council. In 1949, when it came time for Balmer to rotate, Erhardt complained, but Keyes chose not to interfere with the transfer. Erhardt relented. Balmer was ready to move on, and Erhardt did not have the heart to stand in his way.[33]

The Balmer incident was reflective of a larger confrontation: the State Department's campaign to displace Keyes. In 1947, the department had drafted a proposal to turn the high commissioner position over to a civilian, but then decided to wait until a resolution of the state treaty negotiations before making its case. Francis Williamson of the Central European Division wrote Erhardt, reminding him that if relations with Keyes became too bad, "we will take the memorandum out and wave it under the noses of selected people in the Department of the Army."[34] Before the treaty negotiations in 1949 collapsed, State decided try again. Acheson saw the move as part of the effort to kill the idea that policy should ever be driven by a "purely military view."[35]

The Pentagon reaction to State's initiative was equivocal. When first approached, the JCS had offered no objection. Likewise, Keyes raised no specific complaint, but instead renewed his overall concern with policy, arguing that it was overly focused on appeasing Austrian desires at the expense of national security interests. Keyes continued to believe that the real problem was the State Department's tendency to go soft on the Austrians. When the treaty negotiations completely collapsed, he vigorously renewed his attack. Now that the treaty seemed to be a dead-letter issue, Keyes declared, "It is essential that we have singleness of purpose, united effort and unified control."[36] The State Department and the army were pulling at cross-purposes. The general complained that Erhardt was supposed to work through him, but "he feels he is justified in withholding or acting upon, certain matters, thus limiting or restricting his value to the High Commissioner in his capacity as political advisor." Solving the problem by curtailing the high commissioner's authority would only worsen the problem. "The success of the West in holding the line in Austria these past five years should invite grave study," Keyes declared, before a decision was made to change the current command relationship. Rather than replace him with a civilian, the general believed his position should be strengthened and the army's policy of "firmness and benevolence" endorsed. Keyes believed that a choice had to be made: "My only desire is for the matter to be settled on a cold and factual basis free from personalities and inter-departmental jealousies. I have absolutely no interest in a personal row with either Erhardt or his organization. I do hope in the solution, the factor of National Defense is given its rightful weight."[37] The answer, he concluded, was to leave the generals in charge.

Winds of War

Although he continued to win the war over policy, Keyes lost the battle for command. On May 5, 1950, the NSC agreed to the State Department's request to shift all commissioner responsibilities to civilian authority. This motion carried, in part, because the other Allies also agreed to replace their military commissioners, a decision confirmed when the Council of Foreign Ministers convened in London on May 8. General J. Lawton Collins, the army chief of staff, wrote to Keyes explaining the conditions for his relief and that Hickey would also be moved out. Keyes wrote back, requesting that the transfer be delayed until autumn.[38]

Half a world away, on June 25, 1950, North Korean communist forces swept across the 38th Parallel and invaded South Korea. President Truman rushed backed to the White House from his home in Independence, Missouri, and immediately ordered U.S. troops in Japan to respond. At the Pentagon, the normally unflappable Lem Lemnitzer tried to explain to a quaking secretary of defense how the United States could have been caught so off-guard.

On July 5, troops from the 1st Battalion, 34th Infantry Regiment reached Pyongtaek in the dark before dawn. One soldier proclaimed, "As soon as those North Koreans see an American uniform over here, they'll run like hell." Lieutenant Herman Driskell, leading a group of seventeen men, established a roadblock north of the town. It would be his first test in combat. Up the hill, his sergeant was eating a can of beans and watching when their flank was swept by a mass of charging enemy soldiers and a wave of mortar fire. Driskell asked the noncom what they should do. "Well Sir, I don't know what you're going to do, but I'd like to get the hell out of here." America's first hot war of the Cold War was under way, and it looked like it would be a long, hard fight.

While the USFA commander glanced fretfully toward Asia, another wave of riots struck the Austrian capital during September and October. Spearheaded by communist labor activists, the Austrians feared another putsch attempt. After weeks of public disturbances, Keyes was gratified that the government endured the crisis without the intervention of occupation troops. On the other hand, events, particularly in light of the situation in Korea, made him more confident than ever that he had been right all along. Real danger existed, and without force Keyes doubted Austria could resist the threat of communism. On October 12, 1950, as the streets returned to normal, President Truman transferred the high commissioner's authority to the State Department. Keyes promptly retired.

Clausewitz Turned Upside Down

William Stearman, who served in the political directorate of the Allied Council, recently wrote, "the idea that the Pentagon dominated our Austrian policy is clear balderdash."[39] Kennan's remembrances of the period offer a similar conclusion. Their observations fail on one important point, however. While the army did not *dictate* policy, it certainly contributed to the *making* of policy in fundamental and important ways. United States Forces Austria provided the intelligence and threat assessments on which the policy was based, and the high commissioner championed his own policy recommendations while actively engaging with Austrian officials and representatives of the other occupation powers.

Keyes had succeeded in putting his stamp on the conduct of the occupation, and his legacy reflected both the strengths and weaknesses of the army's contribution. Geoffrey Keyes was a man of determination and conviction, serving in a critical, sensitive overseas post at a time of transition and turmoil in U.S. foreign policy. It is not surprising that a military commander played an important role in such an environment. What is disturbing is that in the policy vacuum of the early Cold War years, strategy in Austria appeared to emerge from below rather than emanate from above.

In normal times, following the long-held tradition of civilian supremacy over the military, the army would have eschewed attempting to play a role in making foreign policy. However, given Europe's uncertain postconflict conditions and the transitional character of the national security decision-making process, wartime habits proved far stronger. The army of occupation needed an identified threat, a clear strategy, and a decisive plan. Keyes, supported by Hickey, his loyal and equally aggressive chief of staff, provided them. But Keyes's strategy was the product of a singular viewpoint shaped by the training and traditions of military service. All the critical mechanisms for harmonizing civil-military affairs and extracting the best capabilities of each were lacking. The failure to provide coherent strategic guidance at the outset added ambiguity and confrontation to the already difficult tasks of meeting the challenges of the postwar world.

Keyes's conviction that the occupation merited commitments and strategies on a par with, and in some cases exceeding, those applied to the German question was an example of how a field commander's perspective could yield a skewed and totally unrealistic assessment of national priorities. From the outset of his appointment, Keyes never acknowledged that his role did not compare strategically to that of his northern counterpart. The consequences of the decision to merge the U.S., British, and French zones in Germany were profound. A united West Germany had the resources and, with American support, the potential to rapidly reestablish itself as a formidable, independent European power. No prospect was more abhorrent to the Soviet Union, and by 1948 Germany's future had become the most important and contentious issue dividing U.S. and Soviet interests in Europe. Strategically, Austria's value was meager in comparison, and USFA could not expect a commensurate commitment of America's national power in support of its operations.

Ironically, the fact that USFA was not the central sticking point for U.S. foreign policy provided Keyes a tremendous degree of autonomy. General Douglas MacArthur is often singled out as having unprecedented power and independence in shaping the course of the first years of the occupation of Japan, but in comparison to other commanders his power seems less remarkable. Germany was the exception to the rule. As the high-profile military mission overseas, it received constant scrutiny and direction from Washington. The German occupation, true to the Clausewitzian canon, was an extension of policy. Other commanders had greater freedom, at least through the initial postwar years. No one worked harder to exploit this authority than Keyes, who used his position to push for radical changes in Austrian policy. Keyes's views triumphed because he moved quickly and forcefully to fill a policy vacuum at a time when the apparatus used to develop and implement national security policy was in transition. There were few second thoughts as the United States proceeded to implement his plan for the militarization of Austria.

CHAPTER 6

FROM OCCUPIERS TO WARRIORS

At 5:30 P.M. on September 19, 1950, Gen. Mark Wayne Clark returned to Salzburg. He was a man with a mission. As chief of the Army Field Forces, his responsibilities included training and equipping troops in the United States, as well as inspecting the readiness of overseas commands. The Korean War had given new importance to his assignment. A counterattack employing the last of the U.S. strategic ground force reserve had taken place at the port of Inchon outside the capital of Seoul only days before his arrival. It was still unclear if the bold maneuver, an amphibious landing far behind enemy lines, would prove successful. There were other dangers as well. The United States was not only concerned about the fighting in Asia. The JCS remained fearful that the Soviets would use the war as a diversion, a precursor to aggression in Western Europe.

Clark was no stranger to the dangers of war. Born to a military family stationed in New York, Clark had followed his father into the service. Commissioned as an infantry officer after graduating from West Point in 1917, he joined the American Expeditionary Force in France. He saw only a little action before being wounded early in the summer of 1918 while leading a company of the 11th Infantry Regiment in the Vosges Mountains. Clark passed-up an opportunity to serve with the occupation forces in order to seek a *real* command assignment elsewhere. During the interwar years he gained a reputation as a demanding and energetic leader. Both Marshall and Eisenhower thought highly of him, and Clark went on to become the most well known, and perhaps most controversial, combat leader in the Mediterranean—a man destined for continued high-level leadership positions after the war.

His wartime record and postwar career made Clark a prominent public figure. After his experiences in Austria, Clark became a rabid anticommunist, preaching frequently about the need to meet force with force wherever American and Soviet interests clashed. His tour of USFA would give him an opportunity to see how his old command was standing up to this new challenge.

Transformation

A wave of defense, political, social, economic, and racial issues attended the command's transition from occupiers to warriors. The response to these challenges further fueled the momentum for militarizing the occupation, tested the Americans' relationship with the Austrians, and sharpened the confrontation with the Soviet Union.

Initially, U.S. forces had scant means and little incentive to improve their military preparedness. As a result of the rapid demobilization, troop readiness plummeted drastically. United States Forces Austria was chronically short of people, turnover was constant, and there were limited opportunities and resources for conducting combat training. Nevertheless, the occupation forces proved more than adequate to deal with the security aspects of implementing the disease and unrest formula. There were no official threats meriting an armed response.

In the wake of the Czech coup, Keyes began a concerted effort to restructure USFA into a combat command. He ordered the troops put through an expanded regimen of training. In 1949, he disbanded the constabulary force and reformed it into conventional combat units. All of the combat forces were grouped under the Tactical Command, which was headed by a brigadier general, and directed to conduct winter and mountain warfare exercises. Tactical Command also conducted joint training with British, French, and U.S. troops in Germany, although these contingents had little to offer.[1] There were only a handful of divisions in Germany. The British had seventy-five hundred troops in Austria, including three thousand combat soldiers organized into four infantry battalions. These troops were so involved in occupation duties that they had no opportunity for military training. The French had sixty-nine hundred soldiers grouped into battalions of infantry, five troops of mechanized cavalry, and two companies of engineers. They had conducted some training, but were prepared only to defend key terrain in their zone.[2]

Pass in Review

As for the Americans, when Clark arrived he saw how dramatically things had changed since his departure. The Keyes-Erhardt war had flared and subsided. Keyes was preparing to leave, and Erhardt had been appointed ambassador to South Africa. Meanwhile, Walter Donnelly, a career diplomat whose greatest expertise was in Latin American affairs, was slated to take over as the first U.S. civilian high commissioner for Austria, and Lt. Gen. Leroy Stafford Irwin had been tapped to succeed Keyes as the USFA commander.

Irwin, by training and experience, was more of the Keyes mold. Born in 1898 and graduating from West Point in 1915, he, like Keyes, served in the Punitive Expedition in Mexico. Missing out on combat after being assigned as an instructor during World War I, Irwin went on to command the 5th Infantry Division in World War II. Unlike Keyes, Irwin would enjoy good relations with his State Department counterpart. Confrontations subsided in part because personalities were changing, but also because with negligible progress on the treaty, the State Department could offer little objection to sharpening military preparedness.

United States Forces Austria's transformation impressed Clark. His inspection team rated the quality of training as excellent. On the other hand, despite the progress and positive developments, several areas of concern remained. The command lacked many essentials that prevented it from acting realistically in the manner of a true fighting force. The most serious shortfall was a lack of people. A moratorium on personnel transfers as a result of the Korean War temporarily abated the problem of rapid personnel turnover, but the command still suffered from significant manpower shortages. United States Forces Austria was short a hundred officers and a thousand sergeants.

Equipment was another problem. The command had no gear for mountain operations and no field hospital. Most vehicles were rickety holdovers from the European campaign. The command lacked long-distance radio communications to cover the wide frontages envisioned in the war plans. The troops had no antitank weapons. All these shortfalls would prove significant if U.S. forces were called upon to conduct a fighting withdrawal in the face of superior Soviet forces.

Even worse, the command had no air support and no contingency plans for employing air cover. The troops had not even conducted training in air-ground operations. War plans envisioned that the U.S. Sixth Fleet would provide air support, but the fleet had not been formally tasked. Even if the navy had been assigned the mission, it would have been impossible to execute. The ground troops had no tactical air support control parties, teams that had the equipment and expertise to coordinate air attacks. Nor did the fleet have aerial reconnaissance assets, an air warning system, tactical air defense, navigational aids, or air-to-ground radios. Making matters even more anxious, neither the French nor the British occupation troops had any planes.[3] This was deadly serious. A withdrawal under pressure, without air

Lieutenant General Leroy Irwin *(left)* meets with French officials during Operation Mule Train, a joint U.S.-France training exercise, September 11, 1951. Courtesy National Archives.

attacks to slow the enemy or protect friendly troops from enemy planes, would have been a desperate venture.

The logistical situation was also a nightmare. Most personnel shortages were in support units. Supply and maintenance operations relied heavily on civilian employees. They were dependable in peacetime, but they could not be counted on in war. Also troublesome was the fact that the supply line ran through Germany. United States Forces Austria assumed this would be quickly cut by a Soviet offensive. Wartime maneuvers would require a different route. Before leaving Italy, occupation troops established the infrastructure for a wartime supply line that could be reoccupied in the event of an emergency. This alternative proved less than ideal, running from the port of Leghorn, Italy, through Verona and the Brenner Pass to the Camp Drum storage depot at Innsbruck, and then to the troops in Salzburg—a torturous, mountainous route of over three hundred miles. For the most part, supply points were exposed, highly vulnerable to attack, and not well positioned to support the tactical movement of combat troops to either link up with forces in Germany or fall back toward the Italian border.[4]

Over the next three years, as USFA pushed for a more prominent role in the defense of Europe, the state of forces continued to improve. Army Field

Forces command inspections noted steady progress. The United States opened negotiations with the Italians to make USFA's new supply line functional. The 7617th Support Command set up port operations in Leghorn, and the whole route became operational in 1951. By 1952, critical depots had been relocated and for the most part the supply lines matched the planned routes for operations. A year later, combat stocks were reported to be in relatively good shape. The command had a sixty-day level of prepositioned ammunition in the hands of combat units and more was stored along the Innsbruck–Brenner Pass–Po Valley line. The depot at Leghorn included ammunition reserves for both USFA and forces in Trieste.[5]

Other shortfalls suggested there was still a long way to go, however. Limitations were significant and there is serious doubt that any military effort would have actually succeeded. Air support was a case in point. United States Forces Austria eventually worked out some of the most pressing problems by organizing its own air support platoon to provide air-ground coordination with radios borrowed from the navy, and entering into local training agreements with the Twelfth Air Force and Sixth Fleet. Still, air-ground support was woefully inadequate. Peacetime arrangements with other commands could not be counted on in wartime, and reliable air-ground support and aerial photoreconnaissance for the command was never considered adequate.[6]

Nevertheless, despite the army's limited resources, ground operations showed steady improvement. In 1951, the command conducted Exercise Rebound, a joint training maneuver with troops from 351st Infantry Regiment in Trieste, and Operation Mule Train, a joint training exercise with French troops. In November, 1952, Exercise Frosty employed USFA's 350th Infantry Regiment to defend mountain passes. Two hundred soldiers received mountain warfare training at Camp Carson, Colorado, before deploying to USFA. The command also set up its own mountain training school and sent soldiers to a French military alpine school. The regiment then organized special mountain warfare platoons made up of the most physically fit men who had received the additional training. These units were armed with light weapons and minimal equipment so they could more easily negotiate the key terrain dominating likely invasion routes.[7]

When Brig. Gen. Paul Freeman was appointed commander of Tactical Command, he found it well prepared to execute wartime operations. "We had a secret mission which was to protect the right flank or the Southern flank of the Seventh Army [Germany] and we had battlefield positions extending from Degensburg [Regensburg?], I believe it was, in Germany all the way down to Salz-Kammergut," he recalled. "We were to hold those mountain passes and delay into Italy."[8] United States Forces Austria was ready for

American troops dressed as the "enemy" during Exercise Frosty. Courtesy National Archives.

war. Over a span of five years the command had been remade from an occupying army into a small but credible combat force.

Soldiers and Civilians

The transformation from occupiers to warriors did not go unobserved. The increased emphasis on readiness did not escape the notice of the civilian Austrian press, though USFA did not anticipate its activities would cause much concern. After the first harrowing years of dealing with every form of privation from food and housing shortages to violent crime and rioting, conditions seemed to improve, thus allaying the most serious fears. Commanders were content with the state of cooperation. Official Austrian sources were equally positive. Local police provided periodic reports on the state of local security and public safety, and up to 1950 they generally suggested that collaboration with American occupation forces was satisfactory.[9]

The outbreak of the Korean War, followed by a violent wave of strikes fanned by the KPÖ that lasted from late September to mid-October, dramatically changed the Austrians' thoughts of the future. Before Korea there had been vegetables and meat in stores. There was coal to burn. Men had gone back to work. The outbreak of war changed everything, drying up

American and French troops conducting joint training in the Austrian Alps, September 7, 1951. Courtesy National Archives.

supplies of raw materials and fueling inflation. Fear of being caught in a battle between GIs and Russians swelled.

On February 10, 1951, Donnelly wrote, "Feeling here is that pressure for treaty and withdrawal has noticeably eased since Korea."[10] The presence of U.S. troops, Donnelly argued, was reassuring to the man on the street. The Austrians knew they had not been abandoned. But in truth, Donnelly's assessment did not grasp the depth of unease in the nation. Complaints and fears about the occupation were persistent and endemic in the period following the tumultuous summer and autumn events of 1950.

Even Donnelly acknowledged that one of the major issues preventing harmonious relations was the cost of the occupation. The Allies had agreed from the outset that the Austrians should house their troops and pay the cost of maintaining the occupation forces. The burden was one the Austrian government did not bear silently. In 1947, the United States, responding to Austrian complaints, assumed its own occupation costs. Donnelly contended that if the British and French joined the Americans they could further distinguish their efforts from those of the Soviets. But the British and French, facing fierce pressure to control defense spending, wanted to raise Austrian payments. The British believed that increased occupation costs would not be intolerable for Austria and would still be smaller than the amount other Western countries were devoting to defense.[11] The best of all possible worlds, they argued, would be to figure out how to raise expenses while camouflaging the increases to make the public expenditures appear lower than those going to the Soviets. They dithered over the issue for the next two years, losing any potential propaganda advantage when the Soviets dropped the demand for occupation payments months before the cash-strapped British and French ended the practice. What is more, Donnelly's assessment was disingenuous. Rather than representing the only problem, the issue of occupation costs was a reflection of the growing friction between occupiers and occupied. The United States, of course, came in for its fair share of criticism.

The 1952 Austrian film *1 April 2000*, directed by Wolfgang Liebeneiner, was a stinging reminder of how Austrians viewed the Americans. While the revival of the film industry was a sign of returning normalcy, the subject of this movie was telling. The setting is nearly half a century in the future. After 2,859 unsuccessful negotiating sessions, the four Allies—portrayed as doddering, white-bearded old men—still preside over the occupation. A frustrated Austrian president declares the nation's independence, only to have the "World Union" proclaim it is a menace to global peace. Austria gets a brief reprieve when the union fires its secret weapon at Australia by mistake. While koala bears cower, a delegation is dispatched to Vienna, where the president is put on trial by the world government.

Although billed as a musical comedy and science fiction epic complete with dancing and spaceships, the picture's antioccupation sentiment is thinly disguised. The United States appears just as much at fault for Austria's troubles and as oblivious to the people's sentiments as the other occupying powers. For their part, the Austrians are a happy, singing, pastoral people. The streets of Vienna are pristine, swept clean of wartime destruction. Every scene is bright and sun-filled, far removed from the dark, shadowy images of Orson Welles in *The Third Man*. In Liebeneiner's film, Austria is a country that does not deserve to be occupied.

Jim Crow

The tension between Austrians and Americans was nowhere more apparent than over the issue of race. In the summer of 1952, a local newspaper reported that two black soldiers had attacked three Swedish tourists. An editorial in the *Salzburger Nachrichten* declared: "We abstain from describing what would happen for instance in the Southern states of the USA to such colored rowdies. But we have a good right to demand that the guardians of our liberty protect at least our foreign guests. When the U.S. Army cannot forego using Negro soldiers, and said Negro soldiers are unable to give up their Congo-mentality, the uniformed highwaymen should not be let loose anywhere. . . . Our foreign guests come to Salzburg in good faith but not to find new Africa here!"[12] Donnelly and Irwin complained bitterly about such reporting, but sensational racial comments continued to pop up in the Austrian papers. The *Salzburger Volksblatt* published an open letter complaining about the behavior of U.S. troops. The communist paper *Der Abend* protested that American occupation forces treated Austrian civilian employees like "Negroes" with low pay and unfair labor laws.

On July 25, Donnelly met with a group of Salzburg newspapermen in an attempt to stem the wave of critical articles spotlighting incidents involving black soldiers. One editor suggested the troops' behavior was the result of bringing black soldiers with "a social manner more suggestive of primitive [i.e., African] origins" into the more sophisticated European setting.[13] Donnelly was flabbergasted. The meeting ended in an uproar, and the press continued to pillory the behavior of occupation troops at every opportunity.

That the army often appeared inconsistent in its attitude toward race only complicated the Austrian response. The use of Negro manpower in the postwar military establishment was a contentious issue that extended back to problems encountered during World War II. During the war, blacks were assigned to segregated commands, although the pressing requirement for infantry forced some frontline units to integrate during the closing year of the war in Europe. One battalion commander, voicing a common opinion held by white leaders, said, "The discipline among colored troops was deplorable." The approach to the colored problem was wrong, he argued, as long as colored soldiers were banded together in segregated units, where they were able to evade discipline on the grounds that they were being picked on because of their color. If they had been put in white units in the proper proportion from the beginning, they would have had to stand up and compare themselves with the white soldiers. Finally, he added, "probably the colored people were not advanced enough for this treatment [assignment to integrated units], but if that is the case they should have been given a special uniform and used as service troops."[14]

Official army policy reached similar conclusions. Black troops had limited utility and required special handling. When the War Department polled army commands on the future employment of black soldiers one commander recommended: "units composed of Negroes should be stationed within the continental limits of the United States so as to ensure that there will be an adequate Negro population close by to provide necessary social life for the troops and to ensure that causes of racial friction in the locality will be at a minimum."[15]

On October 1, 1945, Marshall appointed a board under Lt. Gen. Alvan C. Gillem Jr. to develop a policy for employing blacks in the postwar army. The Gillem Board concluded that blacks should only be stationed outside the United States "on the basis of military necessity and in the interests of national security."[16] The army argued that if blacks proliferated throughout the force, racial tensions within the military and in civilian communities at home and overseas would seriously detract from military efficiency.

Europe was a special problem. Rapid demobilization, coupled with high recruitment and retention among blacks, caused the percentage of segregated units in Europe to increase rapidly after 1946. The army responded with a deliberate plan to thin the ranks of such units.[17]

Although blacks had been a prominent part of the force in Europe, they represented, in many respects, an invisible arm of the occupation. There were no blacks in military government. The army concluded that because of the Germanic peoples' views toward race it would be detrimental to assign Negro personnel to the constabulary.[18] In July, 1946, the Negro Newspaper Publishers Association, reporting on conditions in Europe, informed the War Department that, "the very people whom the Army of Occupation seeks to democratize are aware of the Army's policy of separation of Negro and white, and they, both our allies and the natives of occupied countries, question us strongly for seeking to teach what we fail to practice, both at home and abroad."[19]

The report had a point. Army racial policies ignored issues of tolerance, fairness, equal opportunity, and equality before the rule of law—exactly the kinds of values that should have been emphasized in reconstructing civil society in a country whose former government had built its foundations on policies suffused with racial hatred. This was typical of the American efforts. Few of its measures to influence social, political, and cultural developments penetrated to the taproot of the problems of building a tolerant civil society. The United States worked for the creation of a democratic, consumer-oriented, capitalist state, but completely ignored such issues as race and ethnicity. United States Forces Austria's social focus was on denazification efforts, and later offering support for anticommunist groups.

In trying to ignore the race issue, the army was again falling back on its rhythm of habits and wartime experiences. Commanders had been brought up in a tradition that argued integration detracted from military effectiveness, a conclusion reinforced by all of the military's internal reports and studies since World War I. In addition, despite the fine combat record of some segregated commands, the army viewed black units as a liability. Much was made of reports on race conflict, riots, higher venereal disease rates, and poor discipline at posts in the United States, North Africa, and the staging areas in Great Britain. Finally, army leaders saw race relations as a political issue and the military traditionally did not play a prominent role in shaping public policies.[20]

As for Austria, Clark had set the tone during his tenure. He his command in Italy had a number of segregated combat units, most notably the 92d Infantry Division. In a postretirement speech in 1956, Clark concluded, "My World War II experience persuaded me that Negro units in combat tended to be undependable under fire."[21] He argued that the army had little responsibility for their failure. In his memoirs he attributed their poor performance to "our handling of minority problems here at home."[22] Clark endorsed the Gillem Board's findings, especially the recommendation to limit the number of blacks overseas for the sake of military efficiency. Keyes had also lobbied to have excess black soldiers shipped back from Germany.[23]

Clark elected not to have colored troops assigned to USFA. This prohibition was codified in an official U.S. policy prohibiting the assignment of Negroes to units in Austria. Similar policies governed assignments in Trieste, Frankfurt, and Berlin.[24] In light of the army's overseas personnel problems, such policies were self-defeating. In June, 1946, USFET had 17,469 more soldiers than authorized. Given the turmoil in USFA's ranks caused by rapid demobilization, the assignment of Negro units would have quickly alleviated personnel shortfalls. However, rather than assign black troops to USFA, USFET tried to redeploy them to the United States even though the gaining units were 25 percent overstrength and many black troops preferred to remain overseas.[25]

In October, 1946, Clark had to be persuaded by Marcus Ray, a civilian aide to the secretary of war, to accept the assignment of a railroad company of selected Negro personnel. Whether this initiative was ever actually undertaken is unclear. Black troops were not assigned to USFA in any appreciable numbers until 1948. Even then, by November 30 there were only 289 black soldiers in the command—none of them from the Women's Army Corps (WAC), although black WACs were assigned to Germany.[26]

On July 26, 1948, President Truman issued an executive order that created the President's Committee on Equality of Treatment and Opportunity in the Armed Forces, known as the Fay Committee. The committee issued a groundbreaking report calling for the expanded employment of blacks in the military. The army's response was to form another board—this one chaired by Lt. Gen. S. J. Chamberlin—which concluded that "increased opportunities for colored soldiers would adversely affect the fighting spirit and morale."[27]

Despite the service's reluctance to implement Truman's policy, blacks became an increasingly important part of the U.S. forces in Europe. In practice, arguments that black soldiers decreased efficiency withered under the pressure of manpower requirements to enhance the U.S. military presence. Lieutenant General Clarence Huebner had tremendous success improving the training and discipline of black units and soldiers in Germany. In 1951, Lt. Gen. Manton Eddy concluded that integration was the only way to increase the quality and efficiency of the force in Europe. Turning the army's traditional view on its head, Eddy argued that integration was essential to achieve military efficiency. Army Chief of Staff J. Lawton Collins, mainly because of the manpower demands generated by the Korean War, ordered worldwide integration in December, 1952.

The increase in Austrian complaints about black soldiers coincided with the desegregation of the forces in Europe, and the army suddenly found itself in the awkward position of criticizing Austrian attitudes that the service had itself espoused. But commanders quickly became enthusiastic supporters of integration. First, and most important, integration contributed to the buildup of combat forces. Second, it allowed leaders to counteract communist claims that Americans did not really believe in social equality. Almost overnight the army had become a leading proponent of desegregation.

Dread of War

As the issue of race revealed, many Austrians, in contrast to Donnelly's assessment, increasingly saw the American presence in Austria as a threat. Some feared that the outbreak of the Korean War was only a precursor to drawing the country into a Europewide conflict. In fact, the Soviets frequently cited U.S. military initiatives as the reason for slow progress on the state treaty. The Soviets accused the other powers of encouraging the revival of National Socialism and decried remilitarization as a tool of Western aggression. They also argued that by not withdrawing U.S. and British forces from Trieste, the Western powers had violated the Italian peace treaty. The Soviets suggested that Trieste proved there was no guarantee the United States would withdraw from Austria after a state treaty was signed.[28]

The latest voice of Soviet concerns was Andrei Andreyevich Gromyko. Gromyko was the coldest of the cold warriors. He entered the foreign service in 1939 at the age of thirty and served in the Soviet government until 1988, outlasted by the empire by only a year. He was at both Yalta and Potsdam. From 1946–48 he served as Soviet's permanent representative to the United Nations, where he earned the moniker "Grim Grom."

He returned to Moscow to serve as Andrei Vyshinsky's deputy, a post he held for several years except for a brief interlude as ambassador to Britain in 1953. His wide knowledge of foreign affairs was considered legendary.

His capacity to survive the Kremlin's internecine politics was unprecedented. He was loathed in the West. At the 1949 Council of Foreign Ministers in Paris, when the hopes for an Austrian State Treaty still lingered, Gromyko called Vyshinsky from Moscow with blunt instructions that the negotiations had to be reopened. The talks collapsed. Acheson said they could "go to hell." Few Americans could stomach this brand of brutal Cold War diplomacy. Little wonder that, after hearing reports of Gromyko and Vyshinsky's diatribes, American generals always expected the worst from the Soviets.

Threats were a staple of Stalinist diplomacy. Gromyko and other Soviet leaders never failed to point out the West's belligerent acts to the Austrians. They claimed the United States was preparing to instigate a war to seize the Soviet zone in Austria using Yugoslavia as a base for operations. When Gromyko met with Gruber in April, 1951, he charged that the United States was already committed to war. Gromyko then proceeded to lecture the Austrian foreign minister on the Americans' aggressive intentions. Berating Austrian officials over cooperation with the West was a popular Soviet tactic.[29]

Despite Gromyko's harangues and the communist scare during the 1950 riots, some Austrian leaders stuck to a pro-Western orientation, albeit often for the purpose of advancing state policies. Gruber argued that because of security developments in Italy, Germany, and Austria, the priority for further enhancing Western defenses should be to agree to a treaty as quickly as possible so as to obtain the withdrawal of Soviet forces.

Contrary Austrian views on the occupation, however, gained equal prominence. One leading voice for a more neutral foreign policy was liberal politician Bruno Kreisky. A Jew, Kreisky evaded the Nazi concentration camps by fleeing to Sweden. After the war, the young politician rose to prominence in the SPÖ. In 1950, he became a political adviser to Renner's successor to the presidency, Theodor Körner. Kreisky was appointed state secretary in the foreign ministry, giving the socialists a balancing force for Gruber's dominance over foreign policy.

Kreisky had no illusion that the country could openly curry favor with the West and at the same time obtain its independence from Soviet influence. He once told U.S. representatives that he had "a wish to have the security of NATO if that were possible,"[30] He concluded it was not. Kreisky proposed military neutrality as a device to appease Soviet concerns and obtain the long sought state treaty. While Austrians might covertly rely on the West, publicly, the country needed a more independent policy.

It would, however, be wholly incorrect to suggest that, even late in the occupation, the Austrians looked on the presence of U.S. forces as entirely negative. Measures of American support and generosity were never far from conscious memory. In July, 1954, heavy rains caused catastrophic flooding throughout the Danube River basin. Floodwaters wiped out crops and destroyed already scarce housing—a devastating setback to a people less than a decade out of war. The United States contributed military manpower, relief supplies, and emergency economic assistance. The Austrians reacted with sincere appreciation. Some wept recalling the moment. American forces contributed significantly to mitigating the scope of the disaster, which could have strained the fragile republic's resources to the breaking point. Even Austrians who opposed the continued occupation had to admit that over the course of the years U.S. troops had significantly contributed to suppressing disease and unrest in the fledgling postwar state.

The Home Front

In the United States, most Americans had little appreciation for antioccupation sentiment. At the outset, the U.S. government and military did much to encourage the narrative of Austria as victim. A history of the war written exclusively for veterans concluded authoritatively that the country was the "first testing ground for the gigantic Nazi conspiracy."[31] As a result, many Americans had a relatively positive, sympathetic, and tolerant view toward Austrians and the U.S. role in the occupation. America's attention occasionally was drawn to Austria by sensational news articles on issues of race, armed shootouts between Soviet and U.S. troops, the abuse of displaced persons living in holocaust-like conditions, and profiteering or inefficiency in the conduct of military government. But America before the Korean War was self absorbed with its own concerns: finding a job, starting a family, buying a house and a car, going to school. The public attention span on foreign matters was short. Americans relied on their politicians, diplomats, and generals to manage overseas affairs.

In turn, congressional interest was also minimal, with primary attention given to monitoring the use of the more than $1 billion that had been provided for economic reconstruction. Congress's oversight had its greatest impact on the occupation through inquiries over the use of military forces in Europe, debates on NATO's formation, and the effort to legislate military assistance programs. This influence was characterized by considerable ambivalence that in the end contributed significantly to militarizing the occupation.

Following the Brussels Treaty and the establishment of the Western European Union, focus quickly shifted to building a transatlantic military alliance. In June, 1948, the Senate overwhelmingly passed a resolution proposed by influential senator Arthur Vandenberg, which provided a mandate for participation in the creation of NATO. The resolution later enshrined in article 3 of the NATO treaty articulated the principle of self-help. Congress expected the United States to supplement but not substitute for European self-defense. This compromise paved the way for formalizing a long-term commitment not to support the postwar settlement, but to defend against a Soviet invasion. Willingness to deter the Soviet Union with military force became a matter of bipartisan consensus. Even reluctant internationalists like Sen. William Fulbright were unwilling to abandon Europe to the "tender mercies of the Kremlin" and supported U.S. military engagement in the region.[32] Anticommunism was becoming a powerful force in American politics.

In October, 1949, the communists won a bitter civil war in China and seized control of the government. Some Republicans charged that the Truman administration's policies had *lost* China, creating further pressure for the president to take sterner measures in enforcing the containment of Soviet power, and lessening the possibility that there would ever be a serious debate questioning the militarization of foreign policy with regard to Austria. On September 9, 1950, only three months after committing forces to the fighting in Korea, Truman announced a substantial increase in European troop strength, providing the manpower for the transition of the army in Europe from an occupation constabulary to a combat force.

This transformation did not take place without a modicum of congressional debate. Republican senator Robert Taft opposed military commitments to Europe on the scale envisioned by the administration. Trying to hammer out a distinctly "America first" foreign policy in preparation for a run for the White House in 1952, Taft introduced a resolution to remove the troops because the president lacked constitutional authority to deploy them overseas without congressional approval.

The Taft resolution sparked what proved to be the swan song of opposition to militarizing the occupation. His support came primarily from a remarkable alliance of isolationist-minded conservative Republicans, mostly from the Midwest, and a group of blue-dog southern Democrats intent on limiting presidential power that proved short-lived. The troops were not removed, and subsequent "great debate" bills requiring congressional approval before increasing overseas troop strength failed. Congress remained an ally in militarizing Europe as long as the cost of defense remained reasonable.

Crisis in Command

In the wake of Korea, as the Cold War came to "Main Street, U.S.A.," Congress and the American public had little use for Austrian complaints about the burden of occupation or for fence-sitters like Kreisky who were reluctant to take sides. They expected Europeans to act as full-fledged partners in the defense of the West and were deeply suspicious of any lack of resolve. Anxiety was fueled by the many charges of communist conspiracy levied by Sen. Joseph McCarthy. As chairman of the Senate subcommittee on investigations, "tail-gunner Joe" launched a highly publicized effort to identify and remove communists from public office. He was censured by the Senate in 1954, and his political influence diminished rapidly—but not before further heightening anticommunist sentiments.

Commanders in Europe found themselves caught between a Congress and people who expected the army to be tough on both the communists and America's increasingly anxious European partners. There was little sympathy in any quarter. The Europeans were particularly uneasy. At worst, the military was accused of attempting to provoke World War III; at best, many felt annoyance over efforts to compel rearmament at the expense of pushing European economies, domestic politics, and civil society to the breaking point. While the European Allies looked for areas in which to economize, the United States constantly goaded them to increase defense investments.

It is remarkable that USFA remained a viable combat force at all given the pressures building against it. Here, perhaps the command's greatest advantage was that Congress and the public remained largely disengaged from the militarization process. There was no serious effort to question whether traditional military approaches were appropriate for this situation. The first shots of the Korean War focused America's attention on the global confrontation between East and West. There was a predisposition to back up the policy of containment through the increased application of military force and a renewed willingness to contest the Soviet Union at every point, attitudes that complemented USFA's campaign to promote building up conventional defense capabilities in Austria.

In February, 1954, Donnelly's temporary replacement, Acting High Commissioner Charles Yost, reported that although U.S. officials had given some thought to additional troop withdrawals, they had determined that an effective defense of the alpine area would not be possible if there were further reductions. "However, with the forces on hand," Yost added, "the military planners felt that a Soviet attack could be contained for a time to conform to overall strategic defensive plans."[33] The reason for USFA's continued optimism and the plans they were designed to support were the command's most closely guarded secrets.

CHAPTER 7

THE SOUTHERN FLANK

Of all the generals who influenced the occupation, none was more renowned than Matthew Bunker "Matt" Ridgway, a man Dwight Eisenhower called "one of the finest soldiers this war has produced." A 1917 West Point graduate, he was greatly disappointed when assigned to teach Spanish at the academy rather than join the American Expeditionary Force. He could not know that his future held a lifetime of war and visions of war. After Pearl Harbor, General Marshall assigned him to serve as Omar Bradley's deputy in the newly activated 82d Infantry Division. When Bradley moved on, the army chief of staff named Ridgway to succeed him.

As the 82d's commander, Ridgway became one of the leading proponents of airborne operations, which consisted of dropping combat troops behind enemy lines via parachute or glider. As division and later XVIII Airborne Corps commander, he led GIs in harrowing combat during the Sicily, Salerno, Normandy, and Germany campaigns, finishing the war as a three-star general with a reputation as a tenacious combat leader.

During the postwar years a series of political-military positions added to his qualifications for high command. Ridgway served as a military representative to the United Nations and as commander in chief of U.S. forces in the Caribbean. During the dark days of the Korean War he was sent to take over the Eighth Army after Lt. Gen. Walton Walker's tragic death in a jeep accident. Ridgway assumed command at a time when UN troops were retreating in the face of massed Chinese counterattacks. Often seen at the front wearing his trademark combat harness laced with hand grenades, he successfully directed the effort to halt the communist advance, further embellishing his reputation as a fighting general.

Ridgway proved less skilled at negotiating a truce. He left the front in 1952 after having fought the enemy to a stalemate, but failing to secure peace. Mark Clark replaced him, and Ridgway moved to the other side of the world to buck up the Europeans as commander of the newly established NATO alliance's forces. Arriving in Paris to assume his duties, he immediately proved a controversial figure. He was greeted at NATO headquarters by screaming, banner-waving French rioters protesting the alleged use of biological weapons in Korea. The demonstrations were reflective of larger worries: Many people feared that the Asian conflict could lead to a general war or a protracted confrontation between the superpowers, with Europe as the contested ground.

Despite the war in Korea, Europe still topped America's list of national security interests. Ridgway's task was to turn NATO into a credible deterrent. One of his most pressing duties would be developing plans that might actually work in time of war. As he looked for advantages that could speed his efforts, one place he turned an eye toward was Austria, where he hoped to benefit from the militarization of the occupation and use the country to defend NATO's most vulnerable front: its southern flank.

The Sum of All Fears

By the time Ridgway arrived to energize NATO, war plans had already evolved significantly over the occupation's course. Initially, USFA's only contingencies reflected its first priority to "dispel riots, maintain law and order, [and] protect military and civilian personnel."[1] United States Forces Austria and USFET also made arrangements to provide task forces in support of each other during civil emergencies. In December, 1945, thanks to the success of the disease and unrest formula, these contingencies were considered unlikely and the plans were scrapped. No potential threat was considered worthy of a defense plan.

While USFA gave scant consideration to the challenges of armed conflict, military leaders in Washington had already begun to think the unthinkable. On March 12, 1946, shortly after becoming army chief of staff, Eisenhower complained, "no one was thinking about the enormous problems involved in the unlikely case of a major outbreak of hostilities."[2] But his staff surprised him, producing a plan titled "Pincher," drafted by the armed services' Joint War Plans Committee. Pincher assumed that conflict with the Soviet Union was unlikely, but offered contingencies if Moscow's hubris inadvertently sparked a shooting war.[3]

Pincher, recognizing the paucity of strategic options, called for a complete withdrawal in the event of conflict. The plan envisioned that the first priority would be to protect the British Isles as a base for air attacks on the mainland and a staging area for an amphibious invasion. Remembering the difficulties and perils of fighting their way ashore on D day, the planners also wanted to hold a lodgment area on the continent to receive the invasion force. Pincher thus called for troops in Germany and Austria to withdraw to footholds in Italy, Spain, or France. Nowhere would the Yanks conduct a forward defense. Austria was not considered to be "a factor of consequence."[4] The planners even doubted that the United States would be able to hold its position there for very long in peacetime. Pincher left little room for optimism that the country could or should be defended.

A number of senior generals in Europe had misgivings about Pincher's pessimistic assessments. The USFET commander, Gen. Joseph McNarney, questioned whether an organized retreat was possible. He estimated that it would take thirty divisions to hold the hundred-mile front needed to cover the withdrawal, and USFET had less than five. Making matters worse, coalition planning was in an appalling state. Cooperation with the British would be essential for a successful withdrawal, but there was no ongoing joint U.S./British planning. Nor was there any coordination with the French. Even U.S. forces had no joint planning capability. After the creation of an independent air force in 1947, the army and its new sister service each maintained separate European commands reporting directly to Washington. Prospects were bleak. McNarney agreed that the only option in the event of war was to "run as quickly as possible."[5] McNarney's headquarters drafted "Totality," an action plan to be implemented if forces in Austria and Germany were threatened by "other powers."[6] Totality envisioned consolidating USFA with the troops in Germany and withdrawing to Bremen or the Cotentin Peninsula or Marseille in France.

In 1947, the Joint War Plans Committee prepared a contingency plan code-named "Broiler" for a global conflict intentionally initiated by the Soviet Union. Like Pincher, Broiler envisioned withdrawing the occupation troops from Austria. Running away was a foregone conclusion. The U.S. and British chiefs also authorized commanders in Trieste and Austria to conduct secret joint planning for troop evacuation.[7]

Given the military's state at the time, even the most pessimistic plans were overly ambitious. Pincher, Totality, and Broiler all relied on the promise of air attacks to slow a Soviet advance and give the troops time to conduct an organized withdrawal. Such a hope was illusory. The United States lacked the weapons, planes, and accurate targeting intelligence required to mount an effective air campaign with either conventional or atomic bombs. With such limited capabilities, the military saw the need for a more credible ground deterrent lest the Soviets believe they could seize Europe in one quick, decisive stroke. The Joint Strategic Plans Committee, a component of the new Joint Staff established by the National Security Act of 1947, called for options that did not abandon the allies. What was needed, planners suggested, was a scheme that "strives for a common defense which holds the reasonable prospect for future military security."[8]

Keyes believed that if the defense of Austria was assigned a place in these new plans it would ensure continued commitment to the occupation. However, while he had little difficulty persuading an increasingly wary JCS of the magnitude of the Soviet danger in Austria, contemplating the country's defense was an entirely different issue. Most planners considered occupation duties as little more than a burdensome diversion of manpower. Making the case to invest more resources in a region long considered peripheral to U.S. interests was akin to cleaning the Stygian stables.

Before being ousted, Keyes made a forceful case for Austria's strategic importance by highlighting its potential role in defending NATO's southern flank.[9] The loss of the country, he argued, could lead to Italy being isolated—and losing Italy meant forfeiting the Mediterranean and access to Middle East oil and the Suez Canal. Keyes also argued that the southern flank was important for Germany's defense. The Soviets could not overlook the desirability of holding a salient into the West providing access to the Danube River corridor. An advance there would be quicker than a march across northern Germany, and it could be supported by lines of communication through Hungary and southern Germany, while allowing for an easy linkup with Czech and Yugoslav forces.

Keyes acknowledged that holding the country would be no easy task. His intelligence sources described a substantial threat. The Soviets had more than twice as many troops as all the other Allied commands put together. Over the first three years of the occupation, Soviet ground forces in Austria had been reduced from over 200,000 to 54,500—including 7,500 air force personnel with 350 aircraft. While the number of Soviet troops in Austria had declined significantly, USFA still found their force levels troubling. Only 9,000 Soviets were directly involved in occupation duties. Intelligence classified the remaining as well-trained forces. Despite being understrength, the command pointedly added that Soviet units were "hardly emasculated for the eventual conflict."[10] United States Forces Austria concluded that the Soviets were prepared to support a communist coup or attack, seizing all of Austria, and, if reinforced, capable of continuing westward. Reinforcements were not far away in Hungary and Romania, where, by Allied agreement, the Soviets were permitted to maintain military lines of communication into Austria.

There was some cause for optimism. After three years of drawdown, the United States began to rebuild its European military structure. The air force deployed additional units to England and West Germany. American divisions in Germany were reinforced. The navy shifted the Sixth Fleet to the

Mediterranean. The United States also established the Mutual Defense Assistance Program, dispensing training and equipment through Military Advisory Groups (MAGs) under the Joint American Advisory Group (JAMAG) in London. At the same time, the United States advocated a collective European defense framework that included rearming Germany.

The military also began to reorganize its operational forces, although achieving only limited success in that quarter. The European Command (EUCOM), established in 1947 and headquartered in Germany, was assigned responsibility for Western Europe. In reality, EUCOM's commander in Chief, Europe, was simply a different title for the commander, USFET. While the new scheme gave EUCOM broad responsibilities, it was still primarily an army command and did not integrate all theater forces under a single headquarters. The JCS also named the top European commanders of each service as representatives to NATO rather than designating EUCOM as a single point of contact for the Americans.[11] This reorganization left much to be desired. The European forces had no joint staff, and service staffs were shorthanded.

Despite being hobbled by a fragmented organization, the United States still sought collaboration with its Atlantic partners. From April 12–21, 1948, the United States, Britain, and Canada held their first postwar planning conference and on May 11 the Joint Strategic Plans Committee offered a revised version of Broiler code-named "Crankshaft." The group also adopted another plan, "Halfmoon," as a companion to Crankshaft and a basis for coalition war planning. Similar to previous plans, both envisioned the withdrawal of occupation forces, but they differed by proposing, if possible, a fighting retreat to the Pyrenees or French ports. American forces in Austria would still merge with troops in Germany, or, if a Soviet offensive made that impossible, withdraw to Italy or, as a last resort, Switzerland.[12]

In addition to expanding coordination with the Canadians and British, the United States sent unofficial representatives to the Western European Union. In July, its military committee produced a scheme that envisioned a forward defense with U.S., British, and French forces. The three powers willingly took on the responsibility, which is not surprising since the plan had been drafted by their representatives and then turned over to the committee.[13]

The following year, the focus shifted to the newly established NATO alliance. On November 23, 1949, NATO's Defense Committee adopted a short-term plan that envisioned holding on a general line from the Rhine River to the Italian Alps and the Adriatic. The alliance also adopted a midterm plan that looked forward to 1954 when NATO, after a period of rearmament by member countries, was supposed to have up to fifty divisions—a force with which NATO hoped to hold a forward line in Germany.[14]

Although NATO at last had a defense scheme, there was little optimism. Field Marshal Montgomery, the alliance's deputy commander, concluded, "We have plans and committees and paper and talk . . . the ugly fact is that Western European defence is today a pure façade."[15]

Taking Sides

Austria's place in this new security arrangement was equivocal. Some State Department and military officials recommended fully integrating Austria into NATO, but the United States never seriously considered pushing the country to join the alliance, fearing the reaction such moves might prompt from the Soviets.[16] The Austrians were also reluctant to openly declare for NATO, although there were strong and influential advocates for throwing Austria's fate in with the West. One of the most persistent was Ludwig Kleinwaechter. A lifelong conservative, he had been ousted from the First Republic's Foreign Office for criticizing policies that favored relations with Italy's prewar fascist government. Persecuted by the Nazis during World War II, he was interned in the infamous concentration camp at Dachau. These credentials made him an ideal candidate to be the country's first envoy to the United States.

Kleinwaechter was one of the architects of Austria's pro-Western foreign policy. He persistently lobbied Gruber on the importance of taking sides. When the foreign minister first visited the United States, Kleinwaechter encouraged him to forge personal ties with American leaders and publish an article on the Austrian situation in the influential journal *Foreign Affairs*. These efforts took root. A new administration under Figl was assembled in November, 1949, and Gruber was reappointed.

Even the Americans bore watching, however. After years of talking up the West, Kleinwaechter may have thought he made his case too well when he learned that U.S. military leaders were more interested in integrating the country into NATO's defenses than concluding the state treaty. The ambassador lodged a heated protest.[17] Still, despite Kleinwaechter's concern over the generals' antitreaty sentiments, he was even more worried about the threat of Soviet influence. Though he continued to push for close cooperation, he nevertheless recognized the difficulties in publicly siding with NATO. Such a move might jeopardize obtaining the withdrawal of Soviet troops. With the establishment of the Federal Republic of Germany (FRG), the Soviets suspected that it would not be long before West Germany joined the alliance. Under these circumstances, the notion of Austria also aligning with NATO would have been intolerable. Opting for the alliance might prompt the occupation forces to divide Austria in the same way they had split Germany—although the fact that the country had a single, legitimate government would make such a move more problematic for the Allied powers and produce little additional strategic benefit for either side. Nevertheless, the country's leadership remained cautious. Austria was not openly discussed in NATO contingencies. There was not even a mention on occupation troop employment.

The Austrian's predicament, however, did not stop the Western occupation powers from thinking about what would happen to their forces in wartime. In 1949, commanders in Austria and Trieste secretly formed a planning staff under the overall direction of USFA. The focus was still on coordinating a rapid retreat, but drawing on its authority as war plans coordinator, the command objected that linking up with troops in Germany was thoroughly unrealistic; any withdrawal in that direction would expose the force head on to Soviet invasion. The Americans also continued to argue that fighting in Austria had strategic value. More could and should be done.[18]

Keyes was pleased when, on May 23, 1949, the JCS finally detached his command from EUCOM. However, he was disappointed when he received formal instructions in September regarding his role as a wartime commander: If the Soviets launched an attack upon his occupation forces, Keyes could only exercise "existing emergency plans,"[19] which meant he was to retreat as rapidly as practicable. Such a move was still a subject of debate. British plans called for withdrawal to the Rhine while their troops in Trieste were evacuated by sea and deployed to the Middle East. Yet there was still some enthusiasm for not immediately retreating. Montgomery suggested that Trieste might be held as a bridgehead for a counteroffensive. The French high commissioner, General Béthouart, thought the key was control of the Austrian Alps. His forces made serious preparations to defend passes in the Tirol, guarding the routes toward their homeland.[20]

Keyes found less enthusiasm for defending Austria in the Pentagon. In November, 1949, the Joint Strategic Planning Committee submitted a new plan called "Offtackle." Offtackle reflected an interest in fostering alliance solidarity with a promise of fighting forward along the Alps-Piava line. The plan acknowledged, however, that this would be impossible without the massive buildup of European forces promised by the NATO member states. Offtackle included several alternatives, including a fighting retreat to the Pyrenees to hold northwestern Europe, withdrawal to French ports to secure lodgment areas, or evacuation to England or North Africa.[21] Austria, meanwhile, was completely written off. The planners concluded that although the Austrians were sympathetic to the United States, they were unable to contribute anything toward their country's defense. When Truman asked General Bradley, the new JCS chairman, to what extent the United States should commit to the defense of Europe, Austria was not included in the general's list of priorities.[22]

Wild Card

Bradley's ambivalence proved short-lived. Austria's southern neighbor, Yugoslavia, changed the strategic calculus for saving Europe. Initial postwar relations with Tito's regime had been troubled and reinforced the case that in the event of war the entire southern region was indefensible. On December 20, 1946, when the Joint War Plans Committee released "Cockspur," a situation estimate on Italy's security, Yugoslavia's two-hundred-thousand-man army was considered a major threat.[23] Tito's support for the Slovene separatist movement in British-occupied Carinthia was another major concern. The Americans and British also clashed with the Yugoslavs over Trieste, and Yugoslav support for communist separatists in Greece. Souring relations even more, in August, Yugoslav fighter planes attacked U.S. aircraft bound for Austria. On October 22, two British ships struck mines laid by the Yugoslavs in northern Corfu Strait.

Apprehension heightened after the September 15, 1947, peace treaty with Italy requiring withdrawal of all occupation forces from the peninsula. Both the United States and Britain assumed that if general war broke out, both Yugoslav and Soviets forces would attack Italy. American intelligence officers concluded that the peninsula would be overrun and Austria isolated. The Italian situation appeared so glum that the country was not included in any defense plans. With no guarantee against Italy electing a communist government or renouncing NATO in time of war, few were optimistic of the chances for holding the southern flank. In turn, an undependable Italy and a hostile Yugoslavia made any thought of a defensible Austria little more than wishful thinking.

Then, in 1948, the USFA intelligence staff noted a growing rift between Yugoslavia and the Soviet Union. Western military leaders began to speculate about the consequences of falling out of Stalin's camp. Within a year, Tito resolved most of the longstanding territorial disputes (except Trieste), including claims on Carinthia, and turned to the West for economic and military support. These overtures had breathtaking strategic implications. In 1949, Italy joined NATO. With Yugoslav support in defending the approaches along the Austrian frontier, integrating Italy into the alliance defense regime would be a much easier task.[24] Keyes, who had already been thinking along these lines, now argued against the state treaty on the grounds that the absence of occupation troops would allow Stalin to put more direct pressure on

Tito.[25] Political and military leaders were quick to acknowledge the changing situation. In November, 1949, Truman approved a plan to support Yugoslavia if the Soviet Union attacked the country. The JCS in turn declared that Yugoslavia was directly important to the defense of NATO.[26]

American interest in the country dovetailed well with the drafting of NSC-68 by the National Security Council, which argued for a significant investment in the conventional defense of Europe, and the outbreak of the Korean War, which prompted the administration to follow through on the document's recommendations. Following the Soviets' development of an atomic bomb, the Pentagon also began to envision a period—soon at hand—when the United States did not enjoy nuclear superiority. Creating a credible conventional NATO defense seemed both possible and necessary.

In 1951, as part of upgrading the alliance, NATO established the position of Supreme Allied Commander Europe (SACEUR), which had operational command over all NATO forces in Europe. General Eisenhower was appointed to serve as the first SACEUR, a demonstration of America's commitment to the alliance. Within a year, the JCS reorganized EUCOM as the American component of NATO, making it responsible for all of the army, navy, and air force units in the theater (less Austria and Trieste). At the same time, the JCS designated the SACEUR as the EUCOM commander.

In addition to his other responsibilities, Eisenhower was given covert authority to plan operations in Trieste, Yugoslavia, and Austria. A strategist at heart, he immediately began to consider his options. British generals revised Montgomery's proposal of holding an Italian-Austrian bridgehead in Southern Europe. The United States had also changed its plans to reflect the withdrawal of occupation troops into Italy, demonstrating confidence in the republic after communist electoral defeats. Further, the JCS directed USFA to undertake secret joint planning with the Italians and covertly establish liaison with the defense command for the northern region at Verona.[27]

As cooperation with Yugoslavia improved, the United States began to send military aid and initiated discussions on a key region, the Ljubljana Gap, a strategic passage at the intersection of Austria, Italy, and Yugoslavia. The gap presented a major invasion route for both entering Italy and bypassing Austria. Establishing defenses in Ljubljana would block an advance into the Villach area through the Sava River Valley and keep the Soviets from circumventing Italy's forward defenses and outflanking Austria.

Whispers of Promise

While the Americans plotted the defense of Europe, Austria's foreign minister, Karl Gruber, traveled far and wide in an attempt to resurrect the mori-

bund state treaty negotiations. During his trip to the United States in the autumn of 1950, he crossed paths with one man who could, perhaps more
than anyone, provide a hint of Stalin's plans for Austria's future. He was
Andrei Yanuarievich Vyshinsky.

A jurist and diplomat, Vyshinsky was born in 1883. He studied law at the
University of Kiev before joining the Bolshevik ranks during the civil war. After serving as a professor of law at the University of Moscow, he became the
chief prosecutor of the Soviet Union. Vyshinsky served as Stalin's legal aide
during the Communist Party purges, and he was chief prosecutor at the
Moscow treason trials from 1936–38. During World War II, Vyshinsky became deputy commissar for foreign affairs and represented the Soviet Union
on Allied commissions for the Mediterranean and Italy. In 1949, he replaced
Molotov as foreign minister, although it was thought he never entered Stalin's
inner circle. Famed for his biting wit and vitriolic denouncements of American foreign policy, he was a formidable figure and stubborn negotiator.

Gruber more than once had been on the receiving end of Vyshinsky's
barbs. However, when he met with the foreign minister at a palatial private
residence in Glenn Cove on Long Island, the tenor of the conversation was
unusually restrained. Vyshinsky repeated his charges that the United States
was preparing for war against the Soviet Union. The American attitude had
poisoned every aspect of international relations. Yet, he offered that, in the
case of the Austrian question, Soviet policy would follow the status quo for
the present. While the minister offered no new hopes for the treaty, he appeared to imply that the Soviets had no interest in further heating up the
Cold War with a confrontation in Austria. At a time when many believed
that the great powers were on the verge of declaring World War III, Gruber
found Vyshinsky's remarks reassuring and hoped for the best.[28]

Fortress Austria

Military leaders were less sanguine about the future. The promise to defend
Ljubljana Gap and the possibility of holding Italy as well as the backdoor
into Austria galvanized military planning. This thinking was reflected in the
latest war plan, "Dropshot," which envisioned—with a significant expansion of the U.S. armed forces—the real possibility of forward defense.[29]

The Austrians had their own secret military appreciation of the strategic situation. They anticipated that Western forces would withdraw to an Alpine defense zone, leaving the Austrians to act as a poorly equipped and inadequate rearguard. The Austrian appreciation argued that this made no
sense because it left the Soviets an uncontested avenue into Italy, access to
the Mediterranean, and the opportunity to encircle Yugoslavia. It recom-

mended a forward defense in Carinthia, where, the study argued, a force equipped with an ample supply of antitank weapons would have good prospects.[30]

Allied commanders also desired to fight forward. On February 2, 1951, the U.S., British, and French commanders in Austria met to discuss the status of war plans. They agreed to propose defending the country as far north and east as possible.[31] This stand, they argued, was more in line with NATO's desire to fight forward, rather then willingly abandon Europe's heartland in the face of a Soviet invasion. The commanders added that stiff resistance in Austria would allow additional time for the Italians to organize their defenses. They suggested a defensive line from Arlberg to Kufstein to Salzburg to Tarvisio. This could be accomplished with an American infantry division, a French alpine division, and two British combat brigades, while the Italians, working in conjunction with U.S. forces in Trieste, held from Tarvisio south to the Adriatic, and a German regiment defended the Kufstein Pass.

Senior military officials were still unenthusiastic about the notion of dedicating more troops to Austria. The recommendation received a hostile reception at JAMAG, which forwarded it to Washington with a sharp critique. It seems NATO's initial defenses were not designed as a true forward defense, but rather as a "couverture" to hold sufficient ground for an alliance buildup and eventual counterattack. While there were advantages to holding NATO's southern flank as far forward as possible, providing additional troops could only be accomplished at the expense of weakening other areas. The JAMAG planners preferred "Flatiron," a new plan that envisioned a withdrawal to northern Italy.

Faced with an increasing demand for forces to fight in Korea, the Pentagon was reluctant to take on any extra commitments until the prospects for that war improved. Although four additional divisions had been earmarked for Germany, EUCOM declared it could not spare a regiment to help Austria, but Gen. Thomas Handy agreed to look at the possibility of stationing a battalion from Germany adjacent to the Kufstein Pass.

The command relationship between the occupation forces and NATO also remained unsettled. Eisenhower had no formal authority to direct organization, planning, or training of the Austrian occupation forces in peacetime. He did, however, have a secret war plan for employing the forces in Austria. All the troops would fight under the USFA commander, who would serve as the commanding general of Allied Forces Austria. When they retreated across the border they would come under the Italians, but they would remain a unified force. Eisenhower also hoped to provide some reinforcements, which he concluded "should have a very great effect in strengthening that [the southern] flank."[32]

As for the proposal for making a stand in Austria, it was put on hold, although the JCS directed USFA to coordinate with British and French commanders and develop a plan for implementing a possible forward defense of Austria—most likely in the mountain passes near the northern Italian border. Meanwhile, on July 3, 1951, the JCS published their latest draft war plan, "Ironbark." Ironbark called for USFA, in conjunction with forces in Trieste, to take defensive positions in northern Italy or, if that was impractical, retreat to southern Italy. If no defense was possible, the plan called for withdrawal to western Italy or southern French ports.[33]

In addition to Ironbark, USFA was also addressed in a number of other draft war plans: "Mantleshelf," "Manward," and "Pilgrim Dog" (the latest in a series of "Pilgrim" plans).[34] These plans assigned the command three major responsibilities: evacuating noncombatants; coordinating combat operations with NATO; and drafting plans for a withdrawal to Italy. The problem with each, as far as the U.S. forces in Austria were concerned, was that they did not acknowledge the importance of making a stand in the country. Further developments proved equally disappointing. In February, 1952, the JCS produced an outline plan to support NATO titled "War Plan EDP 1–52." In the event of a Soviet breakthrough, the directive ordered USFA to conduct a withdrawal.

Lack of progress on the state treaty reenergized the debate over broadening defense planning to include Austria. On March 13, 1952, the United States, Britain, and France proposed the so-called short treaty. This accord included only the seven articles of the draft treaty already agreed on by the Soviets, and omitted disputed reparation claims, which had been one of the main sticking points in previous talks. The Soviets rejected the proposal, leaving the state treaty negotiations at their lowest point.[35]

On June 2, 1952, NATO secretly designated the USFA commander to serve as wartime commander in chief, Allied Forces Southern Europe.[36] The name implied greater authority, but there was still strong resistance to the notion of a defensive line in Austria. One source of irritation was the French, who had no enthusiasm for fighting anywhere but in their version of the Alpine Redoubt. With limited combat power, the French had little manpower left. They did not think it possible to hold the Austrian front in a conventional battle. Instead, the French favored Pilgrim Dog, a plan drafted at their insistence, which emphasized an Alpine defense scheme. In the summer of 1952, USFA outlined its own coalition war plan, which suggested a more ambitious scheme that would have required holding positions far forward of what the French generals considered prudent. The proposal fueled a bitter dispute. The generals appealed to SACEUR and then to their ministry of defense. The French government referred the issue back to NATO, which refused to approve Pilgrim Dog because of U.S. and British opposition.[37]

The commanders also fretted over whether to retain "Renault," a secret plan to come to the aid of the Austrians in the event of an attempted coup. The commander of the British garrison in Vienna complained that it was unnecessary and unrealistic. The police, he said, could handle anything short of Soviet intervention. If the Soviets did interfere, the forces available would be inadequate to stop them. These arguments made sense, but others, convinced that a show of Allied resolve might blunt Soviet aggression, kept the plan.[38]

Emboldened, USFA renewed its bid for expanding defense commitments in October, 1952. Planners outlined field fortification requirements for the defense of Austria and the Ljubljana Gap and asked NATO to approve defense of the Villach area with both Austrian and Trieste forces. This would dovetail well with a Yugoslav force covering the southern and eastern flank of Travisio-Villach and the Italians deploying some of their own forces forward in Yugoslavia.[39]

United States Forces Austria found little enthusiasm for this idea. Wanting to place more emphasis on central Germany, Eisenhower became hostile to the notion of expanding the command's wartime role. Before Ridgway replaced him, he streamlined and consolidated EUCOM in order to improve its integration with NATO.[40] In December, 1952, control of occupation forces in Austria and Trieste was transferred back to EUCOM, and USFA lost its authority to make its case for the strategic importance of Austria directly to the JCS. The command then received another blow when NATO revised its wartime command and control scheme. United States Forces Austria was now assigned at the outset of conflict to the operational control of the commander, Land South, whose intent was to use the occupation forces to bolster other areas. The French were to withdraw along the Scharnitz-Resia-Brenner axis to a line along the Austro-Italian border. United States Forces Austria would retreat to the Brenner Pass, and the British to Tarvisio, unless directed to defend the Dobiacco and Plocken Passes. Both would come immediately under Italian command. Meanwhile, American and British forces in Trieste would withdraw to Italy or assemble in reserve near S. Giorgio Di Nogaro. United States Forces Austria offered a strong dissent. Instead of this static "Maginot line" defense, the command wanted to conduct a mobile defense in the Austrian passes, an alternative the Italians dismissed out of hand.[41]

Playing the Yugoslavs

When General Ridgway took command, he placed the issue of securing NATO's southern flank high on his agenda. In November, 1952, he dispatched General Handy to conduct exploratory talks. Ridgway also noted approvingly that the Greeks and Turks had shown an interest in coordinating defense plans with Yugoslavia and had initiated parallel discussions. The following autumn, General Collins visited Belgrade for a series of meetings. He was encouraged when Tito declared that the Yugoslavs would defend the Ljubljana Gap.[42]

While prospects for cooperation were improving, Ridgway found himself embroiled in a serious dispute with Collins. Collins also had high hopes for the southern flank, but he wanted to give priority to northern Yugoslavia because it offered the potential of holding the approaches to Italy. On the other hand, he had no interest in southern Yugoslavia, which would have supported the defense of NATO's newest members, Greece and Turkey— both of which joined the alliance in February, 1952. The alliance lacked the means to defend these countries, and investing troops in there would simply be throwing good money after bad. "Anything the Jugs [Yugoslavs] do in the south," Collins argued, "is infinitely less important than their effort in the north."[43] Ridgway disagreed. He wrote to Bradley, "I know, for instance, how widely Joe's [Collins] personal views diverge from mine, and how vigorously he advocates his views." Collins's philosophy, Ridgway argued, is one "of defeat. It would, in my judgment, have serious repercussions among both the Greeks and Turks, if it should become known to them."[44]

The dispute hinged in part on the real value of Yugoslavia's forces in a shooting war.[45] To evaluate the role they might play, the United States needed not only complete understanding of how Tito planned to defend, but also a frank assessment of the country's combat potential. But military talks proved problematic, in part because Italy remained embroiled in a dispute with Yugoslavia over Trieste. Italian war plans still included defending the country against an attack from Yugoslavia. Others were equally unsure of NATO's new ally. Handy recalled that the negotiations were "kind of a forlorn hope. We always worried about that flank in NATO. . . . We could tell the Jugs [Yugoslavs] nothing . . . the Jugs were terrible. They weren't the nicest of people in the world but, that's what you got [sic] to deal with the commies."[46] He had little confidence that the discussions would amount to anything.

Although the talks produced no formal war plans, the Yugoslavs restated their resolve to defend Ljubljana Gap. In turn, the United States established a military mission that resulted in a 1953 staff study recommending the Yugoslavs hold their northern territory and with ten divisions establish a defensive line extending from the Austrian-Yugoslav border, twenty miles west of Dravograd, southwest to the line Ceje–Sava River–Karlovac–Primislje. The JCS approved the study as the basis for future planning.[47]

On February 24, 1953, the chiefs dispatched Collins to meet with

British and French representatives to forge a consensus approach to the Yugoslav military rapprochement. In a series of meetings lasting from March 5 to April 21, they debated new strategic concepts. Collins pressed for his approach. He wrote: "at our tripartite meetings I stated that, in my judgment, any future meetings with the Yugoslavs would be unproductive and pretty useless unless we were prepared to discuss some details of possible coordination between the defenses of Northern Italy and Austria and the defense of the Ljubljana area."[48] The meetings produced a joint policy for integrating Yugoslavia into the defense of the West that leaned heavily on Collins's proposals, but diplomatically did not ignore the southern question. In April, NATO's Standing Group authorized the SACEUR to synchronize plans with the initiatives being developed by the trilateral military talks and the three Balkan powers. Washington invited the Yugoslav government to participate in formal military discussions. Parallel talks with Greece and Turkey were also progressing nicely.[49]

With Yugoslavia now apparently in the camp, USFA's view soon gained ascendancy in the Pentagon. Another factor bolstering the case was the progress on European rearmament, particularly with regard to the German question. For three years, the United States had been working for the implementation of the European Defense Community (EDC). First proposed by French prime minister René Pleven on October 24, 1950, the initiative called for an integrated European army and defense ministry. While the idea of rearming Germany had been anathema to many countries, the proposal had permitted a dialogue on allowing the country to make a military contribution to the West, raising higher the Pentagon's expectations for a credible defense of Europe.

The JCS began to consider Austria as part of NATO's new front line, and they were less enthusiastic than ever about the prospects for a state treaty and troop withdrawals. The new chairman, Adm. Arthur Radford, argued that any weakening of the current situation would create a "military vacuum" in the critical linchpin between NATO's southern and central defenses. "Maintenance of the status quo," he concluded, "would be preferable to acceptance of a treaty which would deny to the United States its security objectives with respect to Austria."[50] The National Security Council concurred, formally reaffirming Austria's strategic importance in a new directive, NSC-164/1.[51]

The Austrians were not excluded from knowledge of this shift in military strategy. A serious defense of their country would have required their cooperation, as well as that of the other occupation powers. Although there is nowhere near a full accounting, documents suggest that plans were coordinated with Austrian leaders. The Military Advisory and Assistance Group

(MAAG) in Italy, after being briefed by USFA on its defense plans, cabled the Department of Defense its support of joint covert U.S.-Austrian contingency planning.[52] Still, while planning a forward defense began in earnest, it remained a closely guarded secret. Even the tactical commander of USFA's combat forces was not briefed. When he asked about the status of planning with the Austrians, he was told it was "none of his business."[53]

In addition to looking at conventional forces, USFA also considered employing weapons of mass destruction. Though there was no consideration of chemical weapons, the command prepared two studies on nuclear arms, one for offensive and one for defensive purposes.[54] Planning was clearly in an embryonic stage. United States Forces Austria did not have any operational plans, nor did the command include nuclear operations in its field maneuvers, though it did have trained nuclear planning officers assigned to the staff. It was remarkable that USFA even considered the idea, given that NATO had not yet approved the concept of deploying tactical nuclear weapons in Europe. The United States did not even *have* any such weapons in the theater until it deployed air-delivered weapons to Verona, Italy, two years later. But the fact that commanders had thought about employing them at all was another demonstration of their commitment to creating a viable forward defense.

The Stand

United States Forces Austria's initiatives reflected General Ridgway's aggressive approach to European defense, pressing the alliance to build up its capabilities as quickly as possible. All of the NATO members had been slow in meeting their commitments to support a fifty-division force. The SACEUR's relentless pursuit for a rapid military buildup and a lack of diplomatic finesse unsettled many European leaders. Such tensions had much to do with abbreviating Ridgway's controversial tenure: He had proved exceedingly blunt when demanding that countries increase their defense forces. At the Lisbon conference in February, 1952, the Europeans had agreed to have thirty to forty combat divisions ready at all times by 1954. When Ridgway tried to collect on the "IOU,"[55] he quickly grew frustrated, writing Bradley: "I find indications of some thinking along the line that 'We have been occupied before. Let's take a chance of occupation again, rather than knuckle-down to meet the costs which present military programs impose.'"[56]

Ridgway tried to avoid the diplomatic aspects of NATO and focus on defense and rearmament. Ignoring European politics, however, only exacerbated alliance complaints. The European press became so rife with rumors of his removal that the SACEUR issued a statement declaring he had no intention of resigning. Bradley, in turn, had to ask Truman for a statement of support. When Eisenhower became president he defused the controversy by appointing Gruenther as SACEUR and recalling Ridgway to the United States to succeed Collins as army chief of staff. Two years later, Ridgway retired.

Although Gruenther became popular among alliance leaders, he shared Matt Ridgway's passion for creating credible NATO conventional forces. After returning to the United States, Gruenther had remained engaged in the debate over European strategic issues as assistant commandant at the newly established National War College in Washington, D.C. His approach to the European situation was brought into stark relief by his relationship with a well-known member of the college faculty, George Kennan, the former State Department representative in Moscow and author of the famous "long telegram." Although the two became good friends, Gruenther and Kennan disagreed on matters of strategy. Kennan argued for limited containment, the qualified use of force, selected engagement with the Soviets, and the expansion of neutral states in Europe. In contrast, Gruenther lobbied for what Kennan called the militarization of the Cold War, confronting the Soviets at every opportunity.[57]

Gruenther continued to hold a hard line when he reported back to Europe as deputy SACEUR. On one occasion, while briefing Dean Acheson, he tried to impress upon the secretary the magnitude of the Soviet threat, gesticulating in front of a map covered with broad red bans and menacing arrows, each depicting likely invasion routes. The briefing prompted Acheson to remark to Eisenhower, "this arrow man of yours is, I think, going to destroy the morale of NATO."[58] A heated exchange followed. Gruenther argued that the secretary did not appreciate the seriousness of the military situation. Acheson, on the other hand, found the "military view" far too narrow. In his mind, NATO's importance was not its ability to fight a shooting war, but its ability to promote Atlantic solidarity. That was not how Gruenther saw it.

As SACEUR he built on Ridgway's proposal for contesting the southern flank. As for Austria, he argued that withdrawal "surrenders without a struggle vital terrain needed for further offensive action."[59] In September, 1953, however, he faced a serious obstacle when the French and British announced plans to eliminate all of their occupation forces with the exception of the detachments in Vienna.[60] Gruenther saw the reductions as a bad sign.

The United States had worried about the possibility of Allied troop curtailments since 1947. The British, in fact, had made a significant investment in drafting Operation Curfew, a plan for the removal of occupation troops.

At the time, USFA had estimated that if the British opted out the command could assume their mission, although it would require significant augmentation.[61] This, however, was before the Soviets had become a declared threat. A year later, the United States considered all Allied troops indispensable. The British, meanwhile, abandoned their withdrawal plan when it became apparent that the Soviets would not approve the state treaty. Nevertheless, facing the pressure of austere defense budgets, commanders endeavored to shrink force requirements as much as possible. Although the United States had also drafted plans in the event of a treaty, military leaders remained wary of a premature reduction in troop commitments.[62]

The new troop redeployment plans angered Gruenther. The withdrawals made any emergency war plans for Austria completely unworkable. The removal of British and French forces not only made defense impossible, it also brought into question the capability of USFA forces to successfully retreat. The alliance, Gruenther complained, might have to give up the thought of ever presenting a coherent defense.[63]

The British and French, Gruenther concluded, had violated a standing agreement not to change the composition of forces earmarked for NATO before consultation. This point served as the basis for a JCS decision paper issued on September 11, 1953, in which the chiefs viewed the reduction decisions "with utmost and urgent concern."[64] The paper identified no less than eleven major strategic problems and urged that the secretary of state and the president take up the matter with the British and French governments.

In a sense, the United States had precipitated the crisis by pushing for the upgrade of NATO forces. European countries, facing the dual pressures of funding both guns and butter, sought to prioritize troop deployments to meet the most pressing demand: the forward defense of Germany. Britain and France also required additional troops to reinforce rebellious portions of their empire from Indochina to Africa. Gruenther, who found this rationale cold comfort, pressed the French to retain at least one battalion in Austria to help guard the lines of communication into Italy, but they would have none of it.

The United States made a last ditch attempt to forestall the withdrawal by setting up special military talks. The Americans wanted these meetings to take place in Washington, but eventually settled on neutral ground at SHAPE headquarters in Paris.

Gruenther made an impassioned case for garrisoning Austria. Sir John Harding argued that the troops were there for political rather than military reasons, and complained that the British forces were isolated and insufficient to defend the key area in their zone, the Tarvisio Gap. Harding even disputed that the gap was of any strategic worth. It was far more likely, he argued, that if the Soviets attacked, they would do so through the Ljubljana Gap, which could be held by the Yugoslavs. As far as he was concerned, the current situation no longer required British troops. A token contingent would serve just as well. The French concurred, and the talks failed.[65]

Gruenther came up with a new proposal. He wanted to preposition USFA forces in Germany prior to an emergency, while shifting U.S. forces in Trieste into the British zone in Austria, where they would be used with Austrian forces to defend the approach into northern Italy through the Tarvisio-Villach area. On December 22, 1953, he forwarded this scheme to the National Security Council. The potential loss of Austria was described as a grave danger. The JCS argued that it might constitute such a serious risk that without the country plans for a forward defense in Germany might have to be abandoned. Austria was equally critical to the Yugoslav defense of Ljubljana Gap and the Italian frontier.[66] This was exactly the kind of strategic thinking for which USFA had been hoping.

In early 1954, the British and French reduced their forces from reinforced regiments to battalion-sized elements. Gruenther hoped to compensate for the disappointing turn of events by reinforcing USFA with troops from Trieste who were due to withdraw after the termination of their mission. The force—consisting of almost five thousand men, including an infantry regiment, artillery battalion, a tank company, and a cavalry troop—was earmarked for the defense of Tarvisio-Villach. Washington was initially skeptical of the idea, but, after being reassured by Gruenther and the JCS, the civilian leadership accepted the proposal.[67]

The recommendation to redeploy forces to Austria hit a snag, however. The issue was housing. United States Forces Austria had anticipated a howl of complaints if it demanded additional quarters from the civilian populace for military dependents, so the command decided to quarter dependents without requisitioning new houses by constructing housing at Camp Roeder near Salzburg. Troops moved in quietly under the guise of being replacements, not new units—a cover story intended to diffuse adverse criticism.[68]

Meanwhile, NATO finalized its first forward defense plan, which included holding the southern flank. That same year, hopes for a Yugoslav contribution rose when the issue of Trieste was finally resolved, and the U.S. and British occupation of the territory was scheduled for termination. Approval of the Balkan Pact—a formal entente between Yugoslavia, Greece, and Turkey—also appeared imminent.

In the spring of 1955, the strategic situation again changed abruptly when Yugoslavia responded to overtures from the post-Stalin Soviet government to improve relations. Dreams of expanding the Balkan Pact into full-blown military cooperation collapsed. Even teamwork between Turkey and

Greece was in jeopardy over the issue of Cyprus. Joint training exercises were cancelled, and the United States phased out military assistance to Yugoslavia. The promise of an integrated defense along the Yugoslav-Italian-Austrian border vanished. These developments did not lessen USFA's belief in its strategic importance or in arguing for the necessity of defending the southern flank. Without Yugoslav support, however, it was clear that the occupation troops alone could not conduct a forward defense in Austria. In the future, military planners would look for other ways to provide for a fighting stand.

Remarkably, the dynamics of Cold War national security concerns convinced Washington to take a stake in defending a country that could add little real security to the West's defenses. The Austrian borders with strategically important Germany and Italy were, after all, defensible. While a forward stand in Austria could provide a useful buffer zone for slowing a Soviet invasion, any preparations came, as a number of skeptics noted, at the expense of investing in other more critical areas. Furthermore, defending the country might have made some sense if the Soviets had planned to invade. But while the Warsaw Pact did develop plans for an advance against NATO by way of Austria, there is no substantial or credible evidence that during the occupation period the Soviet Union intended an assault on the country.

This is not to say there were no dangers—or that picking a prudent course was not difficult. The most important lesson of the Korean War was that Stalin was willing to exploit strategic weakness on his periphery whenever the risks seemed sensible. The United States could not be wholly passive. Still, there was a difference between demonstrating commitment—as shown by the presence of the occupation troops and investments through the Marshall Plan—and sacrificing transparency to undertake secret preparations against shadowy fears. Nevertheless, USFA war planning pushed the notion of containment to its extreme, prompting considerations for defending a country of marginal strategic utility against a questionable threat and completing the transformation that turned Austria's occupiers into frontline warriors.

SECRETS

ew American fighters led a more colorful life than Lt. Gen. George P. Hays. Born in 1892 to a missionary couple in China, he returned to the United States for his education and eventually graduated from Texas A&M University. He gained considerable combat experience as an artillery officer with frontline infantry units during World War I. At the second battle of the Marne he had seven horses shot out from under him while ferrying vital messages to his unit's command post. Hays received the Medal of Honor. During World War II he fought in several battles in Italy, landed on Omaha Beach, campaigned across Europe to the Siegfried line, and ended the conflict as commander of the 10th Mountain Division.

Hays also had considerable experience as a cold warrior. His division had faced off against Tito's troops in 1945, and two years later he joined the occupation force in Germany as U.S.-Soviet relations there rapidly spiraled toward their nadir. In early 1952, Gen. James Van Fleet requested Hays for a combat assignment in Korea, but John McCloy, the high commissioner for Germany, found the general to be indispensable and refused to release him. Finally, in April, McCloy agreed to allow Hays to replace Irwin as the USFA commander since the assignment included promotion to three-star rank.

Officers like Hays represented a third generation of occupation commanders: leaders who possessed a balance of the military skills needed to prepare for the next shooting war and an ability to work in tandem with their State Department counterparts in waging the Cold War. Although he got along well with McCloy, Hays was less than buoyant over the U.S. diplomatic effort in general and Austria in particular. The process of civilianizing the occupation was already under way when he returned to Europe, and the general saw little that was good in it. In his opinion, allowing the State Department to negotiate with the Soviets had been a mistake. "They have had plenty of opportunity to exercise their talents at the United Nations, Council of Foreign Ministers, etc.," Hays wrote to Albert Wedemeyer, "Although

Lieutenant General Matthew B. Ridgway *(center)* and Gen. Thomas T. Handy *(right)* honor Maj. Gen. George P. Hays on the occasion of Hays's retirement, April 30, 1953. Courtesy National Archives.

I don't believe the military leaders will do much better, I can hardly see how they can do worse."[1] Hays believed the priority had to be creating a credible defense for Europe. As the USFA commander he would have the chance to put that conviction into practice. He would bring some unique ideas to the job.

Ancillary Tasks of Doubtful Utility

Covert warfare was not part of the army tradition. Senior commanders had limited confidence and little practice in conducting shadow wars. This did not, however, prevent USFA from dabbling in the instruments of unconventional combat, experimenting with a range of secret activities from stockpiling supplies to arming refugees. These efforts stretched the limits of Austrian cooperation and the Pentagon's support for clandestine activities. They also added another dynamic to the complicated effort to conclude the state treaty.

Although the United States had conducted covert operations during World War II, it entered the postwar period without an organization or clear strategy for either carrying out these activities or integrating them into an overall campaign. Mainstream military leaders, who had scant interest in such tactics, considered pioneers in unconventional warfare like William Donovan, founder of the OSS, anathema.

Nevertheless, with limited conventional forces available, the military had to consider other ways to shore up its tenuous position in Western Europe. In 1947, the first postwar battle plan, Broiler, called for underground activities, support for anticommunist movements, and providing aid to guerrilla forces. Nor was the United States the only power thinking about unconventional warfare. High Commissioner Béthouart of France often talked about "how possible Soviet aggression might be resisted in Tirol-Vorarlberg by arming ex-members of the Wehrmacht from pre-arranged dumps of equipment and ammunition presumably supplied by U.S. or British elements."[2] The French heavily favored the Pilgrim war plans, in part because of the prominent role given to employing Austrian guerrillas in harassing the Soviets along Germany's flank.

At the time, USFA scoffed at the suggestion that readying the Austrians to take part in guerrilla war was more important than focusing on providing internal security and police forces for the fledgling state. Another reason the army showed little interest in these preparations was that they were outside its area of responsibility. The National Security Act of 1947 assigned the newly created CIA responsibility for "additional services" and "other functions." Included in this vague descriptor was responsibility for the conduct of covert operations. Although senior military leaders on occasion argued that they should have oversight for these activities, the armed services generally were happy to be relieved from performing what they considered ancillary tasks of doubtful utility.

Outpost Vienna

One area where USFA differed from the Pentagon and was anxious to engage in secret preparations concerned the Austrian capital. Like Berlin, Vienna was occupied by all four powers, and the country's most important city sat squarely in the Soviet zone. When the Soviets began to interfere with road and rail traffic to West Berlin on April 1, 1948, the situation in Austria became extremely tense. For twenty-four hours, Kurasov's border troops stopped traffic and flights moving in and out of Vienna. The Soviets had interfered with transit before, but the Berlin blockade unsettled everyone. Army engineers set out across the city, searching for a suitable area that could be used as an emergency landing strip so the city would not be completely stranded.[3]

Soviet troops march in review in Vienna's international sector, August 31, 1951. Courtesy National Archives.

Although the standoff ended the next day, it had served as a powerful reminder of Vienna's vulnerability. Things got a lot worse at 10:45 A.M. on June 17 when the Soviet representative at the twelfth meeting of the Allied commandants of Berlin abruptly rose to his feet. He quickly gathered his papers and, talking rapidly, began to awkwardly shake hands with the startled delegates. The translators could not keep up. Confusion reigned. As the Russian headed for the exit, the chairman called out, asking him to stay and discuss the date for their next meeting. The Soviet colonel replied, "*nyet*," and was gone. A few days later the Soviets instituted a total blockade of West Berlin including cutting off electricity as well as all land and water traffic. Europe was stunned. The Americans in Vienna were beside themselves. They might be next.

Beginning that summer and through the autumn, USFA began to stockpile food, fuel, and critical supplies in case the Soviet's attempted to interfere with the delivery of goods and services into the city. "Squirrel Cage" was the code name for amassing an eighty-two-day food supply for Vienna— enough for 1,550 calories a day for each resident. "Jackpot" was a covert horde of petroleum for both Austria and Trieste. The command also assembled a sixty-day stockpile of key commodities produced or procured in the Soviet zone that might be withheld during a blockade. That operation was code-named "Project Skip."[4]

The United States was not the only power concerned about the city's prospects. In July, the British directed a survey of requirements and assets in their portion of Vienna in case the Soviets tried to enforce a more serious blockade. Over the course of the summer the British stockpiled a sixty-day supply of food and fuel for their personnel alone, after deciding not to follow the Americans' lead and cache supplies for the civilian population, too. If a blockade occurred, they reasoned, the responsibility for trying to starve the Austrians should fall squarely on the Soviets.[5]

In contrast, USFA wanted to confront Kurasov head-on. On October 25, the U.S. Legation presented Washington a long memorandum on the implications of a Vienna blockade and the possibility that the Soviets might partition the country. Should this occur, the paper argued, there would be no option but to continue to maintain the city and support the local government. Military action might even be needed.[6]

The Austrians were more cautious. When a group of Austrian ministers was briefed on Squirrel Cage, Figl thought there was little likelihood of a blockade. Gruber agreed, but counseled that it was worth taking precautions anyway. In the end, the Austrians agreed that the secret stockpile was a prudent measure.[7] The government, which took the secret precautions seriously, not only readied for a possible blockade, they also considered the worst-case scenario: having to abandon the city. Figl designated Innsbruck as the emergency capital and coordinated contingency plans for redeploying the government with USFA.[8]

Dollars, rather than politics, proved to be the major obstacle to these plans, particularly with regard to Squirrel Cage. The cost of periodically rotating stocks of perishable foodstuffs caused the United States to have second thoughts. Stocks were reduced to forty-two days, then just fifteen. After three years the United States liquidated the stockpile altogether and used the proceeds to help fund quarters for U.S. forces coming from Trieste.[9]

Rather than the costly process of hoarding supplies, USFA would have preferred having the ability to constantly replenish the city's food and energy reserves. This strategy, however, raised another serious problem: airfields. In 1945, the Allies—concerned about the logistics of supporting their forces during the first hectic months of the occupation—had argued over possession of the airfields surrounding Vienna. The Americans, British, and French eventually agreed to accept two airfields located several kilometers outside the city proper that were accessible only by passing through the Soviet zone. There were also two small strips in the city center where light liaison planes could land. The U.S. field was by the Danube channel, and the British strip outside their headquarters at the Schloss Schönbrunn. Those landing sites, used primarily to shuttle officials between the city and the larger airfields outside of it, would be totally inadequate for transporting supplies into Vienna.

In addition to championing Skip, Jackpot, and Squirrel Cage, under Keyes's direction USFA drafted an antiblockade plan that included building an emergency airstrip in the U.S. sector. United States Forces Austria hoped to establish an airhead in the city that would allow Vienna to hold out indefinitely. European Command rejected the idea. If the routes to Vienna were blocked, the command argued, it would be likely that the Soviets would have also cut off Berlin, and the United States did not have sufficient airlift to deliver supplies to both cities simultaneously. Air commanders were also skeptical. A showdown with the Soviets would have required the air force to husband its resources in case war broke out, leaving few spare planes for delivering groceries. In addition, surveyors concluded that there was no feasible location in the U.S. sector that could accommodate transport planes.[10]

United States Forces Austria was reluctant to abandon the idea, however, and eventually found a satisfactory location in the British sector. At the command's urging, Washington and London agreed that if the Soviets blockaded the city they would build an emergency airfield at Site Swallow in the British zone. This secret plan called for first jointly constructing a runway for the Americans, then building a second strip for the British. Even after a scheme was agreed on, USFA's problems were far from over. The command entered into a running battle with EUCOM and the Pentagon over requisitioning and stockpiling the nine hundred thousand feet of steel planking needed to construct the runway. When Hays became the USFA commander, he advocated creating a permanent airstrip, but nothing came of it. The outbreak of the Korean War placed a worldwide strain on U.S. planes and crews, leaving the feasibility of a Vienna airlift extremely doubtful.

An annex to NSC-164/1 outlining policy guidance in the event of a Soviet blockade reflected the Americans' caution. The directive called for no military action whatsoever. The most stringent requirement was that all preparations or considerations for a blockade had to remain absolutely secret, kept from both the Soviet authorities and the Austrian populace. After the anxious experience of the Berlin blockade, the United States did not want to provide a pretext for another test of resolve while its position in Europe was still tenuous.[11]

Underground Warriors

Although the prospects for the success of USFA's antiblockade plan were not encouraging, the effort was reassuring to both the command and the Austrian leadership, a sign of Vienna's relevance. United States Forces Austria felt the secret bonds were particularly important as public calls for a more neutral Austrian policy became increasingly frequent and pronounced. Yet, despite the overt drift toward neutrality, prominent Austrians leaders secretly continued to cooperate with the West on security matters. One of America's most loyal partners was Franz Olah. The trade union boss and socialist politician had a well-earned reputation as an *SPÖ* strongman. In 1948, Herz described him as a party leader "who at age 41 has spent nearly a quarter of his life in concentration camps, who has dedicated his life to the struggle against dictatorships and who could at any time could call upon a body of disciplined and fanatical followers."[12] Olah was vehemently antifascist and anticommunist.

A member of Parliament, Olah also headed the Construction and Woodworkers' Union. In October, 1950, he helped break up demonstrations by ordering his men into the streets to do battle with the communists. Supported by CIA funding, Olah organized the *Österreichischer Wander Sport und Geselligkeitsverein* (*ÖWSGV;* Austrian Defense Sports and Friendship Association). The organization had its own intelligence network, communications equipment, and weapons caches. It also undoubtedly trained and armed an anticoup group that might possibly have been used to conduct guerrilla operations in the event of war.[13]

In addition to funding clandestine Austrian activities, the CIA, probably using a portion of the assets allocated to the military assistance program, stocked a number of arms caches throughout the country that were intended to be used by the Austrians to conduct guerrilla warfare either to help fend off a Soviet invasion or to counter a communist coup. Under a secret agreement with Austrian officials, the agency established *Waffenposts* — more than seventy hidden caches of small arms and ammunition distributed throughout the country. The military was a silent partner in the CIA's operations. In the wake of the 1950 riots, the CIA's stockpiling of weapons, as well as funneling money and supplies to Olah, most likely went on with USFA's full knowledge and support.[14]

The Soviets also had some inkling of the existence of covert assistance programs. The Soviet-controlled press, for example, took every opportunity to rail against the alleged use of thugs armed and paid by the West to suppress the workers. All this haranguing may not have been the product of conjecture: "Moles" in British intelligence provided the Soviets much information on NATO and matters related to Austria.[15] As a result, not all of the covert operations may have been as secret as USFA assumed.

Soviet Secrets

The Western allies were not the only ones engaged in secret activities with the Austrians. The Soviet Union's meddling in local affairs through overt intimidation and covert programs had a commensurate effect in breeding distrust. The September-October, 1950, upheavals reinforced USFA's fear that shadowy designs lurked behind all Soviet-sponsored organizations. One of the command's most well documented concerns was the Werkschutz, an industrial security force armed and trained by the Soviets and commanded by Soviet officers. They were used mostly to guard industrial sites, such as the *OROP* oil enterprises.[16]

There were other less visible activities as well. Although unknown to U.S. authorities at the time, in 1955, before the Soviets withdrew from Austria, they also decided to leave behind secret arms caches for their supporters. The KGB was ordered to fill a series of depots, including several villages, a monastery, and two ruined castles. Like the American *Waffenposts,* the sites mostly held small arms, ammunition, and explosives.[17]

While U.S. intelligence officers doubted that the Werkschutz comprised a significant military force, USFA feared Werkschutz personnel were being trained to serve as a secret army with the capability of carrying off a putsch. The command shared this concern with Washington on numerous occasions, and senior Pentagon officials often cited the Werkschutz as evidence of an overt Soviet threat. While military leaders actually knew little about the group, they held up the Werkschutz as proof the United States should expect the worst from the Soviets. In addition, though the Werkschutz alone was hardly justification for a military buildup in Austria, Hays and other argued for that as well. The Austrians also exploited the existence of the Werkschutz. The government pointed to its existence as proof of the requirement to beef up the police forces.[18]

The driving force behind the Werkschutz and other mysteries of Soviet mischief in Austria remained the great engine of Soviet foreign policy, Joseph Stalin—a short, stout, ruthless man who rose to command a vast empire. Initially disliked and dismissed by most of the revolutionary leadership, he steadily rose through the party ranks until he was elected secretary general of the Central Committee at Lenin's suggestion. In 1923, Stalin began a campaign to eliminate his political rivals and by 1927 was the sole leader of the party. A round of bloody purges in 1934 further consolidated his control over the state, command that was unshaken during the turbulent war years. During those decades, Stalin earned a justified reputation as a supreme dictator and mass murderer.

Stalin's postwar policies remain a subject of controversy and debate. Recent revelations from the Soviet and Chinese archives over his role in the Korean War offer some important insights into the goals and tactics of Stalinist foreign policy. He initially rebuffed Kim Il Sung's requests to invade South Korea. Only after carefully laying the groundwork for the invasion, and believing North Korea could achieve unification before the United States could respond, did he give the go-ahead. Stalin believed this support would reaffirm his position as the leader of world communism and enhance Soviet security in Asia at little risk. After UN forces successfully counterattacked, Stalin encouraged the Chinese to intervene, and then encouraged a negotiated settlement.[19] Like the Soviets' half-hearted support for the two attempted *KPÖ* coups in Austria and the show of a blockade of Berlin, Korea suggests that Stalin was cautious in pushing beyond his declared sphere of control and risking a direct confrontation with the United States. Despite the frequent belligerent rhetoric, intimidations, and obstructionist treaty negotiations, Stalin's chief objective seems to have been to secure his empire behind an ironclad security zone of bordering states and a neutralized Germany. Generations will continue to debate this, as well as the meaning behind such shadowy initiatives as the Werkschutz. What is not in question is that Stalin remained fully in control almost until the end. He died of a stroke in 1953.

Preparing for War

The events of the last Stalin years—the activities of the Werkschutz, North Korea's surprise invasion of the South, and the Austrian riots—led USFA to be increasingly worried about being caught off guard. One of the most serious concerns was that the Soviets might launch a preemptive attack with little or no warning, even though CIA strategic estimates showed no indication of an imminent invasion. Regardless, in 1951 USFA initiated a program called "Checkmate." The command conducted monthly reviews of all indicators to determine the imminence of hostilities, with particular emphasis on monitoring events in Austria, Czechoslovakia, Hungary, Rumania, Bulgaria, and Yugoslavia.[20]

Early warning would have done little good if USFA lacked the capacity to fight back, and when Hays assumed command, he found the situation wanting. The Achilles' heel of U.S. efforts to militarize the occupation was the army's lack of manpower. Although USFA had trained and reorganized its troops and revised its war plans, there was little hope that Hays's meager command and a few Austrian guerrillas could successfully defend against a Soviet-led offensive. With the many demands for forces on every front, and the administration carefully weighing the value of each defense investment against its impact on the domestic economy, there was little possibility of garnering additional resources.

Hays argued that defense was still a realistic option if a well-organized and supported conventional force were combined with Austrian manpower. On this point he had an advantage over efforts to rearm Germany: the French and British were opposed to arming the Germans, as were the Soviets, because they feared a resurgent German military power so soon after the Nazis' defeat. The European Defense Community proposal had been an attempt to arrive at an arrangement that would make an armed Germany appear less threatening, but negotiations over the proposal proved protracted and difficult. In contrast, Austria was officially a victim of Nazi aggression, and had very limited military potential. There thus was less concern in the West over arming the Austrians.

United States Forces Austria already had secret plans for mobilizing the Austrians in wartime. In 1949, Washington had authorized the command to prescribe standards and procedures for the volunteer enlistment of Austrian civilians, and USFA began to quietly negotiate with officials for a scheme to register men for wartime service. In February, 1952, the Austrians agreed to begin the secret registration (Aufgebot) of qualified personnel. Intelligence estimated that Austria had a manpower potential of 750,000 men of military age fit for service that could be augmented by another 250,000 nominally fit for duty.[21]

American commanders were comfortable with the idea of a mobilization program since it closely mirrored their own methods. Since the Spanish-American War, mobilization, the rapid expansion of a small professional force in time of war by supplementing units with citizen soldiers, had become an accepted tenet of the American way of war. The United States had relied heavily on mobilization in World Wars I and II. Although many leaders in the regular army dreaded the task of mobilizing and training National Guard and reserve soldiers, even they recognized that nations could not afford to keep a large citizen army under arms in peacetime. Mobilization was the only realistic option. Hence, the army's enthusiastic support for adopting Universal Military Training (UMT) in the United States, which would have required all young men to perform a period of national service and be available for call-up in the case of a national emergency. Congress ultimately failed to adopt UMT, but the United States did retain the draft, and army plans remained based on mobilization in the event of future wars. It took little imagination to extend a similar concept to the Austrian situation. It was, after all, a tried and proven rhythm of habit.

The Austrians organized a very efficient system for identifying and calling up recruits in the western zones. The recruitment program proved an impressive success. On October 22, 1952, USFA reported that 15,000 Austrian volunteers, all with previous military experience, had been registered and that sufficient arms were available to train and equip a regiment within ninety days. Within 180 days, 27,000 troops could be equipped with the remainder of the arms on hand, and another 53,000 outfitted if material were available. Austria had the capability of mustering 200,000 men in the western zones, and estimated that another 100,000 would escape from the Soviet zone.[22]

The only problem, as Hays saw it, was that these numbers were not included in alliance war plans, nor did he have sufficient gear to equip all of the forces available. These were significant issues. With all the other competing demands for resources to rearm Europe, the likelihood that the United States would provide arms for three hundred thousand Austrians was remote. Nor could Austria's fragile economy support such expenditure. Even if the country had been able to afford it, the Soviets would not have allowed it. Finally, if USFA somehow had obtained sufficient weapons and supplies for mobilization, it would have done little good without the organization, training, and planning required to turn a mass of men into a credible fighting force. In short, the practical utility of this ambitious secret program was highly suspect.

Recruiting Europe's Stateless

While USFA remained anxious to enlist the Austrians as cold warriors, there was one scheme for which the command had no enthusiasm: a highly classified project initiated by Eisenhower after his assumption of the presidency. Eisenhower's proposal looked to an available source of manpower, but also a potential cause of serious trouble. Postwar Western Europe contained an enormous stateless population, almost half of which had either fled the Soviet Union or lands under Soviet control. After the war ended, 950,000 displaced persons passed through the U.S. zone in Austria alone.[23]

From 1945 to 1947, the Allies resettled or repatriated the bulk of officially classified displaced persons, including resettling or returning 757,000 in Austria's American zone. However, processing grew more difficult with the advent of the Cold War. Fearing that they might be persecuted, imprisoned, or killed, many of the refugees did not want to be returned. In 1947 the United States still had 47,396 displaced persons in custody in Austria, 90 percent of them considered "irrepatriatable."

In his first meeting with the National Security Council, Eisenhower proposed a solution for dealing with Europe's stateless that meshed with his vision for fighting the Cold War.[24] As a military commander, Eisenhower had been directly involved in European security issues for over a decade. His experience led him to conclude that Europe eventually would have to provide its own cooperative defense regime. "I have come to believe," Eisenhower wrote, "that Europe's security problem is never going to be solved satisfactorily until there exists a U.S. of Europe."[25] With that in mind, the president concluded that there was "a great deal of sense in the whole idea" of raising a legion composed of displaced foreign nationals. Enlisting Europe's unwanted displaced ethnic and national groups to fight together in a common cause would serve as a powerful demonstration of Europe's potential to provide its own collective security.

He proposed a Volunteer Freedom Corps of 250,000 stateless young men from countries behind the Iron Curtain. The refugees would be organized in battalions by nationality, each with its own distinctive flag, uniform markings, and insignia. Units would be officered by Americans and used to augment U.S. infantry divisions.[26]

The president's proposal actually originated with Henry Cabot Lodge Jr., who had attempted to legislate the corps during his tenure in the Senate. Although the corps proposal failed in Congress, Lodge saw the passage of a bill that allowed the army to recruit aliens, a measure sponsored by Rep. Charles J. Kersten to spend $100 million to organize "Iron Curtain nationals" in defense of the "North Atlantic area."[27] The programs enjoyed little success. When the army tried to extend recruitment to Austria, for example, USFA refused to permit it for "political reasons," undoubtedly reflecting the government's concerns over the Soviet response and Austrian attitudes toward the displaced populations.[28]

Lodge managed Eisenhower's presidential campaign, and then joined the administration as the ambassador to the United Nations after losing his own bid for reelection to John F. Kennedy. Soon after Eisenhower took office, Lodge proposed the Volunteer Freedom Corps to the president.[29] Lodge's timing was propitious. Eisenhower was intensely interested in European security and determined to demonstrate activism in foreign affairs. Not only would sharing the defense burden hearten American morale, the president argued, but the corps would also be a cost-saving measure for the United States, since it would employ less well-paid East European refugees rather than more expensive U.S. troops. Reducing defense spending would allow the United States to focus on economic growth, while the corps would also increase Europe's contribution to fighting the Cold War. At the same time, promoting the corps was consistent with the president's election-year pledge to "roll back" the communist threat in Eastern Europe. Small, inexpensive, low-risk initiatives like the Volunteer Freedom Corps would help create the appearance of an active but fiscally responsible presidency.

The president cast aside tepid opposition to his proposal in the National Security Council, but there were, in fact, many serious problems with arming stateless Europeans. In Austria, for example, mistrust of and animosity toward displaced people ran high. Many Austrians saw these them as

Jewish displaced persons at the Salzburg airport preparing to leave for Palestine, November 25, 1948. Courtesy National Archives.

sources of disease, crime, competition for scarce housing and jobs, and potential recruits for revolutionaries intent on triggering another European conflict. Initially, some felt the preeminent threat in postwar Europe was lawlessness by bands by displaced persons. United States Forces Austria went so far as to report that "Displaced Allied personnel caused more concern to the military than did the local civil population."[30]

The shadow of anti-Semitism also hung over everything. Both the Austrians and occupation troops expressed anti-Jewish sentiments. Without question, the issue had strained relations. Since Jews made up a significant portion of the stateless, they would undoubtedly provide a large contingent for the corps—which most likely would lead to additional confrontations.

Harsh postwar conditions further diminished European sympathy and tolerance of displaced groups. One official report concluded frankly that the Austrians did not want "to increase their population with people who were foreign in culture, tradition, language, and morals nor did they want politically dissident groups like Yugoslavs, Poles or White Russians."[31] Arming refugees would only exacerbate fear and ethnic hatred.

Displaced person receiving a free issue of coal at a camp outside Salzburg, February 19, 1953. Courtesy National Archives.

Austrians were already resentful of the occupation by Allied troops. Well-paid, fed, housed, and armed displaced men in uniform, regardless of the corps' announced purpose, would be viewed as a burdensome and oppressive mercenary force. Even as economic and internal security conditions improved in later years, stateless groups could still threaten postwar Europe's new and untested republics. Armed camps of expatriates could become potential breeding grounds for destabilizing revolutionary movements. Belgium offered a case in point. After the war, the government did not even trust native resistance fighters who had fought with the Allies. Fearing such groups might devolve into private militias, the resistance groups were disbanded rather than being integrated into Belgium's postwar army. The Volunteer Freedom Corps presented an even graver potential danger for a fragile democracy like Austria, whose civil society was still far from tolerant.[32]

There was also concern about the reaction of the Soviet Union and other Eastern bloc countries. The Nazi and Italian fascists' use of expatriate populations as a pretext for aggression was still fresh in Europeans' minds. An initiative like the Volunteer Freedom Corps might provoke the Soviets to abandon the state treaty negotiations, divide the country, launch a coup, or even invade. Indeed, Stalin found American initiatives that threatened Soviet power in his own backyard particularly irksome and threatening. In short, any U.S.-led defense proposal that looked to organize displaced Europeans was laced with potential danger.

While Eisenhower showed little regard for these concerns, he conceded that he needed cooperation from European governments. The president told the NSC he wanted to do what was right, and "cause the enemy every possible difficulty." On the other hand, he did not want to "kill our friends."[33] Implementation was deferred until the diplomats obtained concurrence from their European counterparts.

Opposition built quickly. United States Forces Austria lobbied against the program, in part because by 1953 the number of displaced persons had declined to the point that there were virtually no qualified individuals. In fact, most of the last million of Europe's stateless people emigrated or resettled between 1947 and 1951. The command preferred the Austrian Aufgebot, a more conventional use of manpower, and was reluctant to endorse any program that might conflict with this effort. The State Department also argued against the country's participation in the program, concluding that the Soviets would probably view Volunteer Freedom Corps troops stationed in Austria as a violation of the four-power occupation agreement. The department determined that the Austrians could not, and would not, agree to the program.[34] Events in Germany soon justified their fears.

The Uprising

On June 18, 1953, two Soviet representatives sent a secret "telephonogram" to Molotov. There had been rioting in East Berlin and confrontation with the West appeared likely. "At 9:30 A.M. at the Brandenburg gates, employees of the people's police of the GDR were fired upon from the direction of West Berlin. The people's police made several shots in return, as a result of which one West Berlin policeman was killed." While tensions remained high, after two days of discord, calm seemed to be returning. "Representatives of the intelligentsia took almost no part in the strikes and disturbances. Many well-known representatives of the intelligentsia spoke publicly stating their trust in the government and condemning the West Berlin provocateurs. Classes in schools and in institutions of higher learning [and] rehearsals in the theaters of Berlin continued in a normal fashion yesterday and today."[35]

This turmoil stemmed from long simmering troubles. Economic conditions in the East had worsened rapidly after the irrevocable split between the two Germanys. There were food shortages all over the country. Worker strikes erupted across East Berlin early on June 16, and by midmorning sixty thousand people were in the streets. By day's end, hundreds of thousands were demonstrating throughout East Germany. Martial law was declared and Soviet tanks rolled out the next day.

The uprising was quickly put down, but it had shaken Soviet leaders. A spate of intelligence reports suggested that Western efforts to funnel in propaganda, secret agents, and weapons were behind the strikes. It was an attempted "fascist" coup. The reports were unfounded. Despite Eisenhower's rollback rhetoric, the United States had done nothing to provoke the events in East Berlin. American leaders were, in fact, stunned by the events of June, 1953, and unprepared to respond to instability in the Soviet sphere. The uprising demonstrated the limits of the rollback. If the United States had intervened, the result might have been a direct confrontation with the Soviet Union and perhaps nuclear war—the one outcome that Eisenhower was determined to avoid at all costs. Caution was warranted. Berlin gave the president the first indication that an initiative like the Volunteer Freedom Corps might prove more trouble than it was worth.[36]

Indeed, no European country volunteered to participate in the corps. One White House staff member advised that it would be best to put the plan "in a file cabinet and cease to worry about it."[37] Still, while the corps remained on hold, the NSC approved an interim covert program that called for expanding the army's civilian European labor service organization (which provided workers on U.S. bases serving as employees of the U.S. government) to include non-German Soviet escapees. They in turn would provide a pool of future Volunteer Freedom Corps enlistees.[38] As for the corps itself, the proposal remained under consideration until canceled in 1960, long after Eisenhower had lost his enthusiasm for the program.

Call to Arms

The demise of the Volunteer Freedom Corps did little to slow the development of covert initiatives. United States Forces Austria felt its other manpower programs were producing promising results. Hays believed the Aufgebot had tremendous potential and fully expected that the Austrians would participate in the European Defense Community. Anticipating approval of the EDC, USFA intensified efforts to determine how its forces could be quickly organized and equipped as combat divisions. The Army Staff even prepared a position paper on how the command planned to utilize Austrian manpower in preparation for the Churchill-Eisenhower talks in Washington in June, 1954.[39]

In September, 1954, the French rejected the EDC proposal, essentially killing the initiative. Undaunted, the United States proceeded with its plans to utilize Austrian manpower. United States Forces Austria even reached an agreement with the British and French on how these forces would be employed in time of war. The Austrians would be responsible for conscripting and mobilizing forces. Where feasible, the troops would come under the occupation commands and be equipped to the maximum extent possible. After reaching a consensus, the occupation powers presented their plans to the Austrian leadership. The American, British, and French high commissioners communicated their proposal to Felix Raab and Schärf in a private meeting on June 11, 1954. The Austrians later declined to make even an oral commitment, although the commissioners were encouraged by the fact that the Austrians had already conducted covert registration and the framework for mobilization was in place.[40]

Decisions, Doubts, and Deceits

While the army generally thought of covert operations as a nontraditional and inefficient use of resources, USFA was willing to consider the weapons of secret war. The command's enthusiasm for these activities reveals a good deal about the character of the latter period of the occupation. Once Washington had decided to engage in the Cold War in earnest, USFA had considerable influence in determining the nature of military activities. Covert operations demonstrated how commanders in the field could drive the process of militarization. While the JCS had little taste for clandestine methods, USFA managed to push through a number of programs. The anti-blockade plan for Vienna was approved, even though some leaders in EU-COM and the Pentagon thought it impractical. Likewise, Washington approved the proposal for the Aufgebot. Central Intelligence Agency operations, which USFA also encouraged, encountered little interference from the Pentagon. On the other hand, the Volunteer Freedom Corps and alien recruitment programs, which the command did not favor, were never seriously pursued.

The command pushed most actively for the one initiative that most closely conformed to traditional military methods. Mobilization had become a mainstay of U.S. military practices, and USFA pressed for developing a similar capability in Austria. Hays proved a particularly forceful and relentless advocate of this approach. The command's emphasis on mobilization demonstrated that while it was willing to consider covert war, it was reluctant to stray too far from its familiar rhythm of habits.

United States Forces Austria's support for other covert activities also revealed how the pursuit of militarization crowded out other concerns. Arguably, the programs initiated by the command would have provided little real security in the event of a determined Soviet effort to take over the country. Without an air bridge, Vienna could not have been held. Guerrilla operations would not have prevented a coup backed by Soviet troops, much less a full-scale invasion. Nor were there sufficient resources to employ Austrian manpower, even if it could be mobilized.

In turn, these activities garnered only a small measure of support from the Austrians. Staunch anticommunists like Olah would have opposed the Soviets with or without U.S. aid. The government participated in covert activities in part to demonstrate a pro-Western orientation, and in part out of genuine fear of communist coup attempts. But if the Soviets invaded, the Austrians had little doubt that, except for perhaps the westernmost region, the country would quickly fall. The Austrian government saw some good, but much risk, in participating in secret preparations with the West. It always remained a cautious partner, although even in providing a modicum of cooperation the Austrians may have exacerbated the confrontation between the superpowers.

There is little question that covert operations fueled Soviet mistrust and suspicion. The United States knew that the Soviets presupposed aggressive designs were behind every action. Frequent complaints in the Soviet-controlled press demonstrated that they were aware of, suspected, or at least imagined the scope of U.S. covert efforts. Post–Cold War revelations also suggest that U.S. covert activities were more transparent than military leaders assumed. We now know that hardliners like Molotov used U.S. military preparations as evidence in arguing against reaching accommodations with the United States.

By attempting to achieve operational secrecy, the U.S. effort to militarize the occupation may have seemed even more ominous to the Soviets. In addition, covert efforts placed the United States in a predicament. Actions by Hays and other U.S. commanders exceeded the authority agreed upon under the terms of the occupation. The United States thus sacrificed the moral high ground in negotiating with the Soviets, and forfeited its integrity as a fair and honest broker in the Austrian occupation. Covert operations undercut the links between force and diplomacy. America's stated policy was to negotiate a treaty in good faith, but its covert military strategies were intended to ensure U.S. security interests above all else. When the secret use of force runs counter to the stated intentions of foreign policy, both suffer in terms of credibility. United States Forces Austria's clandestine activities thus made the effective linkage of U.S. diplomatic efforts and military operations shaky at best.

While the U.S. position was fraught with inconsistencies, the Soviets were not blameless in this downward-spiraling cycle of mistrust. Through their acts of intimidation and their own covert operations, such as Werkschutz military training, the Soviets fueled Allied suspicions. The United States reacted by pushing initiatives that exceeded the immediate needs of the occupation. In sacrificing transparency of policy for military necessity, the army created as many problems as it solved. To Hays and the other USFA commanders, however, any security gained at the expense of U.S. credibility was well worth it if it speeded the pace of militarizing the occupation.

CHAPTER 9

ARMING AUSTRIA

T he year 1953 was a fateful one. The death of Stalin, the uprising in East Germany, and a surprise Soviet diplomatic peace offensive that appeared to offer the promise of détente unsettled the Europeans. Meanwhile, Raab became chancellor after the ÖVP won the election. One of his first changes was to force the resignation of Gruber, the country's pro-Western foreign minister, and move Austria toward a more neutral public foreign policy. In the midst of this turmoil and change, General Hays abruptly announced his retirement. The State Department fretted over a potential replacement. One candidate was Thomas Hickey, who had served as USFA's chief of staff for Clark and Keyes. Francis Williamson at the State Department took a dim view of this proposal. Hickey, he pointed out, "was more or less the key person in the long dispute between the civilian and military elements in Austria which led to the appointment of the civilian High Commissioner."[1] Nor was Williamson enthused with any of the army's other proposed candidates. He preferred Brig. Gen. Jesmond Balmer, a USFA veteran, or Lem Lemnitzer. Lemnitzer had served as Gen. Harold Alexander's deputy chief of staff in the Mediterranean during World War II, was widely respected in Washington, and had worked with State Department on military assistance programs. Both were old hands at dealing with postwar Austrian affairs and popular in the department, but Balmer was only a brigadier general, and Lemnitzer was not available.

Instead, the army and the State Department settled on Lt. Gen. William H. Arnold. Born in 1901 at Dyersburg, Tennessee, he attended West Point and was commissioned as an infantry officer. Arnold commanded a division in the Pacific during World War II and participated in some of the most difficult and exhausting battles of the island-hopping campaigns. After the war he was among one of the first to land in Japan as part of the army of occupation. He remained until November, 1945. In 1950, after a series of stateside assignments, he took over a difficult job as chief of the Joint U.S. Military Advisory Group to NATO's newest member, Turkey. His outstanding combat record made him a worthy candidate as far as the army was concerned. He took over USFA, on May 1, 1953, ready to carry on the important work of shoring up NATO's southern flank.

Origins

Although Keyes had been the architect of militarization, Irwin, Hays, and Arnold were its builders, implementing the strategic plans drafted by their predecessor. The most important of these schemes was Keyes's vision for secretly rebuilding Austria's army. No initiative garnered more attention and resources. As the last USFA commander, it would be Arnold's task to bring this most critical piece of the plan to fruition.

Organizing the country's army was a decade-long process. After the Anschluss, Germany had amalgamated Austrian troops into its own forces, so at the end of the conflict the country had no independent military service. In the immediate postwar period, a number of paramilitary organizations sponsored by French, British, Yugoslav, Slovene, and Austrian communists claimed some kind of lineage and legitimacy. In the British zone, there was the Rogôzin Corps, the Aldrian Brigade, and British-run labor units referred to as "war establishments." The French had formed a battalion of about five hundred men, Wehrmacht deserters and Austrians who had fought with the resistance. After establishing their occupation zone in the Tirol, the French moved the battalion to Innsbruck. Such groups proved short lived, however. The Soviets objected to any organized local military force, arguing that denazification and pacification demanded total demobilization. At their insistence, and with little complaint from the other powers, the Allies disbanded all such organizations.[2]

Despite Soviet concerns, the Austrians almost immediately began to think about creating a new army. When Karl Renner formed the provisional government in 1945, he appointed Franz Winterer as undersecretary for army affairs. A Reichswehr lieutenant colonel during the war, Winterer had been assigned a series of minor posts because of his social democratic sympathies, and thus was relatively untainted. On September 24, 1945, the fledgling government created a small army office with Winterer in charge. In addition to dealing with demobilization and pension matters, the office began to plan the future army. The office's Informationsabteilung had responsibility for organizing a new general staff, while the Vorschriftenstelle was designated as the nucleus of a future intelligence branch. Winterer also had a small cadre of personnel scattered in various labor and guard units.[3]

Major General William H. Arnold greets Secretary of Defense Charles Wilson, August 27, 1953. Courtesy National Archives.

The military office soon produced its concept for a future force. Assuming that Austria would never be an aggressive country, the office's planning paper concluded that

> it will not, however, be possible to attain a position of neutrality similar to that of Switzerland, since geographical and world-political situation clearly exclude this. In the formation, as is to be expected of blocs, Austria will be drawn, perhaps unwillingly, into one or the other constellation and with it into participation in a future conflict. It will be the art of Austrian politics to reduce this participation to a tolerable extent. . . . Our armament must therefore be sufficiently great for us effectively to defend the State territory. Not more, but on no account less. Our future military system must therefore, be looked at from this standpoint of view, render feasible the greatest possible display of strength of a defensive nature.[4]

As for potential enemies, the paper saw little danger from Italy, but Yugoslavia and Hungary were identified as possible sources of tension.

The analysis also offered an assessment of the impact of domestic politics on military issues: "The days of the pro-military right wingers, or the equally anti-military left wingers, belong to the past." This appreciation flew in the face of history. In the wake of World War I, the first Austrian republic had faced a similar challenge when it established the Volkswehr. In the turmoil of the postwar years, the leftist Volkswehr devolved into more of a party guard than a true national army. At the same time, paramilitary groups sponsored by other political factions proliferated. The largest and best armed of these was the right-wing Heimwehr. Throughout the First Republic's tumultuous history, these organizations engaged in political intimidation and, occasionally, violent armed confrontations.

Winterer concluded that an agreement could be reached using Renner's corporatist approach, making the post–World War II army an apolitical instrument. Indeed, there was ample evidence that the Austrians' experiment with democracy had proven a success, at least with regard to maintaining unanimity. In practice, the legislature passed most of its acts unanimously. Winterer believed this spirit could be carried into military affairs. Compulsory militia service would force the army to draw equally on all political factions, reducing the possibility that the troops would become the tool of any party. Hence, his plan proposed a force that included a small regular army of about 22,000 men, primarily for protecting the frontier and dealing with domestic disturbances. The army would be supplemented by a militia of about 25,000 to 26,000 men, who would revert to the reserves after their compulsory term of service. Winter estimated that after thirty years the reserves would grow more than large enough to prevent any faction from dominating.[5]

The Allies soon learned of the government's plans. At a September 15, 1945, meeting of Allied Council military representatives, the U.S. delegate reported that the Austrians were contemplating an army of six hundred thousand men. The Soviet representative quipped, "Who are they going to fight?" The rest of the attendees laughed.[6] This news was passed to the high commissioners, who saw little humor in the proposal. Some members of Winterer's staff were known to have strong Austrofascist roots. The Austrians should not have been surprised when the Allies moved to quickly terminate their effort.[7] On December 10, 1945, the Allied Council issued a directive banning the creation of any "department or similar agency [concerned] with military matters within the Austrian government."[8] After being disbanded, the office's administrative functions were taken over by a new department in the finance ministry: Abteilung L.[9] Allied Council oversight remained stringent. In 1946, at Soviet insistence, the high commissioners directed a subsequent investigation and restated the prohibition against planning for a future Austrian army.[10]

The Palace Guard

The occupation powers did allow for the establishment of a national police force. However, its duties were restricted wholly to normal civil functions, it was subordinated to the occupation forces, and it operated under rigorous Allied supervision. The branches of the police included the federal police, which patrolled the major townships, and the *gendarmerie,* which watched over smaller towns and the countryside. While this organization was not meant to be a security force, Soviet anxiety over its operations was a persistent theme. On April 10, 1946, the Allied Council agreed that members of the *gendarmerie* could carry rifles and that the police could have revolvers. Before the arms were issued, however, the Soviets wanted the council to approve all plans for training and use. A satisfactory agreement was never reached. The following December, the Soviets complained that the strength of the police forces had been increased without council authority. In January, 1947, they protested that the Austrian police were carrying unauthorized automatic weapons.

As a result of Soviet resistance, the police and *gendarmerie* — armed with a handful of various kinds of pistols, rifles, and carbines—hardly constituted a credible security force. The Vienna police had only 3,504 pistols for 8,784 men, and barely any ammunition. Meanwhile, the Austrians continued to grumble over public safety concerns. Although the Soviets were the main target of complaints, the United States was occasionally singled out for censure. All of the Allies fretted over and meddled in the affairs, organization, and politics of the police forces.[11] Some of their worries were justified, but progress was slow largely because the Allied Council failed to achieve consensus on reconstituting the force. The Soviets deserve the lion's share of the blame for this impasse.

The British, whose zone arguably faced the most significant security challenges, were most concerned over the state of the poorly trained, ill-disciplined, and inadequately equipped *gendarmerie.* Unlike the Americans, the British did not have sufficient forces to create constabulary troops. Facing declining manpower on one hand, and rising crime rates and continuing confrontations with the Slovenes and Yugoslavs in Carinthia on the other, they were very keen on building up the *gendarmerie.* In fact, British troops were already using *gendarmes* to assist in policing the frontier in Styria and Carinthia.

The British were more concerned about strengthening the country's internal security before the approval of the state treaty than they were in pacifying Soviet worries over denazification. Without waiting for Allied Council approval, the British provided pistols to the police and rifles to the *gendarmerie* and planned a three-phase program to turn all responsibility for the frontier over to the Austrians. The first phase, assigning *gendarmes* responsibility for manning the border posts, was completed by the end of the year.[12]

The British were particularly willing to rely on the police, because they not only had been denazified, but their ranks had been largely purged of communist influence. The police were under the federal jurisdiction of the Ministry of the Interior. The first minister had been Franz Honner, a communist. When the *KPÖ* lost control of the ministry after the November, 1945, election, the *SPÖ*'s Oskar Helmer replaced Honner and reorganized the force, removing many communists from the ranks.

A Post-Treaty Force

Looking to further strengthen internal security, the British engaged in secret discussions with Austrian officials in 1947 regarding the composition of the country's post-treaty army.[13] The Austrians surprised them, delivering a proposal that proved far more ambitious than Winterer's initial recommendation: a legion of five divisions, more than a hundred thousand men, 150 tanks, and a hundred artillery pieces. The British were stunned. The numbers far exceeded what was needed or could realistically be achieved. Gruber, who led the discussions for the Austrians, said he believed "his military experts had decided to err on the safe side, assuming that not all their requirements would be met."[14] But the British were put off, a reaction both to the scope of the proposal and fear that it might be leaked to the Soviets, making the British appear to be sponsors of Austrian rearmament.

Instead, in cooperation with the Americans and the French, the British decided to address the issue in the Allied Council. The draft state treaty included a provision for establishing a fifty-three-thousand-man military force. On March 28, 1947, the British high commissioner argued that denazification had been sufficiently successful to permit the Austrians to establish a Ministry of Defense and begin planning for an army and air force along the provisions outlined in the treaty. The Soviets abruptly rejected the proposal, declaring that such discussions exceeded the council's authority.[15] Any negotiations on the scope of Austrian military forces would have to be part of the state treaty talks.

After treaty negotiations stalled the following year, Leopold Figl proposed that the issue be taken up again. France's deputy high commissioner, Gen. Paul D. R. Cherrière, suggested a new scheme for beginning military preparations before the treaty was approved that would bring the Austrians into discussions on how the initiative could be implemented without antagonizing the Soviets. The USFA staff was skeptical. The Soviets had shown little flexibility in private meetings, so the command sent a cable to the JCS saying that Kurasov was likely to veto any such proposal. By this time the Americans, as well as the British and the French, had begun to conclude that the only way to create an Austrian security force would be to covertly build up the *gendarmerie*.[16]

The Austrian Way

It would be wrong to view the creation of a pretreaty armed force as solely a Western initiative imposed on the Austrians. By 1948, the *SPÖ* and *ÖVP* were troubled over the prospect of a communist coup, as well as the poor state of public safety. They considered the creation of a protective military force to be a covert operation that was worth the risk of raising the Soviets' ire. In fact, they were at times frustrated that secret developments did not proceed with greater speed.[17] On April 20, 1948, Julius Deutsch scheduled a meeting with General Balmer to discuss the issue. Deutsch, a former military officer, had been instrumental in establishing the First Republic's Volkswehr, and eventually became the secretary of state for the army. A socialist, he fought for the Republicans in Spain and escaped the Nazis by immigrating to the United States in 1940. He became a prominent leader in the *SPÖ*'s conservative wing after the war ended. He was also one of his party's principal leaders on military matters.

Deutsch confided to Balmer that, in anticipation of the treaty being approved, a committee including himself and Helmer, and State Secretary Ferdinand Graf and Emil Liebitzky of the *ÖVP*, had been formed to develop a framework for the future military. The *KPÖ*, which had been actively campaigning against creating a standing army, had not been invited to participate. Knowing the Soviets would reject any overt government initiative, Deutsch proposed that the committee continue to work in secret, consulting as needed with U.S., British, and French authorities. Balmer could not have been more pleased. Winterton, the British deputy, shared that he had engaged in a similar conversation with Helmer. The British also broached the subject with the French, who revealed that they, too, had come to the conclusion the Austrians needed a self-defense force sooner rather than later.[18] Shortly thereafter, U.S. and British representatives conferred with an Austrian working group composed of Deutsch, Helmer, Hans Brachmann (the *SPÖ* member of Parliament), and the *ÖVP*'s Graf, Raab, and Vice President Alfons Gorbach to draft a comprehensive national defense law that would establish a ministry of defense, institute a draft, specify the length of enlistments, include provisions for the political rights of the military, spell out the duties of the army, and assign unit geographical locations.

The secret negotiations were paralleled by a public debate on the future military system. In June, 1948, Deutsch wrote in *Die Zukunft* that Austria could either rely on the great powers forever or see to its own responsibilities. The police and *gendarmerie* would be inadequate for operations in the field, and, as lifetime servants of the state, their members would not be true representatives of a democratic military force. While an Austrian army would be of no great importance in a major war, it was essential for the country's self-protection. He advocated forming a conscription army that "will mirror the better tendencies and directions of the mass of the people."[19] In contrast, Graf argued it would be more efficient and appropriate to be defended by a well-armed and disciplined professional force. Graf also feared that socialists would dominate a large militia. Deutsch, on the other hand, lobbied against having only a small force in part because he believed its members would be primarily conservatives. The debate became quite contentious.

Keeping the Secret

As interparty deliberations intensified, secret military preparations and training for the Austrians began in earnest.[20] In a meeting with Helmer on June 16, Balmer offered arms and weapons training for the police. The minister agreed that Figl would write a letter requesting that U.S. training facilities be made available. United States Forces Austria, in turn, would propose to train selected groups in the use of small arms and light machine guns. Armed with this agreement, USFA could report to Washington that the Austrians had *requested* the training. On September 15, the command completed an agreement with the Austrian government and five days later the JCS approved the plan. Operation Kismet would become the catalyst for establishing a nascent military force under the guise of the *gendarmerie*. The British began a parallel effort, Exercise Constable.

Two months later, the U.S. command reported that the Austrian police and special *gendarmerie* in its zone were being trained at the rate of two hundred per week. Based on this success, USFA also started training police in its sector of Vienna. Although the British and French had second thoughts about the program and opted not to participate, USFA still estimated that thirty-two hundred Austrian police and *gendarmerie* personnel would be trained by December. It did not have authority to give the Austrians any weapons, but the following April the JCS approved distributing arms to American units, which stored them for the police.

Notions of creating a secret army quickly proved to be another mark of divergence between the diplomats and the generals. The State Department's Policy Planning Staff was unenthusiastic about the program, arguing that it would accomplish little of practical value and antagonize the Soviets.[21] In fact, all this activity did not go unnoticed. One communist newspaper reported that the police were being trained for use against the working classes. United States Forces Austria's response to complaints was that the occupation agreement made each high commissioner responsible for maintaining law and order in his zone, leaving him free to outfit and train the police as he saw fit.[22]

Training was completed by February, 1949. Meanwhile, in secret talks with the Americans and British, and with French concurrence, the Austrians fleshed out a plan for their future military force, proposing to an organize a unit within the *gendarmerie* that could serve as a cadre for the future Austrian army. Deutsch recommended the formation of battalions from a force of five thousand policemen and twenty-five hundred *gendarmerie,* with the units to be centered around Linz or Graz. The committee settled on establishing a regimental headquarters near Salzburg with one battalion each in the U.S. and British zones and a third planned for the French zone. Each would have a scout, armored car, and infantry company. Based on this proposal, Helmer announced on March 9 the formation of the special uniformed *gendarmerie* under the command of Gendarmerieoberst Dr. Ernst Mayr.[23]

The most significant problem faced by the new force was that it had virtually no equipment. Deutsch suggested that the regiment use old German rather than U.S. gear, which might be less likely to provoke the Soviets. The committee, on the other hand, recommended that the British outfit the regiment from their cache of U.S. equipment. On September 30, 1948, the British reported they did not have sufficient stocks available, although they did offer up a hodge-podge of weapons and vehicles of questionable reliability. United States Forces Austria rejected the proposal on the grounds that, to be effective, the regiment needed serviceable, uniform equipment so it could train and function as a proper military unit. It was more than a matter of simply outfitting a few police units to U.S. leaders; they wanted to build the core of a fighting army. While the United States did not yet have a formal military assistance program to outfit the Austrians, on July 8, 1949, U.S officials agreed to commence training the special regiment with available U.S. equipment—which would remain army property, albeit under *gendarmerie* control.[24]

As preparations progressed, Austrian planners supervised by Figl, Graf, Raab, and Gorbach began to draft a general organizational concept for the post-treaty force. A compromise between the recommendations of the two major parties, the proposal was close to Winterer's initial recommendation.

Enrollment in the armed forces would be based on compulsory military service. Initially, most of the recruits would be drawn from the ranks of those with prior military training. Trained conscripts would serve for six months, whereas untrained recruits would remain in uniform for a year. Only men who had *not* served in the Wehrmacht would be eligible to become officers. The garrison locations would become the nucleus of future combat brigades. The army's initial strength would be between 20,000 and 30,000 troops, eventually growing to the 53,000 authorized in the draft treaty.[25]

At first the U.S. found the British and French generally supportive of the initiative, though they provided little material, financial, or training assistance.[26] The British government was willing to field a post-treaty Austrian air force of five thousand men and ninety planes, and both British and French officials considered providing some surplus equipment. Even this support was tentative, however. In June, 1949, the British high commissioner, Gen. Sir Alexander Galloway, had second thoughts about the plan, fearing it might jeopardize the treaty negotiations.[27] He was concerned the United States was moving too fast. Winterton reported that USFA was determined to begin implementing Austria's military buildup immediately. "It would be a great pity," he added, "if the British who have hitherto taken the lead in these matters are left at the post, and I would like to suggest that you should use your influence with General Keyes to get him to delay a little longer if necessary."[28]

Galloway summed up the British concerns, saying he would "deplore the development of a situation in which the US kept deferring ratification [of the state treaty] in order to form an Austrian Army, and the Soviet withheld their ratification because an Austrian Army was being formed. Such a situation would obviously be fraught with some danger."[29] Instead, he proposed that the *gendarmerie* not serve as a cadre for the Austrians' post-treaty army. In November, 1950, the British withdrew their offer to outfit an air force. The French, expressing similar reservations, said they had little to contribute to the effort.

Both the British and French complained they had neither the resources to follow through on outfitting the army, nor the means to stand up to a severe Soviet response to the operation. Believing there was little likelihood the program could be kept secret, they would have preferred to defer the initiative. However, due largely to USFA's persistence, they agreed not to obstruct U.S. plans to build up the *gendarmerie* regiment.

Guns and Butter

Recruiting an army would be a hollow victory if the force lacked equipment. The real issue for USFA was where it would get the resources required to allow an Austrian army to take the field. With France and Great Britain carefully measuring their military commitments, the United States conceded it would have to carry the lion's share. To provide the necessary gear, USFA intended to make use of a new tool in the Cold War arsenal: the Mutual Defense Assistance Program (MDAP). The formation of NATO had vastly expanded requirements for military assistance, driving the need for a full-fledged MDAP.

The emergence of the MDAP, which eventually grew to encompass half of America's foreign aid, was fraught with difficulty and controversy. General Lemnitzer, a champion for military assistance programs, often found himself in the thick of bitter interagency debates. The Pentagon had many concerns. Much of the initial opposition to the MDAP came from the armed services. Lemnitzer recalled that he "never saw the Army Staff. . . . They were a million miles away from all of this. . . . I used to have a head-on collision with the Army. I had the same collisions with the Navy and the Air Force."[30] The services' intransigence was understandable. The MDAP competed for resources with all the other defense priorities, including prosecuting the Korean War, funding nuclear weapons programs, and rebuilding America's conventional capability in Europe. There was also a question as to how much military aid the Europeans could reasonably absorb. Even if the United States gave its partners free equipment and ammunition, they would have to make their own investments in manpower, maintenance, and administration—costs that would only further strain the economy of war-weary states that were struggling to rebuild. Despite the economic stimulus provided by the Marshall Plan, no Western European country could afford an abundance of guns *and* butter.

The JCS eventually supported the MDAP, but their approval was based on the assumption the administration would request $14.4 billion for defense for fiscal year 1951, the first year of implementation. When the president reduced the defense budget request to $13 billion, the chiefs could have adjusted to the deficit by cutting the $1.4 billion earmarked for the MDAP. The administration, however, insisted on retaining the MDAP funding and instead canceled other defense programs, including the navy's supercarrier. The ensuing acrimony over the budget erupted into the infamous "revolt of the admirals" and a series of House Armed Services Committee investigations and hearings. It took strong congressional support, another one of the few areas where legislative interest in foreign affairs directly affected Austria, to get the MDAP off the ground.

Even here there were challenges. Senator Thomas Connally (D-Texas), a typical skeptic declared: "What I have been fearing about this whole program . . . is that most of the countries in Europe are just going to sit down and fold their hands and say 'well, the United States is going to arm us. The United States is going to protect us.'"[31] Vandenberg, Congress's strongest proponent of a postwar bipartisan foreign policy, who was often at odds with Connally, was equally critical of the plan and declared he would do anything to stop the "'war lord bill' which would have made the President the top military dictator of all time."[32] Despite this rhetoric, Congress approved the program with only a few modifications to the administration's initial proposal.

Austria was not on the list of initial priorities, but USFA lobbied frequently and aggressively for providing materiel assistance. Now that the program was an unavoidable reality, military leaders found that providing arms for Austria offered another opportunity to beef up NATO's troublesome southern flank. The JCS recommended $12 million for the *gendarmerie* and $100 million to equip a future army. The State and Defense Departments in the end added a program for Austria in the bill presented to Congress.[33]

Then another problem arose: the United States could not legally transfer equipment before the treaty's approval. Instead, the administration opted to earmark money in the MDAP for equipment to be dispensed after the signing. Here, too, there were difficulties. In the original MDAP, $93,330,000 was allocated for Austria, sufficient funds to outfit the entire force authorized by the draft treaty. The Bureau of the Budget, reasoning that treaty approval was not imminent, reduced the Austrian program to $11,570,000, enough to equip only the *gendarmerie*. The bureau argued that if the treaty was unexpectedly approved, resources could be reprioritized. But delivery of military equipment required a long lead-time and could be supplied only at the expense of other MDAP accounts, by breaking the equipment retention levels set by the JCS, or by tapping the MDAP's emergency fund. If the treaty was approved, arming Austria thus might prove to be impossible.[34] However, after the outbreak of the Korean War and with renewed momentum for European rearmament, the chiefs pushed to expedite an $82 million program in October, 1950, arguing that "there is an immediate and pressing need to stockpile in Austria and/or Germany the arms and equipment required to equip an initial Austrian security force of approximately 28,000."[35]

To build up the necessary supplies, the "Program for Stockpiling Material for Title I Countries (European MDAP)" was redesignated "Stockpile A (MDAP supplies for Austria)." By the end of 1952, Stockpile A contained about 227,000 tons of materiel (representing almost $70 million in military aid and 87 percent of the requirements for the new Austrian force) stored in U.S. Army Europe depots in France and Germany, the bulk consisting of five thousand vehicles maintained at the Fontenot Ordnance Depot in France.[36]

The Committee War

It would be difficult to overstate how closely USFA and the Austrians worked together in building the state's secret army. *Gendarmerie* files include copies of the voluminous correspondence between the *Österreichisches Wiener Komitee* (Vienna Committee), the Austrians representing the government, and the U.S., British, and French military commanders known as the *Salzburger Komitee* (Salzburg Committee). The Vienna Committee provided periodic updates on the status of the special *gendarmerie,* including ammunition allocations, vehicle maintenance status, distribution of clothing and special equipment, and budgeting. The Salzburg Committee peppered the Vienna Committee with requests for information on everything from training and readiness to how personal records were being maintained. The committee also held approval authority for all officer assignments.[37]

Despite this close relationship, U.S.-Austrian cooperation was often strained over the scope of the rearmament program. When the special *gendarmerie* regiment conducted exercises in September and October, 1951, USFA was thoroughly dissatisfied with its performance and wanted to take over the regiment's reorganization and training. In turn, the Vienna Committee produced its own separate and sharply contrasting set of assessments and recommendations. The committee argued that the regiment should not be preparing for conventional war as practiced during the field training, but preparing to counter attempted coups. After some negotiation, the two sides agreed on a compromise to train the *gendarmerie* as a countercoup force, as the Vienna Committee envisioned, but also to develop a plan for general wartime mobilization.

The Austrians came to rely heavily on the so-called B-Gendamerie as a reaction force, maintaining alarm plans to rapidly call its units into action.[38] Indeed, the *gendarmerie* were called out to deal with riots and a general strike in October, 1950. Communist newspapers complained that they were nothing more than the government's own private army, a combination "*Prügelgarde . . . Terrorgarde . . . Schlägertrupp.*"[39]

Within the *gendarmerie,* however, it is clear that they, like their U.S. counterparts, saw themselves as more than just an anticoup force. The *gendarmerie* files reveal that the future Austrian military was thinking seriously about a conventional defense against the Soviets. In 1952, the Austrians participated in USFA's Exercise Frosty, which practiced a defense of the passes in Upper Austria. In addition, the curriculum in the *gendarmerie* schools included the discussion of conventional military operations, including the study of Russian combat methods on the eastern front in World War II. The Austrians were particularly interested in the conduct of antitank defenses, especially the kind that would be needed to stem a future Soviet armored invasion. Finally, documents from the files make it clear that *gendarmerie* officers wanted to fight a forward defense in Carinthia in coordination with the Yugoslavs. This approach, the Austrians argued, made sound strategic sense. It was unrealistic to contemplate a fighting defense that did not hold on to at least part of the country.[40]

Another indicator of the seriousness of the Austrian effort was its recruitment policies. As the Austrians began to step up recruiting for the special *gendarmerie,* it was clear that they were looking for men with conventional military experience. Buried in the files of the Interior Ministry are the records of the *gendarmerie* administration. This division was responsible for managing a number of posts scattered throughout the U.S., British, and French zones—the homes of the B-Gendarmerie. Most of the files give little hint of the B-Gendarmerie's purpose. There are thick folders of letters: commanders issuing tedious administrative instructions, fretting over the cost of maintaining ramshackle installations, buying windows, bemoaning the exorbitant cost of boots, complaining about the state of plumbing. Also in the files are requests to join the B-Gendarmerie. A typical letter came from a young man in Graz who labeled himself a "*gendarmerie* aspirant." His letter carefully spelled out his background and qualifications. Born in Furstenfeld on December 16, 1925, he underwent military training in 1941–42 and was then assigned as a noncommissioned officer in the 50th Infantry Division. While fighting on the eastern front, he was captured by the Russians on May 10, 1945, and sent to Moscow and then Siberia. Repatriated in 1950, he had joined the *gendarmerie* in 1951 and hoped to obtain a position in the newly established and expanding B-Gendarmerie. As in the other applications in the *gendarmerie* files, the writer's military education and experience are underlined in red. The attention given to military training was understandable given that the B-Gendarmerie served as the secret training ground for the nucleus of Austria's post-treaty army.[41]

Watch on the Danube, Moscow, and the Potomac

United States Forces Austria closely monitored the *gendarmerie*'s progress since its development formed the backbone of the rearmament program. In particular, it kept a watchful eye on the perceived twin great dangers: communist infiltration and Soviet obstructionism. Helmer always maintained that his first priority was to purge communists from the force and not repeat the mistakes of the First Republic by allowing the security forces to become politicized. Nevertheless, U.S. representatives maintained rigorous oversight. At one point, Ambassador Donnelly confronted the Austrians over reports of a renewed presence of communists in the police force. In an effort to intimidate the ministers, Donnelly produced a letter he had drafted himself but purported to be from the State Department, expressing alarm at the communist presence in the police ranks. The confrontation generated a prompt and reassuring response that everything possible was being done to root out *KPÖ* influence.[42]

As for concerns over Soviet obstructionism, a particularly noteworthy incident was the infamous, almost comical, Christmas Eve *Gummiknüppel* incident. Without warning on December 24, 1952, Soviet military detachments began fanning out through their zone confiscating the *gendarmerie*'s rubber truncheons. The Allies were at a loss to explain the behavior, but the U.S. ambassador cautioned that the Soviets "may be releasing trial balloon with intention push control further if unopposed this time. . . . In view customary Soviet technique of moving first against police in any area they intend to take over, we are concerned by possible seriousness Soviet action and propose strong reaction."[43] This response was not untypical. Any Soviet action against the police or *gendarmerie* was a matter of grave consternation.

The United States was far less concerned with purging threats from the right, which had once been the occupation force's principal mission. Two years before, a new right-wing party, the *Verband der Unabhängigen (VDU)*, had been officially organized. Its support came mainly from former Nazi and ultranationalist groups. When the high commissioner reported the party's apparent rise in popularity on the eve of the 1952 national elections, he urged restraint, arguing that the "overt demonstration of dislike or distrust of *VDU* would be imprudent."[44] The occupation authorities were pleased with the Austrians' corporatist government and believed it was strong enough to withstand a pull from the right. In fact, the *gendarmerie* files offer numerous examples of government concern over penetration of the police force by *VDU* members.

The resurgence of the right wing and a surge in *VDU* membership in the *gendarmerie*, on the other hand, elicited a stern response from the Soviets. Soviet occupation authorities also noted disapprovingly the special *gendarmerie*'s training regime. On December 23, 1953, the official Soviet news service *TASS* carried a report that the special *gendarmerie* schools were being used as a nucleus to train the cadre for a future army.[45] In articles such as this, in the frequent lectures that the Soviets dished out to Austrian officials, and in the Allied Council meetings, they continued to rail over the danger of a resurgent fascist threat.

American leaders brushed aside Soviet complaints. In Washington,

USFA had secured the JCS's full support, and they were united in seeing the program through to the end. The chiefs persisted in arguing that the state treaty should not be concluded until provisions for having an adequate defense force in place before the occupation forces withdrew were assured. Friction between the State Department and the military resurfaced in an unusually heated debate played out before Eisenhower at the April 30, 1953, NSC meeting. Secretary of State John Foster Dulles complained that the military "would prefer to see Austria divided and occupied by both western and Soviet troops rather than a unified and unoccupied Austria."[46] General Hoyt Vandenberg, speaking for the chiefs, countered that the military's primary concern was preventing the further encroachment of Soviet power into the West and that they had no problem with any treaty—as long as there was a guarantee that a post-treaty Austrian army would be ready to take the field. While the president seemed sympathetic to Dulles's case for pressing on with the treaty, he showed no inclination to override the military.

Additional pressure to speed preparations came in 1954 in the wake of British and French moves to decrease their occupation forces to skeletal commands. The reductions spurred USFA, with the support of Austrian officials, to request an increase in the special *gendarmerie* from five thousand to eighty-five hundred troops. When Arnold reported in as the new USFA commander, he found that beefing up the *gendarmerie* was his top priority. With the additional forces, the restructured regiment was organized into nine infantry battalions and one engineer battalion, providing almost a division's worth of combat power—as much as was available to the American, British, and French commanders combined.

While Arnold pushed for the accelerated fielding of the special *gendarmerie,* he anxiously tracked internal Austrian activities and debates over the army's formation. One particularly uneasy moment occurred over sudden dissension in the ranks of the socialists. Sources suggested a significant struggle among leaders and members over the influence of former Nazis in the *gendarmerie* and the compromise plan for a mixed professional and conscription force as agreed to by the Vienna Committee. Speaking to a member of the U.S. State Department, Bruno Mitterman, an *SPÖ* parliamentary leader, acknowledged that there was ongoing debate over whether the army should be a professional military organization or one based on conscription and UMT. Helmer also acknowledged the dispute and had already conceded to the proposal, even though he admitted that other party leaders might oppose it.[47] The confrontation was disconcerting in light of sudden and unexpected progress in the state treaty negotiations.

Changing of the Guard

One of the most renowned figures in the sudden Soviet peace offensive was the white-haired, goateed Nikolay Alexsandrovich Bulganin. The son of an office clerk, he rose quickly through the military and political ranks, spending almost thirty years at the highest levels of Soviet leadership. A classic Soviet apparatchik, his chief skill seemed to be not making enemies. Although he lacked military training, he was given the rank of general during the war and served for a while on Marshal Georgi Zhukov's military staff. After failing to distinguish himself, he transferred and performed with distinction in other posts on the front. In 1944, Bulganin became a member of Stalin's war cabinet. After Germany capitulated, Stalin elevated him to the rank of marshal of the Soviet Union and appointed him minister of the armed forces. He became defense minister shortly before Stalin's death and watched as a triumvirate of party leaders—Premier Georgi Malenkov, police head Levrenti Beria, and Moscow party boss Nikita Khrushchev—vied for power. In 1955, with Khrushchev's backing, Bulganin was named prime minister.

One of Khrushchev's proposals was to ameliorate confrontation with the United States while consolidating control over the Soviet sphere, including a rapprochement with Yugoslavia and the integration of East Germany but not Austria. In April of that year, Bulganin met in Moscow with a high-ranking delegation led by Raab. Schärf recorded a remarkable exchange between the two in his diary, claiming that Bulganin conceded the Soviets had avoided serious negotiations over the state treaty during the previous half-decade.[48] There had been hope of using the state treaty and the withdrawal of Soviet troops as a bargaining chip, holding Austria hostage to achieve a more favorable resolution of the German question. Bulganin's confession revealed a position long held by Molotov, who thought that Austria's fate should be deferred until a satisfactory German settlement.[49]

Molotov's hard line had always had a fatal flaw. Although USFA had long argued that Austria was an invaluable adjunct to the defense of NATO's southern flank, its strategic importance to the West paled in comparison to Germany. It is inconceivable that the Americans would have compromised on the most important nation in Europe to obtain an advantage in Austria. It was not a worthy bargaining chip. As a result, USFA had always assumed that the primary Soviet interest in the country must have been *military* (retaining Austria as a launch platform for the invasion of Western Europe), and not *political*. Bulganin's comments suggested that the Soviets' view had been exactly the opposite: it had always been a matter of politics rather than power.

But all of this was guesswork at the time; Soviet intentions for the future of the republic were as obscure after Stalin's death as before. Still, Bulganin's purpose in meeting with the Austrians had been to send a clear signal that, for whatever reason, the Soviets were at last prepared to conclude the state treaty. This dramatic change (after the virtual demise of the treaty negotiations in 1949 and the quick death of the "short treaty" in 1952), along with a blitzkrieg of other Soviet foreign policy initiatives, seemed to signal a clear shift in Soviet tactics, though to what end Western leaders could only conjecture.

Countdown

With a settlement suddenly imminently possible, the ability to rapidly put an Austrian force in the field seemed more important than ever. Soviet attitudes toward the country's post-treaty military also changed with unexpected swiftness. On April 19, 1955, Graf informed U.S. representatives that a Soviet official had told him his country had no objection if the Austrians exceeded the fifty-three-thousand-man treaty force limit. According to Graf, "for all they cared the Austrians could have an army twice that size."[50] In fact, in September the Soviets offered Raab equipment for the new army. This proposal was undoubtedly designed to demonstrate that the post-Stalin leadership was serious about respecting Austria's neutrality and reaching détente with the West. The Soviets eventually transferred a cache of military stocks that included ten thousand carbines, ten thousand machine pistols, twenty-four howitzers, and twenty-eight T-34 tanks.[51] These supplies were mostly symbolic; hardly significant enough to affect the military balance in the region.

Meanwhile, with the time for the treaty's implementation approaching, the United States redoubled its efforts to prepare the Austrian army to take the field. No one experienced the sense of urgency more than Lt. James R. Stephens, who was assigned to the 63d Signal Battalion at Camp Roeder. In the summer of 1955, he was unexpectedly summoned to an audience with his battalion commander, who told him: "I'm putting you in charge of a program to train a handful of highly placed Austrian communications people—residents of the area—who will take the material you give them from the Signal School to form a base for training the Austrian Army Signal Corps. You're to consider this TOP SECRET. If word gets out to the Soviets, Allied Powers' withdrawal and the Future 'neutrality' of Austria can blow up in our faces—and that's the least that can happen."[52]

Stephens left breathless. He had a secret mission: His task was to provide the Austrians everything they would need to learn NATO communications doctrine. With little time to accomplish his assignment, the lieutenant took the thousands of pages of signal material to the Camp Roeder photo lab and ordered copies of everything. The lab supervisor was dumbstruck and flatly refused the request. Stephens asked to borrow his telephone and placed a call to General Arnold. The lieutenant reasoned that the general would want to know that his mission was in jeopardy. Stephens explained the situation to the general, who promptly ordered the flustered lab supervisor to provide everything the young officer wanted. A few days later Stephens met with his Austrian counterparts and handed over the enormous stacks of photocopies. Mission accomplished.

Arnold's command also began to map out secret post-treaty assistance. The United States planned to continue covert military assistance after the conclusion of the state treaty, offering $10 million in annual military aid. Directing this effort would require at least some U.S. leadership. As early as 1951, Gruber had suggested that some way might be found to retain U.S. military advisers. In November, 1955, Raab personally selected five U.S. Army officers to remain in the army attaché's office to serve as secret advisers.[53]

While the Austrians were willing to continue covert cooperation, they still refused to enter into any formal commitments. The Soviets' sudden desire to negotiate a final settlement and unexpected gift of arms and ammunition did not prompt any turn toward the Iron Curtain. Nevertheless, the Austrians remained cautious about antagonizing their soon-to-be-former occupiers. In particular, the Austrian government made no firm security guarantees to the United States before the treaty. In fact, it was this decision that prompted U.S. planners to recommend "as soon as political and military circumstances warrant seek the approval of the president to initiate covert planning in cooperation with the west in case of attack."[54] Likewise, an NSC progress report dated April 6, 1955, stated that the United States had not been able to reach a formal agreement on the employment of Austria's post-treaty military forces.[55]

With the approval of the state treaty, Austria's new army took the field. The special *gendarmerie* troops were reconstituted as the first units in the armed forces.[56] Meanwhile, the United States transferred the bulk of material in Stockpile A to the government. This cache included tanks, howitzers, mortars, trucks, jeeps, antitank weapons, and ammunition. The equipment, along with that recently obtained from the Soviets, became the arms for the new force. Austrian units thus took the field bearing the weapons of the two great Cold War protagonists. Today, on the grounds of the Heeresgeschichtliches Museum in Vienna, one of the army's first U.S. tanks stands side-by-side with a Soviet tank—an enduring reminder of the occupation's final ironic act.

As USFA prepared to case its colors, it looked with some pride on its achievement: leaving an Austria armed and prepared for battle. Despite frequently violating Clausewitz's precept that the military is an extension of the political instrument, in the end the Americans had remained true to another of his iron maxims: "the aim of war should be what its very concept implies—to defeat the enemy."[57] The U.S. Army not only adhered to this dictum in battle, it followed it in the conduct of peacetime operations as well, focusing all of its efforts on opposing the Soviets in every manner possible.

FLAWED TRIUMPH

On May 15, 1955, Llewelyn Thompson stood by John Foster Dulles's side at the formal ceremony for the signing of the Austrian State Treaty. Before his appointment as high commissioner for Austria in 1953, Thompson had planned to resign from the foreign service. Dulles convinced him to stay. The secretary had high regard for the diplomat's talents, and the situation in Europe demanded a stubborn statesman. Dulles selected Thompson to negotiate the final settlement on Trieste. The high commissioner also served as a point man for combating the Soviet peace offensive. When the Soviets began to make overtures to Raab on February 8, 1955, Dulles gave Thompson the task of restraining the chancellor.[1] The high commissioner had safeguarded U.S. interests throughout his tenure, continuing to follow policies that had, in effect, been forged by his military predecessors during the first half of the occupation. Then suddenly, without prompting by the United States, in the wake of Raab's meetings in Moscow, Thompson saw the great powers rapidly move to conclude a treaty.

Although a round of Austrian-Soviet bilateral talks ultimately led to the breakthrough, the sudden progress was due in large part to a dramatic reshuffling in the Soviet government. Nikita Khrushchev had won the post-Stalin struggle for Kremlin leadership. Malenkov was demoted and sent off to manage a power station in Kazakhstan, Beria was executed, and Molotov's influence largely marginalized. Following these victories, Khrushchev's foreign policy initiatives came to the forefront. The new premier brushed aside hardliners opposing the withdrawal of Soviet forces. Much had changed between 1953 and 1955. Khrushchev had healed the breach with Tito. Renewed Soviet-Yugoslav cooperation and the establishment of the Warsaw Pact in May (which allowed the Soviets to retain troops in Romania and Hungary irrespective of the right to secure lines of communication for the occupation troops) significantly improved the situation in Southern Europe, further lessening Austria's strategic value. In addition, ending the occupation would remove the presence of the U.S. military, making the situation even more favorable for Soviet security. The Austrians had also stated their intention of adopting a policy of neutrality.

Not only did Austria hold diminished military importance, a treaty would enhance Khrushchev's stature as a global statesman and might perhaps slow the pace of Western military and political integration. In addition, the Soviets had already seen their hegemony questioned in East Germany and Yugoslavia. Hungary would soon prove difficult as well. Voluntary withdrawal from Austria would put the Soviets' European presence in the most positive light, allowing them to focus on more pressing concerns.

The United States also found itself poised to accept a final settlement. While both Eisenhower and Dulles had abandoned the notion of rolling back Soviet power, they were loathe to sacrifice an inch of the Western frontier and highly skeptical of the growing number of nonaligned states declaring their neutrality in the confrontation between East and West. Nevertheless, they had been impressed by Austria's covert cooperation. Sabotaging Raab's diplomacy, which had paved the way for the final settlement, might diminish U.S. stature abroad and undo the progress and goodwill achieved in promoting the country's self-defense and Western orientation.

At the same time, the United States had already secured the big strategic prize: a firm decision to rearm West Germany, the last essential element required to make the new NATO defense regime viable.[2] Although the United States suspected the Soviet treaty initiative was a last-ditch attempt to unhinge German rearmament (perhaps to suggest to the West Germans that they, too, could cut a deal with the Soviets by declaring neutrality), it was too late. The future of NATO, upon which the United States rested all of its hopes for Europe's long-term security, already seemed assured. Meanwhile, other commitments had strategically overstretched key alliance partners France and Great Britain, both of whom were more than willing to end the Austrian affair. As a result, the United States felt obliged to conclude the occupation.

The night before the treaty signing, Dulles met with Molotov to discuss the ceremony.[3] They agreed, according to Thompson, to offer formal non-controversial remarks. Dulles, who usually wrote his own speeches, retired to his quarters to prepare a brief, courteous address. The next day, May 15, 1955, in the great hall of Vienna's Belvedere Palace, Thompson, who spoke a bit of Russian, acted as Dulles's interpreter. It was a serendipitous moment for the last U.S. high commissioner in Austria. The decision not to resign

had proved a momentous choice. Within two years he had directly participated in resolving two of the Cold War's most intractable disputes.

When the moment came for the foreign ministers to speak, Molotov
launched into a half-hour diatribe extolling the Soviets' leadership role in
concluding the treaty. "What's he saying? What's he saying?" Dulles demanded impatiently as an appalled and flustered Thompson tried to trans-
late. Unflustered, Dulles issued his prepared remarks and the ceremony concluded. The great deed had been done, although the unsettling incident just
concluded suggested that the signing of the state treaty would not signal the
end of U.S.-Soviet confrontation or conclude the peace of Europe that the
Allies had hoped to achieve on V-E Day almost exactly a decade before.

Retreat into Victory

In October, 1955, as required by the state treaty, USFA and the other Allied
forces were simultaneously withdrawn. Redesignated as the Southern European Task Force, the U.S. troops moved to Italy and assumed responsibility
for the strategic Villach-Ljubljana approach. As it redeployed, the army was
generally pleased with the conclusion of operations in Austria, in part because the treaty ended the distraction of occupation duties, allowing greater
focus on combat tasks directly related to NATO defense. Senior military
leaders also felt satisfaction in what they had accomplished. While the military generally disapproved of Austria's declaration of neutrality, it was content with the fact that the country's self-defense forces, principally through
the buildup of the B-gendarmerie and the stockpiling of military supplies,
were ready in time for the treaty.[4]

That Raab had refused to enter into any formal agreements with the
West either overtly or covertly was now of less importance. The truth was, a
well-organized post-treaty Austrian army could offer far more resistance to
a Soviet invasion than the meager Western occupation forces stationed there.
In some respects, it could be argued that NATO's southern flank would be
more secure with an Austrian army in the field and the occupation troops
redeployed to shore up other critical areas.

A progress report on NSC-164/1 issued just a year before the final treaty
was signed reflected America's increased confidence.[5] Although the assessment was far from sanguine, the U.S. military believed it was on the cusp of
achieving a reasonable security situation. Austria seemed relatively secure,
and U.S. observers believed the Soviets would respect the country's borders
unless war broke out. Much like their counterparts in Moscow, military
leaders in Washington found something worthwhile in the treaty.

Wins and Losses

While the U.S. Army was satisfied with the conclusion of the occupation, there is much to debate over how effectively means were applied to ends. Organization, training, and doctrine, as well as the military's routine practices and traditions, largely shaped the conduct of the occupation—and not always to best effect. This was not simply an issue of military efficiency. The outcome had significant influence on U.S. foreign policy both for good and ill.

The army's shortfalls and successes during the course of the occupation demonstrated well the impact of the military instrument on international relations in the early years of the Cold War. Most significant of all, the success of postwar activities allowed U.S. foreign policy to take the initiative. The conduct of occupation operations in Europe, especially Austria, allowed the United States tremendous freedom of action. In part through the disease and unrest formula and in greater measure through its Cold War commitments, the United States made substantial investments in Europe's reconstruction. As a result, Western Europe emerged as a dependable global partner.

On the other hand, the occupation also demonstrated that military forces designed for war are necessary but inadequate and insufficient tools for ensuring peace. The military is not the proper instrument to serve as an unsupported cornerstone for postwar foreign policy. The habits, practices, and traditions of U.S. combat forces were well suited for fighting battles, but poorly adept at peace operations.

Overdependence on the military was nowhere more clearly evident than in the outbreak of the Cold War. Did the army cause the Cold War in Austria? Emphatically not. On the other hand, it did nothing to help ameliorate the confrontation between East and West and, in fact, contributed significantly to accelerating superpower confrontation by promoting the militarization of American policies.

In truth, there was little advantage in attempting to co-opt Austria into a Western defensive regime. From a strategic viewpoint, the country could at best offer only a marginal contribution to NATO's defense. The southern flank could have been held at the Italian and Germans borders, both of which were adequately defensible. From a strategic standpoint, given the alliance's many commitments, arguing for Austria's inclusion in the Western security zone was a proposal of questionable value.

Nor could militarizing operations be justified by the argument that the United States was saving Austria from Soviet expansion. America, by the mere presence of its occupation forces and generous economic aid, had already successfully blocked Soviet penetration and established viable democratic institutions. In addition, the Austrian government had demonstrated in 1948, and again in 1950, that it was both stable and secure enough to withstand popular unrest, and could likely survive anything short of a Soviet invasion—which the Allies could not have prevented anyway. Given the minimal benefits of militarization and the fact that U.S. actions provided added encouragement for Soviet hardliners who wished to prolong the occupation, it is difficult to argue that the course the United States pursued represented an optimal foreign policy.

The military's influence on policy making, driven by its institutional rhythm of habits, was significant. After World War I, the army had also drafted war plans against potential threats. One target of U.S. plans was Great Britain, which at the time seemed one of the few countries with the potential to be a global competitor. The army, however, had scant resources and only marginal influence. The United States and Britain clashed over few matters of vital national interest, so the military's meager preparations made little difference in U.S.-British bilateral relations. In contrast, American military leaders commanded significantly more resources after World War II. They had prestige, international experience, and were active participants in formulating national policy. In this environment, the rhythm of habits became an important factor in shaping international relations between the great powers.

The army's labors are also a sharp reminder that our history of these events has been as imperfect as the efforts they purport to describe. The arguments of the major Cold War paradigms—the traditional, revisionist, and postrevisionist schools—are, in the end, unsatisfying. Odd Arne Westad recently suggested, "It seems to me both our general approaches to how history is studied and the emergence of massive new bodies of evidence lead in the direction of analytical diversity and away from the concentration on the so-called schools of interpretation."[6] In the case of the army's behavior during the first postwar years, his thoughts are appropriate. There can be no simple history of those complicated times.

The Meaning of Victory

On May 8, 1945, Gen. Dwight D. Eisenhower proclaimed to the men and women of the Allied Expeditionary Force, "Full victory in Europe has been attained." He was wrong. The military's task was far from over when the firing stopped at midnight. Yet the sentiments of his declaration persist. Senior U.S. military leaders and some political pundits are fond of saying that the purpose of armed forces is to fight and win the nation's wars. But winning wars is not winning. *Peace* is winning—and establishing peace in the lands destroyed by war requires as determined a military effort as any combat campaign.

   Peace and stability operations cannot be conducted like military maneuvers, they must assume a character appropriate to the task at hand. Leaders who are serious about ending conflicts on the most advantageous terms
possible must be willing to invest the commensurate intellectual and material resources in their armed forces so that they are ready when called. These
are commitments worth making. In the end, the fight for peace is the most
important battle of all.

NOTES

List of Abbreviations

CMH	Center of Military History
DA	Department of the Army
DRS	Declassified Documents Reference System
DDE	Dwight D. Eisenhower Presidential Library
FDRL	Franklin D. Roosevelt Presidential Library
FRUS	Department of State, *Foreign Relations of the United States*
LL	Lauinger Memorial Library
HM	*Heeresgeschichtliches Museum*
MC	George C. Marshall Center
HTPL	Harry S. Truman Presidential Library
HI	Hoover Institution
IWM	Imperial War Museum
LC	Manuscripts Division, Library of Congress
MHI	Military History Institute
MHS	Massachusetts Historical Society
ML	Mugar Library
NARA	National Archives and Records Administration
NSA	National Security Archive
NDUL	National Defense University Library
ÖSA	*Österreichisches Staatsarchiv, Archiv der Republik*
PRO	Public Records Office
RG	Record Group
SL	Seeley G. Mudd Library

Prologue

1. Carl von Clausewitz, *On War,* 87. For more on Clausewitz teaching in U.S. military schools see, Christopher Bassford, *Clausewitz in English: The Reception of Clausewitz in Britain and America, 1815–1945,* 154–60.

2. Quoted in Albert Resis, ed., *Molotov Remembers: Inside Kremlin Politics,* 59.

3. For a comprehensive historiographic survey see, Günter Bischof, "Eine historiographishe Einführung: Die Ära des Kaltenkrieges und Österreich," in *Österreich im frühen Kalten Krieg, 1945–1958: Spione, Partisanen, Kriegs Plane,* ed. Erwin Schmidl, 19–54. See also Günter Bischof, *Austria in the First Cold War, 1945–55: The Leverage of the Weak,* 3–4. Among the most important recent works are Manfried Rauchensteiner, *Der Sonderfall: Die Besatz-ungszeit in Österreich, 1945 bis 1955;* Audrey Kurth Cronin, *Great Power Politics and the*

Struggle over Austria, 1945–1955; Gerald Stourzh, *Um Einheit und Freiheit, Staatsvertrag, Neutralität und das Ende der Ost-West-Besetzung Österreichs, 1945–1955;* Robert Keyserlingk, *Austria in World War II: An Anglo-American Dilemma;* and Bischof, *Austria in the First Cold War.*

4. Herbert Feis, *From Trust to Terror: The Onset of the Cold War, 1945–1950,* 397.

5. Joyce and Gabriel Kolko, *The Limits of Power: The World and United States Foreign Policy, 1945–1954,* 703–704.

6. John Lewis Gaddis, *Strategies of Containment: A Critical Appraisal of Postwar American National Security Policy,* 191.

7. Bruce Cumings, "Revising Postrevisions, Or, The Poverty of Theory in Diplomatic History," in *America in the World: The Historiography of American Foreign Relations Since 1941,* ed. Michael Hogan, 34–44.

8. Melvyn P. Leffler, *A Preponderance of Power: National Security and the Truman Administration and the Cold War.* In reviewing this book, Michael Sherry pointed out that the importance of Leffler's work is that he focused attention not so much on how the United States viewed the Soviet Union, but on how the nation pictured the chaotic postwar world (*Journal of American History* [Sept., 1992]: 726). Howard Jones and Randall Woods also find merit in Leffler's approach. See their essay titled "Origins of the Cold War in Europe and the Near East: Recent Historiography and the National Security Imperative," in *America in the World,* ed. Michael Hogan, 235. See also Robert McMahon, "Credibility and World Power: Exploring the Psychological Dimension in Postwar American Diplomacy," *Diplomatic History* 15 (fall, 1991): 455–72; Günter Bischof, "Der Nationale Sicherheitsrat und die Amerkanische Österreichpolitk im frühen Kalten Kreig," in *Österreich Unter Alliierter Besatzung, 1945–1955,* ed. Alfred Ableitinger, Siegfried Beer, and Edward Stavdinger, 111–36; and Robert Garson, "American Foreign Policy and the Limits of Power, Eastern Europe, 1946–50," *Journal of Contemporary History* 21 (July, 1986): 362.

Chapter 1. The Disease and Unrest Formula

1. "History of U.S. Forces in Austria," Thomas F. Hickey Papers, MHI (hereafter Hickey Papers), 2.

2. R. H. Gabriel, "American Experiences with Military Government," *American Historical Review* 49 (1944): 630–44; Andrew Birtle, *U.S. Army Counterinsurgency and Contingency Operations Doctrine, 1860–1941.* Of related interest are Robert Coakley, *The Role of Federal Military Forces in Domestic Disorders, 1789–1878;* and Clayton Laurie and Ronald Cole, *The Role of Federal Military Forces in Domestic Disorders.* For an introduction to the history of peace operations in general, see Erwin Schmidl, "The Evolution of Peace Operations in the Nineteenth Century," in *Peace Operations Between War and Peace,* ed. idem., 4–20.

3. *American Military Government of Occupied Germany, 1918–1920: Report of the Officer in Charge of Civil Affairs and Armed Forces in Germany,* 64. See also Harry Alexander Smith, *Military Government.*

4. Harry Coles and Albert Weinberg, *Civil Affairs: Soldiers Become Governors,* 153. A postwar army study noted "the historic reluctance of the military" to undertake civil affairs missions (Daniel Fahey Jr., "Findings, Conclusions, Recommendations, and Analysis Concerning U.S. Civil Affairs/Military Government Organization," Feb., 1951, NDUL).

5. U.S. Army, *Field Service Regulations,* 77.

6. *FRUS: Diplomatic Papers: Conferences at Malta and Yalta, 1945,* 536.

7. Edward Peterson, *The American Occupation of Germany: Retreat into Victory,* 33

8. SHAEF, memorandum, Subject: Progress Report on Austrian Planning, May 11, 1944; SHAEF, G5, Subject: Personnel Requirements, Dec. 31, 1944; and Wickersham to McSherry, Oct. 19, 1944, Frank J. McSherry Papers, MHI (hereafter McSherry Papers).

9. Message, SHAEF to U.S. Group CC, Subject: Organization of Nucleus U.S. Group Control Council, Austria, Oct. 11, 1944; SHAEF, Subject: Additional Personnel for the Provisional

Group U.S. Control Council Austria, Oct. 21, 1944; and memorandum, SHAEF, G5, Oct. 23, 1944, McSherry Papers; Donald R. Whitnah and Edgar L. Erickson, *The Occupation of Austria: Planning and Early Years*, 23–24, 26–27; Robert W. Komer, *Civil Affairs and Military Government in the Mediterranean Theater*, NDUL, xxiv–10. By Apr. 23, 1945, USGCC/A included 217 army personnel, sixty-five Army Air Corps personnel, and twelve navy personnel. For a further breakdown of personnel, see *FRUS, 1945*, 3:9.

10. McSherry to Flory, Jan. 20, 1945, McSherry Papers.

11. George Benson, "American Military Government in Austria May 1945–February 1946," *in American Experiences in Military Government in World War II*, ed. Carl Friedrich, 171–72.

12. Hajo Holborn, *American Military Government: Its Organizations and Policies*, 105.

13. Snowden to Hartigan, Oct. 30, 1946, John Doane Hartigan Papers, HI (hereafter Hartigan Papers). See also George Fitzpatrick et al., *A Survey of the Experiences and Opinions of U.S. Government Officers in World War II*, 3.

14. Military Government Course Lecture, Austria Precis no. 1; and AFHQ, Office of the ACofS G2, "Secret Lecture," Jan. 14, 1945, box 7, Hartigan Papers. From February to April, 1945, the British G5 ran the Military Government School for British and American personnel at Portici, Italy. By April 1, 1945, 121 U.S. officers had attended training. Seventy-one had military government experience. Fifty were reassigned from combat duty to civil affairs. Personnel who had no experience in military government attended a two-week course. Others with experience received only a one-week orientation. Most of the graduates returned to their regular duties, but were earmarked for future service in Austria. For an example of the courses taught, see Sqdn. Ldr. P. H. Layton, 93/52/1, IWM. In April, the United States assumed full responsibility for training its personnel. A two-week joint Air-Ground Demobilization School was also established in Caserta (*FRUS, 1945*, 3:80).

15. Coles and Weinberg, *Civil Affairs*, 153.

16. *Infantry in Battle*. See also Paul Gorman, *The Secret of Future Victories*, I-27–II-33.

17. Walter T. Kerwin Jr. Oral History, vol. 1, MHI, 1980. Charles Thayer, who later joined the Foreign Service and served in Austria as part of the OSS, expressed similar views about his West Point education (Charles Thayer, *Bears in the Caviar*, 17). For an overview of the academy's curriculum development, see William Simons, *Liberal Education in the Service Academies*, 62–80. See also Charles Kirkpatrick, "Orthodox Soldiers: U.S. Army Formal Schools and Junior Officers between the Wars," in *Forging the Sword: Selecting, Educating, and Training Cadets and Junior Officers in the Modern World*, ed. Elliott Converse III, 99–116.

18. Scott Koch, "The Role of U.S. Army Attaches Between the World Wars," *Studies in Intelligence* 38 (1995): 111.

19. Benson, "American Military Government in Austria," 171–72.

20. Michael Hunt, *Ideology and U.S. Foreign Policy*, 151.

21. Francis Trevelyan Miller, *The Complete History of World War II*, 4.

22. *American Military Government of Occupied Germany*, vol. 11, *American Occupation of Germany*; Joseph Whitehorne, *The Inspector General of the United States Army*, 271–77, 293–300.

23. Snook to Hartigan, Aug. 14, 1946, box 7, Hartigan Papers. See also *American Military Government of Occupied Germany*.

24. Eric James Bohman, "Rehearsals for Victory: The War Department and the Planning and Direction of Civil Affairs, 1940–1943" (Ph.D. diss., Yale University, 1984).

25. The major difference in U.S. postwar operations was preparation. American operations in Austria and Korea were late in organizing, and hence, more hectic and disorganized in execution. Organizational and operational practices, however, were very similar. See, e.g., studies on Japan: Robert Howard and Sakamoto Yoshikazu, eds., *Democratizing Japan: The Allied Occupation*; Michael Schaller, *The American Occupation of Japan: The Origins of the Cold War in Asia*; John Dower, *Embracing Defeat: Japan in the Wake of World War II*; Nicholas Sarantakes, *Keystone: The American Occupation of Okinawa and U.S.-Japanese Relations*;

Robert Wolfe, ed., *Americans as Proconsuls: United States Military Government in Germany and Japan, 1944–1952.*

26. The British military also exhibited a tradition of forgetting. For a review of Great Britain's peacekeeping operations before the Second World War, see F. S. V. Donnison, *Civil Affairs and Military Government: Central Organization and Planning,* 3–20.

27. This notion dovetailed well with contemporaneous administrative theory, which envisioned a clear delineation between the civilian and military functions of government. See James Stever, "The glass firewall between military and civil administration," *Administration and Society* 31 (Mar., 1999): 28–49.

28. In June, 1943, the Combined Civil Affairs Committee was established to coordinate inter-Allied policy. It was composed of members of the War, Navy, and State Departments and members of the British Staff Mission and Embassy in Washington. See also "The Treatment of Austria: Policy Recommendation, The Inter-Divisional Committee on Germany," PWC-217 (CAC-219), June 8, 1944, box 1, David Harris Papers, HI. For the problems and challenges of planning, see Williamson's memorandum to Riddleberger, Subject: Meeting of Civil Affairs Committee on Dec. 26, dated Dec. 27, 1944, box 2, Records of the Office of Western European Affairs, 1941–54, Subject Files, Austria, RG 59, NARA. In addition to the work of the committee, the army also cooperated closely with the navy's Office for Occupied Areas in the Office of the Chief of Naval Operations. The government also drew heavily on nongovernmental organizations to facilitate postwar planning. The most influential group was the Council on Foreign Relations. From 1940 to the end of the war, the council generated 682 memoranda that were forwarded to the Department of State (Michael Wala, *The Council on Foreign Relations and American Foreign Policy in the Early Cold War*).

29. The OSS's Research and Analysis (R&A) Branch, for example, produced at least eight substantive studies on Austrian affairs. See Box 16C, OSS Files, MHI. "Administrative Separation of Austria from Germany," R&A Study 2110, was reprinted almost word for word as War Department Pamphlet no. 31-229, *Civil Affairs Guide: The Administrative Separation of Austria from Germany,* in March, 1945.

30. Fahey, "Findings, Conclusions, Recommendations, and Analysis."

31. Erhardt to Matthews, June 28, 1945, box 2, Records of the Office of Western European Affairs, 1941–54, Subject Files, 1941–54, Austria, RG 59, NARA.

32. Erhardt to Matthews, Mar. 4, 1945, Lester D. Flory Papers, MHI (hereafter Flory Papers).

33. David Trask, *The AEF and Coalition Warmaking, 1917–1918.* The post–World War I Allied occupation was nominally under the unified command of the French, but in practice each national army ran its zone of occupation independently and enforced occupation policies as it saw fit. For a discussion of the administration of U.S. military government in World War I, see *American Military Government of Occupied Germany,* 63–81.

34. Memorandum by H. Q. Clowder on "Future Special Missions in Austria," Clowder Reports, HS6/17, PRO, 2 (hereafter Clowder Reports).

35. The Soviets showed no serious interest in coordinating the details of occupation until after they captured Vienna in April, 1945. See memorandums, SHAEF, G5, Subject: Russian Participation in Austria Military Government, May 27, 1944; Subject: Austria, May 3, 1944; and Subject: Post Hostilities in Planning Military Government in Austria, July 4, 1944, McSherry Papers. Flory began pushing for direct coordination with the Soviets as early as February, 1945 (*FRUS, 1945,* 3:19–20). On April 25, 1945, the Soviets stated they had no objection to working directly with American officers but never acted on the proposal (ibid., 3:93, 95–96). The State Department also pressed for closer coordination with the Soviets. See, e.g., ibid., 3:27–29, 31, 35.

36. Mack to Henn, War Office, Mar. 16, 1945, "Cooperation with the Russians," FO1020/1026, PRO.

37. Victor Pechnatov, "The Big Three After World War II: New Documents on Soviet Thinking about Post-War Relations with the United States and Great Britain," Working Paper no. 13, Cold War International History Project, Washington, D.C., July, 1995.

38. *Infantry in Battle,* 138–39.

39. Ralph E. Pearson Papers, MHI.

40. Keyserlingk, *Austria in World War II;* Dennis Showalter's review in *Austrian History Yearbook* 22 (1991): 214–15; Robert Keyserlingk, "Arnold Toynbee's Foreign Research and Press Service, 1939–43, and Its Post-war Plans for Southeast Europe," *Journal of Contemporary History* 21 (Oct., 1986): 539–58. See also Günter Bischof, "Die Instrumentalisierung Der Moskauer Erklärung nach der 2. Weltkrieg," *Zeitgeschichte* 20 (Nov.-Dec., 1993): 345–65.

41. Keyserlingk, *Austria in World War II,* 66–67.

42. "Austria Military Government Handbook," 1945, CMH, 2. Two handbooks were used during the early months of the occupation. Initially, SHAEF issued a provisional handbook. After AFHQ assumed command of the area, it issued a slightly different version. See Flory to Hilldring, June 1, 1945, Flory Papers.

43. "Provisional Handbook for Military Government in Austria," 13–15. For U.S. objectives in Austria, see "Austria Military Government Handbook," 2–5; "Provisional Handbook," 16.

Chapter 2. A Far Country

1. John Lamberton Harper, *American Visions of Europe: Franklin D. Roosevelt, George F. Kennan, and Dean G. Acheson,* 98.

2. "Presenting Post-War Planning to the Public," Office of Public Opinion Research, Princeton University, 1943, box 211, John G. Winant Papers, FDRL (hereafter Winant Papers).

3. Enclosure, "Operation RANKIN Revision of the Spheres of Responsibility," Report by the JCS Planners, file 2025, MC. See also memorandum for the president, Jan. 26, 1944, Leahy Files, box 20, RG 218, NARA; and memorandum for the acting secretary of state, Feb. 21, 1944, file 2025, MC.

4. Note for Winant dated May 29, 1942, box 226, Winant Papers.

5. Maddox to Winant, box 215, Winant Papers.

6. Winant's role in the EAC is described in Alan Nevins, *He Walked Alone: A Biography of John Gilbert Winant,* 192–209. Nevins overstates Winant's personal involvement in the negotiations concerning Austria.

7. Eisenhower to Wilson, July 4, 1944, McSherry Papers.

8. SHAEF, Subject: Zones of Occupation Austria, Apr. 12, 1945; and SHAEF G5 to ACOS, Apr. 29, 1945, McSherry Papers; *FRUS, 1945,* 3:98–99.

9. Allen Weinstein and Alexander Vassiliev, *The Haunted Wood: Soviet Espionage in America — The Stalin Era,* 270–71. For the origins of the French participation, see *FRUS, 1945,* 3:73; Klaus Eisterer, "Französische Besatzungspolitik in Tirol und Vorarlberg Spätsommer and Herbst 1945," in *Österreich 1945: Ein Ende und viele Anfänge,* ed., Manfried Rauchenstiener and Wolfgang Etschmann, 229–30; Klaus Eisterer, "Der 'Goldene Westen' zum Aussenhandel der französischen Zone 1945–1947," in *Österreich Unter Alliierter Besatzung,* ed. Ableitinger et al., 431–63; Stefan Zauner, "French Occupation Policies after World War II," in *Austria in the Nineteen Fifties,* ed. Günter Bischof and Anton Pelinka, 274–75.

10. Günter Bischof, "Anglo-amerkanische Planungen und Überlegungen der österreichischen Emigration während des Zweiten Weltkrieges für Nachkriegs-Österreich," in *Österreich 1945: Ein Ende und viele Anfänge,* ed. Manfried Rauchensteiner and Wolfgang Etschmann, 15–52.

11. X to MX, Dec. 9, 1942, Austria Office, HS6/3,PRO.

12. Intelligence Summary no. 3., Feb. 26, 1945, FO1020/1244, PRO. The OSS produced two reports questioning the redoubt. See "The Alpine Redoubt: An Interim Survey of Available Intelligence," R&A Branch, file 1704, MC; and "The Alpine Redoubt: A Second Survey of Available Intelligence," R&A Branch, file 1695, MC. In March, 1945, Ultra reports suggested that forces were withdrawing to the Alps to organize a resistance movement (Perry Biscombe, *Werewolf: The History of the National Socialist Guerilla Movement, 1944–1946,* 267). See

also Timothy Naftali, "Creating the Myth of the *Alpenfestung*: Allied Intelligence and the Collapse of the Nazi-Police State," in *Austrian Historical Memory*, ed. Bischof and Pelinka, 203–46.

13. Intelligence Summary no. 3.

14. For an account of the Clowder mission, see Peter Wilkinson, *Foreign Fields: The Story of an SOE Operative*. For a summary of activities, see Clowder, "Future Special Missions in Austria"; notes by Clowder for his special operations mission in Austria for mid-November, Nov., 1994; Maj. C. H. Villiers, "Report on a Mission to Carinthia (KOROSKO), May to September 1944"; and "Report on Clowder Mission," May 13, 1944, Clowder Reports. See also "Jedburg Missions in Austria, 1944–45," HS 6–1, PR; Martin-Smith, Lt. P. G. B., 86/3/1, IWM; and Fred Warner Papers, 96/23/1, IWM, 56.

15. Clowder, "Future Special Missions in Austria," 1. See also "Austrian Resistance Movements in STIERMARK," Source MASTIFF, FO1020/1262, PRO; and Clowder's notes for his special operations mission in Austria for mid-November.

16. Oliver Rathkolb, ed., *Gesellschaft und Politik am Beginn der Zweiten Republik, Vertauliche Berichte der U.S. Militäradministration aus Österreich 1945 in englischer Originalfassung*, 13–21. For a discussion of the R&A Branch, see Oliver Rathkolb, "Professorenpläne für Österreichs Zukunft. Nachkriegsfragen im Diskurs der Forschungsabteilung Research and Analysis," in *Geheimdienstkrieg gegen Deutschland: Subversion, Propaganda und politische Planungen des amerikanischen Geheimdienstes im Zweiten Weltkrieg*, ed. Jürgen Heideking and Christof Mauch, 166–81. See also Siegfried Beer, "Target Central Europe: American Intelligence Efforts Regarding Nazi and Early Postwar Austria," Working Paper no. 97–1, Center for Austrian Studies, University of Minnesota, Minneapolis, Aug., 1997; Franklin A. Lindsey and John Kenneth Galbraith, *Beacons in the Night: With the OSS and Tito's Partisan in Wartime Yugoslavia*, 174–77.

17. For an account of Greenup, see Gerald Schwab, *OSS Agents in Hitler's Heartland: Destination Innsbruck*; Hqs., Detachment A, OSS Austria, Subject: Greenup Debriefing Report, Aug. 10, 1945, Subject Files, box 1, Records of the Office of Western European Affairs, 1941–54, Austria, RG 59, NARA. For a summary of OSS operations see, memorandum, Subject: Field Teams for Central Europe, Apr. 17, 1945, box 2, ibid.; Lindsey and Galbraith, *Beacons in the Night*, 149–77; Fritz Molden, *Fires in the Night: The Sacrifices and Significance of Austrian Resistance*, 84–93. The number of missions cited varies. Molden notes only seven, whereas Beer's research suggests possibly as many as fifty were planned. See Siegfried Beer and Stefan Kramer, *Der Kreig aus der Luft: Kärnten und Steiermark, 1941–1945*, 76.

18. Naftali, "Creating the Myth of the *Alpenfestung*," 203.

19. *Infantry in Battle*, 16.

20. SHAEF, memorandum, Subject: Interim Directive to AFHQ to Initiate Planning of Civil Affairs, subject to confirmation by the CCS, Apr., 1944, McSherry Papers.

21. SHEAF G5, memorandum, Subject: Post Hostilities in Planning Military Government in Austria, July 4, 1944. For an inventory of the plans generated, see *FRUS, 1945*, 3:86–88, 91–92. In addition to the plans and the military government handbook, the unit also produced twelve specialized manuals addressing such issues as public safety and finance (Komer, *Civil Affairs and Military Government*, NDUL, xxiv–5).

22. AG WAR to Wilson, Sept. 9, 1944, McSherry Papers; JCS 1369/2, "Basic and Political Directive to Commander in Chief of U.S. Forces of Occupation Regarding Military Government in Austria," Flory Papers.

23. AFHQ, Subject: Freeborn-Directive, Policy in Austria, Oct. 11, 1944, FO1020/263, PRO. Initial drafts of the Freeborn plan assigned overall responsibility for the mission to Fifth Army. However, Lt. Gen. Lucian K. Truscott Jr., the Fifth Army commander, argued that it made more sense to assign responsibility for the logistical, personnel, and administrative missions to an army group. As a result, the mission was given to 15th Army Group in May, 1945 (Whitnah and Erickson, *Occupation of Austria*, 47–48).

24. AFHQ issued an occupation directive based on the Freeborn plan on May 20, 1945

(Draft Historical Statement of U.S. Group CC [Austria], January, 1945, box 1, USFA Historical File, RG 260, NARA, 1–3). The first units entering Austria operated under the SHAEF plan for the postwar occupation of Germany, titled Eclipse. See, e.g., Hqs., 6th Army Group, Final Report, G3 Section, July 1, 1945, file 02–6, CMH.

25. Military Government Report of the High Commissioner, Dec. 20, 1945, CMH.

26. *FRUS, 1945*, 3:505, 738, 887.

27. Clowder, "Future Special Missions in Austria." See also "Developments in Yugoslavia, Mar.–Aug. 1945, Summary," Franklin A. Lindsey Papers, box 9, HI; Lindsey and Galbraith, *Beacons in the Night*, 176.

28. Message from Main Eighth Army, Subject: Yugoslav Matters, 8 May 1945, FO1020/42, PRO.

29. 15th Army Group to Eighth Army, Subject: Yugoslav Matters, May 12, 1945, ibid.

30. Message, Eighth Army to V Corps, Subject: Yugoslav Matters, May 14, 1945, ibid.

31. Message, AFHQ to SHAEF, Subject: Yugoslav Matters, May 17, 1945, ibid.

32. Message, Eighth Army to V Corps, Subject: Yugoslav Matters, May 14, 1945; AFHQ to AG WAR for Combined Chiefs of Staff, Subject: Yugoslav Matters, May 17 1945, ibid.; memorandum, Subject: Future Plans, June 7, 1945, Top Secret and Highly Confidential Correspondence, FO1020/1, PRO.

33. Entries for May 17–18, 1945, box 3, Annotated Transcripts, George S. Patton Jr. Papers, LC (hereafter Patton Papers).

34. Morgan to McCreery, June 7, 1945, Top Secret and Highly Confidential Correspondence, FO1020/1, PRO.

35 Entries for May 18, 1945, box 3, Annotated Transcripts, Patton Papers. Patton believed the Soviets were directing Tito to divert the Americans while they either resumed the offensive in central Germany or secured a warm-water port on the Adriatic Sea.

36. D. B. Heuser, *Western Containment: Policies Towards Yugoslavia, 1948–1953*, 99–100; Nebojsa Bjelakovic, "Comrades and Adversaries: Yugoslav-Soviet Conflict in 1948: A Reappraisal," *East European Quarterly* 33 (spring, 1999): 103; Vojtech Mastny, *Russia's Road to the Cold War: Diplomacy, Warfare and the Politics of Communism, 1941–1945*, 282; Richard Dinardo, "Glimpse of an Old World Order? Reconsidering the Trieste Crisis of 1945," *Diplomatic History* 21 (summer, 1997): 365–81.

37. Quotes and documentation on Flory's mission are from "Mission to Vienna," Flory Papers. For the origins of the mission, see memorandum, SHAEF G5, AFHQ Mission, Subject: Austria, May 3, 1944; and "Post Hostilities Planning for Military Government in Austria," July 4, 1944, McSherry Papers. Flory's report, which includes an explanatory introduction, is reproduced in Siegfried Beer and Eduard Staudinger, "Die 'Vienna Mission' der Westalliieren im June 1945," *Studien zur Wiener Geschichte, Jahrbuch des Vereins für Geschichte der Stadt Wien*, Band 50. Additional material can be found in RG 84, NARA.

38. Erhardt to Adams, June 1, 1945, box 1, Records of the Office of Western European Affairs, 1941–50, RG 59, NARA, 1.

39. See Martin Hertz, "The View from Austria," in *Witnesses to the Origins of the Cold War*, ed. Thomas Hammond, 165–67. This view was also held by the Vienna provost marshal, Col. William Yarborough, who recalled that Soviet commanders often did not know where their people were. Discipline and control were extremely lax, contributing to a high crime rate among Soviet soldiers (William P. Yarborough Oral History, CMH, 6).

40. *FRUS, 1945*, 3:26.

41. Churchill had these concerns even before the Vienna mission. See, e.g., *FRUS, 1945*, 3:102.

42. Report on Winterton's Vienna mission, FO 1020/28, PRO, pt. 2, 1. For another positive British assessment of the Soviets during the first months of the occupation period, see "Impressions of Russian-Speaking Liaison Officer on the Anglo-Soviet Line of Demarcation in Austria," May–June, 1945, FO1020/1262, PRO.

43. Memorandum no. 20, Subject: Transmittal of Report on Vienna Mission, June 19, 1945, Political Advisor, box 1, Top Secret General Records, 1945–55, RG 84, NARA, 2.

44. See also Hertz, "View from Austria," 163–65. The report of the British mission was also skeptical of reports of Soviet misbehavior (Winterton's Vienna mission report, 1).

Chapter 3. Shepherding Midnight's Children

1. Erhardt to Matthews, June 3, 1945, box 1, Records of the Office of Western European Affairs, 1941–59, RG 59, NARA, 2–3. One team hid out in filmmaker Leni Riefenstahl's house in the Tirol (Leni Riefenstahl, *The Sieve of Time*, 305–309).

2. Erhardt to Adams, June 1, 1945, box 1, Records of the Office of Western European Affairs, 1941–50, RG 59, NARA, 2.

3. Erhardt to Matthews, June 28, 1945, ibid., 1.

4. Quotations and information on reports are from notes, Salzburg, June 13, 1945, ibid.

5. Memorandum no. 19, Subject: Report of Visit to Salzburg by the Political Advisor on Austrian Affairs, June 18, 1945, signed Erhardt, box 1, Top Secret General Records, 1945–55, RG 84, NARA.

6. Memorandum for the President, Office of Strategic Services, July 7, 1945, box 15, OSS Memoranda, Papers of Harry S. Truman, HTPL (hereafter Truman Papers).

7. Grew to President, May 4, 1945, box 71, President's Secretary Files, Subject Files, Foreign Affairs Files, Truman Papers.

8. Information on the administration of Upper Austria and the Eigl case is from memorandum, Subject: Meeting of Land Officials, June 8, 1945; memorandum, Subject: Inspection of Landeshauptmann Hofrat Dr. Eigl of Wels on June 16, 1945; memorandum, Subject: Inspection with Landeshauptmann Hofrat Dr. Eigl at Gmunden on June 9, 1945; memorandum, Subject: Inspection with Landeshauptmann Hofrat Dr. Eigl at Vocklabruck on June 9, 1945; memorandum, Subject: Inspection with Landeshauptmann Dr. Eigl of Braunau on June 23; memorandum, Subject: Reaction to Removal and Arrest of Landeshauptmann Eigl, Sept. 4, 1945, from Detachment EIA to HQ II Corps, Weekly Report from 2400 Sept. 4 to 2400 Sept. 11, 1945; and memorandum, Subject: Report of Investigation of Land Government Officials Upper Austria, Oct. 16, 1945, Hartigan Papers; Rauchensteiner, *Sonderfall*, 123–24; Martin Herz, *Understanding Austria: The Political Reports and Analyses of Martin F. Herz, Political Officer of the U.S. Legation, 1945–1948*, ed. Reinhold Wagnleitner, 37, 47–48.

9. Military Government, Report of the High Commissioner, Dec. 20, 1945, "History of U.S. Forces in Austria," 19. Reported numbers varied. See Günter Bischof, "Bacque and Historical Evidence," in *Eisenhower and the German POWs: Facts Against Falsehood,* ed. Günter Bischof and Stephen E. Ambrose, 209.

10. Information on disarmament is from Office of the Chief Historian, European Command, "Disarmament and Disbandment of the German Armed Forces," 1947, file 8–3.1 CA7 C1, CMH.

11. Walter Sheppard file, Perry Family Papers, MHI, 18.

12. MTOUSA Directive no. 11 for Austria, "Elimination and Prohibition of Military Training in Austria," May 10, 1945, box 1, USFA Historical File, RG 260, NARA.

13. Walter Anton, "Die Österreichische Bundesgendarmerie, 1945–1955: Ein Beitrag zur Geschichte Österreichs in der Besatzungszeit" (Ph.D. diss., University of Vienna, 1984), 114.

14. Hendrickson to Hartigan, July 15, 1946, box 7, Hartigan Papers.

15. Hqs., 15th Army Group, Intelligence Summaries no. 2, June 2, 1945; and no. 3, June 12, 1945, USFA, United States Allied Command Section, box 6, Historical Files, RG 260, NARA; Joint Intelligence Committee, Sept. 6, 1945, Intelligence, FO1020/40, PRO.

16. Bischof, *Austria in the First Cold War*, 7–18.

17. "Austria Military Government Handbook," CMH, 4.

18. For a discussion on criminal activities in the U.S. zone, see Donald and Florentine Whitnah, *Salzburg under Siege: U.S. Occupation, 1945–1955*, 69–77.

19. "History of U.S. Forces in Austria," 12.

20. Civil Affairs Division Special Staff, DA, "Austria: Problems in U.S. Army Occupation, 1945–1947," Jan. 1, 1948, NDUL, 11–12.

21. Office of the Chief Historian, European Command, "Fraternization with the Germans in World War II," 1947, file 8–3.1 CA10 C1, CMH, 20.

22. *American Military Government of Occupied Germany,* 178–91.

23. Office of the Chief Historian European Command, "The First Year of the Occupation," 1947, file 8–3.1 CA1 V2, C1, CMH, 91.

24. See, e.g., R. L. Crimp, manuscript entries for May 16 and 18, 1945, 96/50/1, R. L. Crimp Papers, IWM.

25. Erhardt to Riddleberger, July 17, 1945, box 3, Records of the Office of Western European Affairs, 1941–54, RG 59, NARA, 3.

26. Erhardt, handwritten manuscript, June 13, 1945, box 1, ibid.

27. Ibid.

28. For U.S. policies, see Jean Malcolm, "War Brides and Their Shipment to the United States," 1947, file 8–3.1, CMH.

29. Petra Goode discusses the positive effects of fraternization in the case of the German occupation. See Petra Goode, "From Villains to Victims: Fraternization and Feminization of Germany, 1945–1947," *Diplomatic History* 23 (winter, 1999): 1–20.

30. "History of U.S. Forces in Austria," 15.

31. Brush to ?, 15 Dec. 1945, Thomas Brush Papers, MHI.

32. Hqs., USFA, Intelligence Summary no. 12, Aug. 24, 1945, box 6, RG 260, NARA, 4.

33. Many examples can be found in *BKA, Verbindungsstelle zum Alliierten Rat (1946–1951), Gruppe 04, Inneres/Justiz, ÖSA.* For the minister of the interior's reports on the state of public security, see *BMI, GD für die öffentliche Sicherheit (1945–51), Gruppe 04, Inneres/Justiz, ÖSA.*

34. See, e.g., Military Government Austria, "Report of the High Commissioner," Jan., 1946, CMH, 24. Not all reports were positive, see ibid., Dec., 1945, 142–43.

35. See, e.g., letter, Sept. 11, 1945, and letter, Sept. 12, 1945, folder 1, Charles Arthur Roberston Papers, HI (hereafter Roberston Papers).

36. 42d Infantry Division Journal, entry for June 1–July 31, 1945, box 10668, RG 94, NARA.

37. Ibid., entry for May 1–30, 1946.

38. The account of the Werfen train is from memorandum, Subject: Orders and Directives received and Actions taken by Property Control Section, July 17, 1947, box 20, RG 260, NARA. For the results of the army's internal investigation of property control, see memorandum, Subject: Report of Investigation, ibid. For the disposition of the train's assets, see a series of JCS messages in ibid.

39. Erhardt, handwritten manuscript, June 13, 1945.

40. Richard B. Moran Papers, MHI.

41. USFA Report, Apr.–June 1946, USFA Historical File, box 1, RG 260, NARA, 59–60.

42. Letter, Dec. 20, 1945, Thomas Stewart Brush Papers, MHI (hereafter Brush Papers).

43. Letter, Sept. 23, 1945, ibid. See also "Resume of Army Roll-Up Following World War II," file OCMH-39, CMH.

44. John Sparrow, "History of Personnel Demobilization in the United States Army," 189–90, 295–96.

45. Letter, Feb. 8, 1945, Brush Papers.

46. Letter, May 2, 1946, Roberston Papers.

47. Yarborough Oral History, 6.

48. Michael Rauer, "Order out of Chaos: The United States Constabulary in Postwar Germany," *Army History* 45 (summer, 1998): 23; United States Constabulary, "Occupation Forces in Europe Series, 1945–1946," file 8–3.1 CA 22, CMH, 3–4. If the army had studied its own history, it might have better anticipated the need for constabulary-like forces. See Erwin Schmidl, "Police Functions in Peace Operations: An Historical Overview," in *Policing the New*

World Disorder: Peace Operations and Public Security, ed. Robert Oakley, Michael Dziedzic, and Eliot Goldberg, 19–26. Information on the development of the constabulary is from "History of the U.S. Constabulary, 10 Jan 46–31 Dec 46," file 8–3.1 CA 37, CMH, 1–2; Historical Subsection, G3, U.S. Constabulary, "The Establishment and Operations of the United States Constabulary 3 Oct. 1945–30 June 1947," 1947, Halley G. Maddox Papers, MHI, 1–2; United States Constabulary, "Occupation Forces in Europe Series, 1945–1946," 6, 10; and James Snyder, "The Establishment and Operations of the United States Constabulary," file 8–3.4 CA, CMH.

49. "Circle C" referred to the circular badge resembling a cattle brand emblazoned on helmets worn by constabulary troops. The red, blue, and yellow insignia of the constabulary corps reminded many Germans of potato bugs.

50. USFA, Jan.–Mar., 1946, box 1, Historical File, RG 260, NARA, 1.

Chapter 4. The Largest Single Industry

1. L. James Binder, *Lemnitzer: A Soldier for His Time,* 145.

2. Ibid., 64.

3. Clausewitz, *On War,* 117.

4. Horace G. Torbert Oral History, Aug. 31, 1988, LL, 5. More documentation on the patterns of U.S. Army intelligence operations can be found in, James Jay Carafano, "Deconstructing U.S. Army Intelligence Operations in Postwar Austria: The Early Years 1945–1948," in *Österreich im frühen Kalten Krieg,* ed. Schmidl, 55–72; James Jay Carafano, "'Waltzing into the Cold War': U.S. Army Intelligence Operations in Postwar Austria, 1944–1948," in *The Vranitzky Era in Austria,* ed. Günter Bischof, Anton Pelinka, and Ferdinand Karlhofer, 165–89.

5. AFHQ G2 Section Counterintelligence Plans Subsection, microfilm no. 438-B, NARA; "History of Allied Forces Headquarters, Aug. 1942–Sept. 1947," pt. 4, "July 1944–Dec. 1945," file 8–4 AD V.4 cy 1, CMH, 194.

6. Hqs., USFA, Intelligence Directive no. 1, July 9, 1945; and idem., Intelligence Directive no. 2, July 31, 1945, box 5, RG 260, NARA.

7. Report of the General Board, United States Forces, European Command, "The Military Intelligence Service in the European Theater," Study no. 12, CMH, 3–4; "History of G-2 USFA: From the Beginning to June 1947," box 5, RG 260, NARA, 1–2, 10, 30; Edwin Kretzman, "Four Powers in Three-Quarter Time: Tales of the Austrian Occupation, 1945–1948" (unpublished manuscript, author's collection).

8. See, e.g., letter, Subject: Propaganda Themes in Red Army and Communist Newspapers in Austria, Apr.–Sept., 1946, box 184, RG 263, NARA.

9. Siegfried Beer, "OSS and SSU in the American Occupation of Austria: Intelligence Between War and Cold War" (paper presented at the Society for Military History Conference, Arlington, Va., 1996); idem., "Early CIA Reports on Austria, 1947–1949," in *Austrian Historical Memory and National Identity,* ed. Bischof and Pelinka, 247–88. For OSS complaints about working under the USFA see, Hqs., USFA, OSS, Subject: Monthly OSS Austria to OSS Washington, Sept. 13, 1945, box 16C, OSS Files, MHI, 1–2, 5.

10. "The Second Year of Occupation," Occupation Forces in Europe Series, 1946–47, Office of the Chief Historian European Command, file 8–3.1 CB1 V7, CMH, 3; G5, USFA, "History of Operations 8 May 1945–30 Sept. 1945," box 10672, RG 407, NARA.

11. "Austria Military Government Handbook," CMH, 5.

12. Hqs., USFA, Appendix A to Intelligence Summary no. 12, Aug. 24, 1945, box 5, RG 260, NARA, 3–4.

13. United States Allied Commission Austria Joint Weekly Intelligence Summary no. 27, Jan. 19, 1946; and ibid., no. 25, Jan. 5, 1946, box 36, RG 260, NARA; G2, USFA, Intelligence Bulletins, "Occupation of Austria—42d Division 8 Dec. 1945—6 Jan. 1946"; and "G2 Journal—Occupation of Austria, 42d Infantry Division, 1 Oct 1945–30 Apr. 1946," box 10665, RG 407, NARA.

14. By then the U.S. Detailed Interrogation Center had amassed over four hundred thousand file cards, which provided an index to the files they maintained on over half a million registered or suspected Nazis. The center was discontinued in June, 1947. Records were shipped to other headquarters or turned over to the Austrians. Up until 1947, denazification also consumed most of the USFA's counterintelligence effort. The Counterintelligence Branch estimated that 90 percent of its workload involved denazification operations. See "Report of Operations," 7769th Military Intelligence Service (Austria), encl. no. 5, Denazification Section, "Historical Report," July, 1947, box 5, RG 260, NARA; and "Short Summary of the history of Austrian denazification legislation," MHI, 2.

15. Hqs., 15th Army Group, Intelligence Summary no. 3, box 6, RG 260, NARA, 1.

16. Ibid., no. 4, 1.

17. Ibid., no. 9, 3.

18. The only information provided was an estimate of troop movements and strength. The summaries also provided information on British and French troop strengths. This information was discontinued after March, 1946. See, e.g., USACA Joint Forthnightly Intelligence Summary no. 3, Mar. 23, 1946, box 36, RG 260 NARA. The U.S. Army G2 estimated Soviet troop strength at 120,000–150,000. Despite these estimates, the secretary of war reported to the secretary of state on December 28, 1945, that an estimated 200,000 Soviet troops in were Austria (probably confusing the number with the recommended figure for troop ceilings). In December, 1946, the U.S. delegation proposed to the Council of Foreign Ministers a ceiling of 200,000 Soviet troops in Austria. See *FRUS, 1945,* 3:691; *FRUS: Diplomatic Papers, 1946,* 2:1466–67.

19. G2 Intelligence Bulletin no. 72, 42d Infantry Division, July 21, 1945, box 10666, RG 407, NARA.

20. S2 Journal, Occupation of 222d Infantry Regiment, 42d Infantry Division, May 1–31, 1946, entry 9, May 1946, box 10697, RG 407, NARA.

21. James Milano and Patrick Brogan, *Soldiers, Spies and the Rat Line,* 37. See also ibid., 19–36, 38–42.

22. See, e.g., USACA, Joint Weekly Intelligence Summary, vol. 1, no. 11, Aug. 18, 1945, box 36, RG 260, NARA.

23. Joint Chiefs of Staff Decision on JCS 1545, Oct. 16, 1945, "Military Position of the United States in the Light of Russian Policy," file 2569, MC.

24. Binder, *Lemnitzer,* 152.

25. War Department, "Basic Intelligence Directive," June, 1946, Reference Guide, NARA (emphasis in original).

26. Beginning in November, 1945, the USFA commander began to submit a series of monthly reports to the JCS summarizing much of the intelligence collected on social, political, and economic conditions. The reports also included a classified annex of economic indicators. See, e.g., Military Government Austria, Report of the High Commissioner, no. 1, Nov., 1945, CMH. At the request of the State Department, the USFA G2 produced a special report on the Soviet zone. The report measured attitudes toward economic and political developments. See Hqs., USFA, Office of the AC of S, G2, Special Report no. 5, "The Soviet Zone of Austria," Nov. 22, 1946, CMH.

27. G2, USFA, "History of the G-2," box 5, RG 260, NARA, 10.

28. Report of the General Board, Military Intelligence Service, CMH, 12; Report of the General Board, United States Forces, European Theater, "Organization and Operation of Counterintelligence Corps in the European Theater," Study no. 13, CMH, 6.

29. Brief for the army chief of staff, Dec. 7, 1945; and memorandum for the secretary of war, Subject: Preliminary Report of the Committee Appointed to Study War Department Intelligence Activities, Nov. 3, 1945, box 9, RG 165, NARA.

30. Herz worked closely with Henry Pleasants and Johannes Imhof on the USFA intelligence staff. Herz claims to have both relied heavily on and contributed to the USFA intelligence summaries. For Herz's assessment on the collection effort, see folder 30, box 1, 6–8, Papers of

Martin F. Herz, LL, 17. Herz also recalled that he felt overwhelmed with all the intelligence available. See Herz, *Understanding Austria*, 11.

31. Office of the Director of Intelligence, Oct. 1, 1947–December 31, 1947, folder 45, box 6, RG 260, NARA. The OSS reported similar problems in Austria. See Hqs., USFA, Monthly Report of OSS Austria to OSS Washington, Sept. 13, 1945, OSS Files, box 16C, MHI, 5.

32. Hqs., USFA, Office of the Director of Intelligence, Information Report, Oct. 31, 1947, box 6, RG 260, NARA.

33. Hqs., USFA, Intelligence Summary no. 38, Feb. 23, 1946, box 6, RG 260, NARA, 6.

34. DA, Staff Plans and Operations Division, Subject: Information related to Subversive Activities for the Period Ending Aug. 27, 1948, box 75, RG 319, NARA.

35. Herz, *Understanding Austria*, 418–19.

36. "Report of Operation," 7769th Military Intelligence Service, box 5, RG 260, 6.

37. Carafano, "'Waltzing into the Cold War'," 174.

38. Hqs., USFA, "Commander's Estimate of the Situation," Mar. 10, 1948, CCS 383.21 Austria (1–21–44), sec. 15, box 2, Records of the U.S. Joint Chiefs of Staff, Geographic Files, 1946–47, RG 218, NARA, 2. The USFA concluded that Soviet forces were a potential military threat despite the fact that they had been reduced from an estimated 150,000 in 1946 to approximately 56,000, and that the Soviets showed no signs of stockpiling supplies or other aggressive activities. Intelligence estimates were primarily based on the reports of Soviet deserters. The CIA's reports for April, 1948, estimated Soviet forces at 46,000, including 33,000 combat troops in two divisions. Their combat readiness was rated high due to reports of extensive training. See CIA, "The Current Situation in Austria," Apr. 28, 1948, The United States Intelligence Community, NSA, 6.

39. See, e.g., "History of the Office of the Director of Intelligence, United States Forces in Austria, Jan.–Mar. 1948," box 6, RG 260, NARA.

40. *FRUS: Diplomatic Papers, 1947*, 2:595.

41. USFA, Office of the Director of Intelligence, report, Jan. 24, 1948, box 6, RG 260, NARA; Military Government Austria, "Report of the High Commissioner," Jan., 1948, no. 27, CMH, 7.

42. Kurt Tweraser, "Military Justice as an Instrument of American Occupation Policy in Austria 1945–1950: From Total Control to Limited Tutelage," *Austrian History Yearbook* 24 (1993): 172.

43. Mark Clark Oral History, file 221.01, CMH, 29.

44. Historical Division European Command, "A Survey of Soviet Aims Policies and Tactics," 1948, file 8–3.1 CC 3, CMH, 364–65. See also ibid., 254–74.

45. Vladimir Pechatnov, "'The Allies are Pressing on You to Break Your Will . . .' Foreign Policy Correspondence Between Stalin and Molotov and Other Politburo Members, September 1945–December 1946," Cold War International History Project, Working Paper no. 26, Sept., 1999; Eduard Mark, "Revolution By Degrees: Stalin's National-Front Strategy for Europe, 1941–1947," Cold War International History Project, Working Paper no. 31, Feb., 2001; Vladislav M. Zubok and Constantine Pleshakov, *Inside the Kremlin's Cold War*. See also William Wohlforth, "New Evidence on Moscow's Cold War: Ambiguity in Search of a Theory," *Diplomatic History* 21 (spring, 1997): 237–40.

46. David Alvarez, "Behind Venona: American Signals Intelligence in the Early Cold War," *Intelligence and National Security* 14 (summer, 1999): 179. See also Robert Jackson, *High Cold War: Strategic Air Reconnaissance and the Electronic Intelligence War, 1949–97*.

Chapter 5. On-the-Job Training

1. George Woodbridge, *UNRRA: The History of the United Nations Relief and Rehabilitation Administration*, 2:301. For operations in Austria, see ibid., 2:295–320.

2. "Mission to Europe to Enquire into the Conditions and Needs of Displaced Persons, June 1945," Office Files, Truman Papers, 8. See also Kindleberger to ?, Aug. 16, 1946, box 4, Papers of Charles P. Kindleberger, HTPL, 6.

3. Sorenson interview, Eleanor Lansing Dulles Papers, DDE (hereafter Dulles Papers). See also George F. Kennan, *Measures Short of War: The George F. Kennan Lectures at the National War College, 1946–1947*, 195–96.

4. Williamson to Erhardt, Dec. 10, 1945, box 1, Records of the Office of Western European Affairs, 1941–50, RG 59, NARA.

5. Memorandum for the State Member, SWNCC, Subject: United States Future Policy Toward Austria, May 14, 1947, box 2, JCS Geographic Files 1946–48, RG 218, NARA.

6. Hickey to Keyes, n.d., Hickey Papers.

7. Alexander Samouce, "I Do Understand the Russians" (unpublished manuscript, author's collection), chap. 21, 3–6.

8. Committee on the National Security Organization, "Schedule of Committee Meetings, Assignments and Tasks," Sept. 9, 1948, U.S. Intelligence Community Collection, NSA, 476.

9. Comments to Keyes, Feb. 11, 1948, Hickey Papers.

10. Keyes to Secretary, memorandum, Subject: The Austrian Problem, n.d., box 7, RG 59, NARA; Keyes to DA for JCS, Sept. 29, 1948, box 11, JCS Geographic Files 1948–50, RG 218, NARA, 2.

11. Unless otherwise cited, information on Keyes's economic plan is taken from State-Army-Navy–Air Force Coordinating Committee, "Neutralization Plan for Austria," App.; and Keyes to ?, Nov. 10, 1947, box 2, JCS Geographic Files 1946–48, RG 218, NARA; and Keyes to Secretary, memorandum, n.d.. Erhardt also believed that the United States needed a more proactive economic policy for Austria. See Erhardt to Williamson, July 26, 1946, box 1, Office of the Assistant Secretary of European affairs, 1941–50, RG 59, NARA. Eleanor Lansing Dulles, a senior economic analyst for the U.S. Legation, believed a plan was required not to block Soviet penetration, but to ensure a viable Austrian economy (Eleanor Lansing Dulles, "U.S. Economic Policy, Austria," July 25, 1946, box 12, Dulles Papers). The analysis in Dulles's report suggests the threat of Soviet economic penetration was far less serious than Keyes suggested. Russian (idem., "Seizures Effects on the Austrian Economy," Mar. 21, 1947, box 12, Dulles Papers). This contrasts with Dulles's recollections in her memoirs, in which she claims to have been thoroughly concerned about the threat of Soviet penetration and stressed as much in her reports (idem., *Eleanor Lansing Dulles: Chance of a Lifetime*, 207–10). See also Bischof, *Austria in the First Cold War*, 196–97 n 155.

12. For example, on Sept. 29, 1948, Keyes sent his own long telegram, a seven-page cable outlining his views on resuming negotiations for a state treaty (Keyes to DA for JCS, Sept. 29, 1948). Keyes's staff also provided a detailed analysis of the pros and cons of the proposed Austrian State Treaty. See Hqs., USFA, memorandum for the Commanding General Subject: Austrian State Treaty, Feb. 11, 1948; "Comments on Memorandum to Commanding General 11 Feb—Austrian State Treaty"; "Advantages and Disadvantages of Concluding a Treaty with Austria and Terminated Four Power Occupation"; and "Strategic Aspects of the Austrian State Treaty," Hickey Papers.

13. Günter Bischof, "'Austria looks to the West': Kommunistische Putschgefahr, geheime Weiderbewaffnung und Westorientierung am Anfang der fünfziger Jahre," in *Österreich in den Fünfzigern*, ed. Thomas Albrich et al., 186–90.

14. London to Secretary of State, Feb. 27, 1948, box 11, JCS Geographic Files 1948–50, RG 218, NARA.

15. The JCS begrudgingly concluded, "although from the military point it was undesirable at that time to withdraw the occupation force from Austria, the Treaty should be concluded if political and economic considerations were overriding." Even so, effective steps had to be taken by Western powers to organize, train, and equip Austrian security forces, forestalling a treaty until Austrian security could be assured (Lovett to ?, Dec. 7, 1948, box 11, JCS Geographic Files, RG 218, NARA). See also memorandum and enclosure, Sept. 21, 1948, box 5, Office of the Assistant Secretary of State for Occupied Areas, 1946–49, RG 59, NARA.

16. Wedemeyer to Hickerson, Mar. 29, 1948, box 98, Albert C. Wedemeyer Papers, HI (hereafter Wedemeyer Papers).

17. Erhardt to Vedeler, Oct. 15, 1947, box 2, Records of the Office of Western European Affairs, 1941–54, RG 59, NARA.

18. Keyes was especially indignant when Clay suggested that troops be withdrawn from Austria (Keyes to EUCOM, Nov. 19, 1947; and Clay to Eisenhower, Nov. 5, 1947, box 2, JCS Geographic Files 1946–48, RG 218, NARA; CSGPO to ?, Oct. 30, 1947, box 3, ibid.). See also Jean Edward Smith, ed., *The Papers of General Lucius D. Clay: Germany, 1945–1949*, vol. 1. Keyes rates barely a mention in Clay's memoirs. See Lucius Clay, *Decision in Germany*, 228–29.

19. Marc Trachtenberg, *A Constructed Peace: The European Settlement, 1945–1963*, 47–48.

20. Wedemeyer to Keyes, Jan. 6, 1948, and Keyes to Wedemeyer, Jan. 28, 1948, box 98, Wedemeyer Papers.

21. Erhardt to Williamson, Oct. 20, 1948, box 1, Office of the Assistant Secretary for European Affairs, 1941–50, RG 59, NARA.

22. Erhardt to Kidd, Jan. 22, 1948, ibid.

23. Memorandum for Holders of SANACC 393, Neutralization Plan for Austria, June 4, 1948; Disposition Form, Subject: Neutralization Plan for Austria, Feb. 25, 1948; and "Neutralization Plan for Austria," Feb. 18, 1948, box 105, RG 319, NARA.

24. For the implementation of the Marshall Plan in Austria, see Wilfried Mähr, *Der Marshallplan in Österreich*; Günter Bischof, "Der Marshallplan und Österreich," *Zeitgeschichte* 17 (1990): 463–74; Günter Bischof, Anton Pelinka, and Dieter Stiefel, eds., *The Marshall Plan in Austria*.

25. "A Report to the President by the National Security Council on the Future Courses of U.S. Action with Respect to Austria," Nov. 17, 1949, file 1574, MC; Cronin, *Great Power Politics*, 76–85.

26. Keyes to Bolte and Maddocks, June 14, 1949, box 10, JCS Geographic Files 1948–50, RG 218, NARA.

27. Handwritten notes, Hickey Papers; ? to MA FRANCE, June 15, 1949, 2; and Keyes to CSGPO, Oct. 19, 1949, box 11, JCS Geographic Files 1948–50, RG 218, NARA. For an overview of Karl Gruber's foreign policy initiatives, see Günter Bischof, "The Making of a Cold Warrior: Karl Gruber and Austrian Foreign Policy, 1945–1953," *Austrian History Yearbook* 26 (1995): 99–127. For an example of Gruber's manipulative approach to the Allied powers, see Cronin, *Great Power Politics*, 65–66.

28. Günter Bischof, "Between Responsibility and Rehabilitation: Austria in International Politics, 1940–1950" (Ph.D. diss., Harvard University, 1989), 711–15.

29. Princeton Seminars, Oct. 10–11, 1953, box 89, Papers of Dean Acheson, HTPL, reel 2, tracks 1, 2, 6, 11, 14.

30. Ibid.

31. NSC-38/1, June 16, 1949, box 11, JCS Geographic Files 1948–50, RG 218, NARA.

32. Memorandum, Oct. 26, 1949, box 65, Memoranda of Conversation August–December 1949, Acheson Papers. See also Cronin, *Great Power Politics*, 77–79, 87–89.

33. Erhardt to Williamson, Nov. 4, 1949, box 7, Records of the Office of Western European Affairs, 1945–1950, RG 59, NARA.

34. Williamson to Erhardt, Aug. 10, 1948, box 1 Office of the Assistant Secretary of State for European Affairs, 1941–50, RG 59, NARA. For a recommendation to shelve the earlier proposal to transfer the high commissioner's authority over the army to the State Department, see "Administrative Responsibilities for Austria," box 5, Records of the Office of Western European Affairs, 1941–54, RG 59, NARA.

35. Princeton Seminars, Oct. 10–11, 1953, box 89, Acheson Papers, reel 4, tracks 1, 7.

36. COMGENUSFA to JCS, Mar. 23, 1950, box 11, RG 218, NARA.

37. Keyes to Gruenther, Mar. 17, 1950, box 2, Alfred M. Gruenther Papers, NATO series, DDE.

38. "The Austrian Transfer," May 24, 1950; and Secretary of Defense Johnson to Secretary of State, July 17, 1950, box 4, Records of the Office of Western European Affairs, 1941–54,

Office of Italian and Austrian Affairs, 1949–51, RG 59, NARA. For a discussion on the transfer of the high commissioner's authority, see memorandum, Subject: Directive to the Civilian High Commissioner for Austria, box 71, G3 Operations Decimal File, RG 319, NARA; memorandum, Subject: Definition of the Term "Military Matters," Oct. 25, 1950, box 41, WHCH: Confidential File, Truman Papers.

39. Quoted in Warren W. Williams, "Review Essay: The Road to the Austrian State Treaty, *Journal of Cold War Studies* 2 (2000): 106. See also Kennan, *Measures Short of War,* 195. Stearman's view of the occupation can be found in William Lloyd Stearman, *The Soviet Union and the Occupation of Austria: An Analysis of Soviet Policy in Austria, 1945–1955.*

Chapter 6. From Occupiers to Warriors

1. The 350th Infantry Regiment was the USFA's main fighting force. The regimental headquarters was at Camp Truscott in Salzburg. The 1st Battalion and the heavy tank and mortar companies billeted at Saalfelden. The 2d Battalion was at Saint Johann. The 4th Reconnaissance Battalion was headquartered at Camp McCauley with the 510th Field Artillery Battalion (equipped with light 105-mm howitzers) and the 77th Field Artillery Battery (equipped with medium 155-mm howitzers). The regiment was also supported by the 70th Engineer Battalion and the 11th Antiaircraft Artillery Battalion.

2. Quarterly Military Survey, Hqs. USFA, Feb. 20, 1949, box 10, JCS Geographic Files 1948–50, RG 218, NARA, 15.

3. "Report of Army Field Forces Inspection of U.S. Forces Austria," Sept., 1950; and ibid., Oct., 1951, file HRC 333, CMH. In 1947, due to critical manpower shortages, the British deactivated the wing that provided air cover to northern Italy. See Air Division to Commander in Chief, May 6, 1947, Occupation Forces Reduction, FO1020/1155, PRO.

4. James Huston, *Outposts and Allies: U.S. Army Logistics in the Cold War, 1945–1953,* 95.

5. Memorandum for Handy, Mar. 17, 1953, Subject: Regarding Ammunition Stock Piles in Europe, SHAPE Correspondence 1951–53, Matthew B. Ridgway Papers, MHI (hereafter Ridgway Papers). See also "Report of the Army Field Forces Inspection of U.S. Army Austria," Nov., 1952, 7–8; and ibid., Oct., 1953, 16, file HRC 333, CMH; Huston, *Outposts and Allies,* 113–14.

6. "Report of Army Field Forces Inspection of U.S. Army, Austria, Oct. 1953, 14; and ibid., Oct., 1954, file HRC 333, CMH, 9.

7. "Report of the Army Field Forces Inspection of U.S. Army Austria," Nov., 1952, file HRC 333, CMH, TAB E-3.

8. Paul L. Freeman Oral History, sec. 2, MHI, 19.

9. Bundespolizeidirektion Salzburg, Monatsbericht für Februar 1950, Feb. 24, 1950, 30344–2/50, BMI, *GD für Öffentliche Sicherheit, Gruppe 04, Inneres, ÖSA;* Lagebericht für den Monat Februar 1947, 26125–2/47, Karton 2, BMI, *GD für Öffentliche Sicherheit, Gruppe 04, Inneres, ÖSA; Sicherheitsdirektion, Lagebericht für den Monat Dezember 1949,* Jan. 1, 1950, 30344–2/50, BMI, *GD für Öffentliche Sicherheit, Gruppe 04, Inneres, ÖSA;* Ekern to Williamson, Independence Day, 1950, box 4, Records of the Office of Western European Affairs, 1941–54, Office of Italian and Austrian Affairs, 1949–51, RG 59, NARA.

10. *FRUS: Europe: Political and Economic Development, 1951,* pt. 2, 4:1107.

11. Ibid, 1119, 1121.

12. Espy to Donnelly, July 3, 1952, Arthur Compton Files, box 3, Records of the Office of Western European Affairs, 1941–54, Austria, RG 59, NARA. See also Espy to Dowling, Aug. 25, 1952, ibid.

13. Weekly Summary no. 3, Office of the U.S. High Commissioner for Austria, Aug. 15, 1952, box 12, ibid., 23–24.

14. Carl I. Hutton, "An Armored Artillery Commander in the European Theater" (unpublished manuscript, U.S. Army Field Artillery School, Fort Sill, Okla.).

15. Bernard Nalty and Morris MacGregor, eds., *Blacks in the Military: Essential Documents,* 181.

16. Ibid., 200.

17. Morris MacGregor Jr., *Integration of the Armed Forces, 1940–1965*, 385, 387. See also Margaret Geis, "Negro Personnel in the European Command, 1 January 1946–30 June 1950," file 8–3 cf3, CMH, 17–18. The State Department declined to argue against the military's reluctance to use black troops for occupation duties. In fact, State followed similar policies. The department, for example, had no black personnel assigned to Europe. See, Michael Krenn, *Black Diplomacy: African Americans and the State Department, 1945–1969*, 31–34.

18. Nalty and MacGregor, *Blacks in the Military*, 211, 217; McGregor, *Integration of the Armed Forces*, 330–31.

19. Ibid., 210.

20. Richard Stillman II, *The Integration of the U.S. Armed Forces*, 34–35.

21. Ibid., 61.

22. Mark Clark, *A Calculated Risk*, 414–15.

23. John Willoughby, *Remaking the Conquering Heroes: The Social and Geopolitical Impact of the Post-War American Occupation of Germany*, 71.

24. Geis, "Negro Personnel in the European Command," 54.

25. Ibid., 18–19.

26. Nalty and MacGregor, *Blacks in the Military*, 209, 219.

27. "Integration of Negro and White Troops in the U.S. Army Europe, 1952–54," CMH, 1.

28. *FRUS, 1951*, pt. 2, 4:1093.

29. Svetlana Savranskaya, trans., *O deiatelnosti organov Severo-atlanticheskogo Soiuza v sviazi s sozdaniem atlanticheskoi armii i remilitarizatsiei zapadnoi Germanii*, Feb., 1951, NSA; *FRUS, 1951*, pt. 2, 4:1114; memorandum for Freund, Subject: First Report of Working Group, NSC-164/1, pt. B, White House, National Security Council Staff, Papers 1948–61, OCB Central Files, DDE.

30. *FRUS, Germany and Austria, 1952–1954*, 7:1133.

31. Miller, *Complete History of World War II*, 93.

32. Randall Bennett Woods, *Fulbright: A Biography*, 167.

33. "Consideration of Troop Withdrawal by Western High Commissioners," Feb 25, 1954, Yost Acting High Commissioner Political Advisor & High Commissioner, Top Secret General Records, 1945–55, box 7, RG 84, NARA.

Chapter 7. The Southern Flank

1. "G5 Protective Security Plan—Minor Uprising, Division Motorized Infantry Battalion Alert Force—Occupation of Austria, 42d Infantry Division," Dec. 14, 1945, box 10672, RG 407, NARA.

2. Memorandum for the Chief of Staff, Mar. 12, 1946, box 78, RG 319, NARA.

3. Steven Ross, *American War Plans, 1945–1950*, 25–29.

4. Memorandum for the Chief of Staff, Mar. 12, 1946.

5. "Changes in NATO Strategic Concepts and Defense, 1949–1966," file 2–3.7 AD.R, CMH, 1.

6. U.S. Forces in the European Theater, G3, "Plan TOTALITY: Alert Plan for Defense in the Event of Aggression, Germany," Jan. 1946, MHI.

7. Joint Strategic Plans Group, BROILER, Feb. 11, 1948, box 104, RG 310, NARA, app. A, 58. See also memorandum for Chief of Staff U.S. Army, Subject: Planning Responsibilities of the Commanding General U.S. Forces Austria, Aug. 21, 1952, box 8, Army Operations Decimal File, RG 319, NARA.

8. Joint Strategic Plans Committee, "United States Military Alliances with Nations of Western Europe," Apr., 1948, box 39, RG 218, NARA, 3.

9. "The Military Significance of Austria," Hickey Papers.

10. "USFA Commander's Estimate of the Situation," May 20, 1948, 38; and ibid., Aug., 1948, box 10, JCS Geographic Files 1948–50, RG 218, NARA, 4.

11. U.S. Army Center of Military History, "Short History of EUCOM, 1947–1974," file OCMH-114, CMH, 3; Ronald H. Cole et al., *The History of the Unified Command Plan, 1946–1993,* 17–19.

12. Ross, *American War Plans,* 89–90.

13. Huebner to Wedemeyer, Oct. 18, 1948, box 9, Army Operations, General Administration, Hot Files, RG 319, NARA.

14. "Changes in NATO Strategic Concepts," 1–5.

15. "Memorandum tabled by Field Marshal Montgomery for his meeting with Western Union Chiefs of Staff on 20 June 1950," June 17, 1950, box 150, Army Operations, General Decimal File 1950–51, RG 319, NARA, 379–80.

16. Ekern to Williamson, Independence Day, 1950; *FRUS, 1951,* pt. 2, 4:1102, 1179.

17. *FRUS: Council of Foreign Ministers: Germany and Austria, 1949,* 3:1115.

18. Chief of Staff, U.S. Army to Joint Chiefs of Staff, Subject: Separation of U.S. Forces in Austria and European Command, JCS1369/18, May 14, 1949, box 10, JCS Geographic Files 1948–50, RG 218, NARA.

19. JCS to Keyes, Sept. 16, 1949, ibid.

20. Bruno Koppensteiner, "Béthouarts Alpenfestung Militärische Planungen und Die Verteidigungsvorbereitungen der französischen Besatzungsmacht in Tirol und Voralberg," Frankreichs beginnt in Tirol," in *Österreich im frühen Kalten Krieg,* ed. Schmidl, 193–238.

21. Ross, *American War Plans,* 103–22.

22. Bradley to Secretary of Defense, memorandum, Subject: Position on Recommendations to be Submitted to the President Regarding A European Defense Force and Related Matters, Aug. 10, 1950, box 1, Records of the Bureau of European Affairs, Subjects Relating to European Defense Arrangements, RG 59, NARA.

23. For an assessment of Yugoslav military capability, see "Yugoslavia Armed Forces, Strengths and Capabilities," Intelligence Review no. 18, June 13, 1946, MHI, 10–15.

24. For the State Department's Policy Planning Staff analysis and recommendations, see *The State Department Policy Planning Staff Papers 1949,* 3:141–43.

25. Keyes to JCS, Sept. 29, 1948, box 11, JCS Geographic Files 1948–50, RG 218, NARA, 6. This view was echoed by Bradley. See, Bischof, "Between Responsibility and Rehabilitation," 754.

26. "Narrative Summary of Major Activities ACofS G3, 9 Sept. 51 through 31 December 1952," file 20–2.3 AA 1951–52, CMH, 17. See also "The Current Situation in Yugoslavia," Nov. 21, 1950; and "Probability of an Invasion of Yugoslavia," Mar. 20, 1951, box 253, Intelligence File, National Intelligence Estimates, President's Secretary Files, Truman Papers; "Possibility of Direct Military Action in the Balkans by Soviet Satellites," July 29, 1950, box 2, Records of the National Security Council, CIA Files, Truman Papers.

27. "Short History of EUCOM, " 3; Cole, *History of the Unified Command Plan,* 17–19; Narrative Summary of Major Activities of AcofS G3"; "Report of the Joint Strategic Plans Committee," Mar. 5, 1951, box 74, JCS Geographic Files 1951–53, RG 218, NARA, 1, encl. B.

28. Karl Gruber, *Between Liberation and Liberty: Austria in the Post-War World,* 185.

29. Ross, *American War Plans,* 124.

30. "Die Bedeutung Österreichs für die Verteidung des Westens, 1952," Gendarmerie Files, HM; "Stellungnahme zu den Vorschlagen der Alliierten bei der Aufstellung von Gendarmerieformationen bei der Besprechung am 17. Oktober 1951," Gendarmerie Files, HM.

31. Information on the proposal for a forward defense is taken from memorandum for Chief of Staff U.S. Army, Subject: Planning Responsibilities of the Commanding General U.S. Forces Austria, 21 Aug., 1952, box 8, Army Operations Decimal File, RG 319, NARA; CGUSFA, Salzburg, Austria, to Director, JMAG, London, England, Feb. 6, 1951; and Kibler to JCS, 281531Z Feb., 1951, box 10, JCS Geographic Files 1948–50, RG 218, NARA; memorandum for the JCS, Subject: Conversations with General Eisenhower and General Gruenther in

SHAPE Headquarters, Paris, France, Oct. 4–5, 1951, box 8, Army Operations General Decimal File, 1950–51, RG 319, NARA, 3.

32. Louis Galambos et al., eds., *The Papers of Dwight David Eisenhower*, vol. 12, *NATO and the Campaign of 1952*, 120.

33. CGUSFA to CSUSA, May 19, 1951, box 10; and "War Plan IRONBARK," box 72, JCS Geographic Files 1951–53, RG 218, NARA, 27–28. For Eisenhower's view of Ironbark, see Galambos et al., eds., *Papers of Dwight David Eisenhower*, 12:592–95, 805.

34. Information on these plans and ED 1–52 is from "Directive for the Implementation of the Joint Outline Emergency War Plan Support SHAPE EDP 1–52," Feb. 26, 1952; and "Report by the Joint Strategic Plans Committee," June 27, 1952, box 71, JCS Geographic Files 1951–53, RG 218, NARA, 12; Political Advisor and High Commissioner, memorandum, Subject: Defense plans in Austria, Aug. 13, 1952, box 5, Top Secret General Records, 1945–55, RG 84, NARA; Hqs., USFA, Subject: Planning Responsibilities of Commanding General U.S. Forces Austria, June 10, 1952, box 8, Army Operations Decimal File, RG 319, NARA. Operations Mantleshelf and Manward were superseded by EDP 1–52. Operation Pilgrim Dog was never approved. See Report by the Joint Strategic Plans Committee, June 27, 1952; and "Directive for the Implementation of the Joint Outline Emergency War Plan Support for SHAPE EDP 1–52," Feb. 26, 1952, box 71, JCS Geographic Files 1951–53, RG 218, NARA.

35. Cronin, *Great Power Politics*, 116–18; Bischof, *Austria in the First Cold War*, 123–29.

36. SACEUR to CINCSOUTH, 1412213Z June, 1952, box 8, Army Operations Decimal File, RG 319, NARA.

37. Espy to Donnelly, July 14, 1952, box 5, Top Secret General Records, 1945–55, RG 84, NARA.

38. To Chief of Staff, HQ, BTA, Subject: Operation RENAULT, Mar. 16, 1950, Operation Renault; and Subject: Operation Renault, Mar. 23, 1950, Operation Renault, FO1020/3458, PRO; Walter Dowling, "Emergency Employment of Vienna Garrison," July 28, 1952, box 5, Top Secret General Records, 1945–55, RG 84, NARA; "Internal Security Scheme," n.d., Civil Disturbance Directives, FO1020/2334, PRO.

39. Hays to JCS, 29110Z Oct., 1952, box 10, JCS Geographic Files 1951–53, RG 218, NARA. See also file no. G3 091 Austria TS, box 8, Army Operations Decimal File, RG 319, NARA, 3. American fortification construction did not go unnoticed by the Soviets (*FRUS, 1951*, pt. 2, 4:1134).

40. "Short History of EUCOM," 5; Hqs., USAREUR, "Annual Historical Report," (U) Jan. 1, 1953–June 30, 1954, file 8–3.1 CK 1 C 1, CMH, 417–18. For Eisenhower's recommendation, see Galambos, *Papers of Dwight David Eisenhower*, 12:1064–68.

41. Ridgway to Carney, Dec. 18, 1952, SHAPE Classified Files June, 1952–June, 1953, Ridgway Papers; Ridgway to Sullivan, n.d., box 7, Top Secret General Records, 1945–55, RG 84, NARA.

42. ACofS, G3, "Narrative Summary of Major Events and Problems, FY 1953," file 20–2.3 AA 153, CMH, 11; Galambos, *Papers of Dwight David Eisenhower*, 12:493–95, 505, 551–53.

43. Memorandum, Subject: Discussions with General J. Lawton Collins, Chief of Staff, U.S. Army, SHAPE, Plans, Policy, and Operations Division, Sept. 6, 1952, SHAPE Classified Files June 1952–June 1953, Ridgway Papers. See also Collins to Gruenther, Mar. 29, 1951, box 17, J. Lawton Collins Papers, DDE. Eisenhower agreed that Collins should talk to Tito about the defense of the Ljubljana Gap. See memorandum for JCS, Subject: Conversations with General Eisenhower and General Gruenther, 2. Collins's claim in an interview that he did not object to spreading NATO's defenses to Greece and Turkey was disingenuous. See J. Lawton Collins Oral History, SL, 17–18.

44. Ridgway to Bradley, Oct. 3, 1952, SHAPE Classified Files June, 1952–June, 1953, Ridgway Papers. See also Montgomery to Chief of Staff, Sept. 8, 1952, ibid.; Matthew B. Ridgway, *Soldier: The Memoirs of Matthew B. Ridgway*, 251–54.

45. Memorandum, Subject: Discussions with General J. Lawton Collins, Feb. 6, 1952. The Yugoslav army had been highly dependent on Soviet assistance. See Bojan Dimitrijevic, "Soviet

Security Relationships: Yugoslav-Soviet Military Relations, 1945–1948," *Journal of Slavic Military Studies* 9 (Sept., 1996): 581–93.

46. Gen. Thomas T. Handy Oral History, sec. 5, MHI, 29, 32–33.

47. "Narrative Summary of Major Events and Problems," 13–14.

48. Collins to Ridgway, Apr. 1, 1953, White House Office, National Council Staff, Papers, 1948–61, OCB Files, DDE.

49. "Narrative Summary of Major Events and Problems," 13–14; Heuser, *Western Containment,* 171; Winfried Heinemann, "The West and Yugoslavia in the 1950s," *Army History* 40 (winter, 1997): 12–15. See also David Stone, "The Balkan Pact and American Policy," *East European Quarterly* 28 (Sept., 1994): 393–407; and James W. Riddleberger Oral History, SL, 20–28.

50. Memorandum for the Secretary of Defense, Subject: U.S. Position with respect to Austria, Oct. 9, 1953, box 11, JCS Geographic Files 1951–53, RG 218, NARA, 2.

51. *FRUS, 1952–1954,* pt. 2, 7:1914.

52. Chief MAAG (Italy) to JCS, 171205Z Sept., 1953, box 10, JCS Geographic Files 1951–53, RG 218, NARA.

53. Freeman Oral History, sec. 2, 20.

54. "Report of Army Field Forces Inspection of U.S. Army, Austria, October, 1953," file HRC 3333, CMH, 15. In December, 1954, a NATO council report concluded that military commanders should be authorized to develop war plans incorporating the use of tactical nuclear weapons "whether aggressors used them or not" ("Changes in NATO Strategic Concepts," 10). See also ibid., 8–9. For the army's view on planning the employment of chemical weapons, see report for Wedemeyer, "Examine the Feasibility of Resorting to Chemical Weapons for the Defense of the Rhine," Oct. 29, 1948, box 9, Army Operations, General Administration, Hot Files, RG 319, NARA, 3–4.

55. Jonathan Soffer, *General Matthew B. Ridgway: From Progressivism to Reaganism, 1895–1993,* 159.

56. Ridgway to Bradley, Dec. 31, 1952, SHAPE Correspondence 1951–53, Ridgway Papers. See also Ridgway to Bradley, "Eyes Only, General Bradley," June 18, 1951, ibid.

57. George F. Kennan, *Memoirs, 1925–1950,* 305–307, 463.

58. Princeton Seminars, Oct. 10–11, 1953, box 89, Acheson Papers, reel 5, track 1, page 8.

59. Gruenther to JCS, 131105Z Oct., 1953, box 11, JCS Geographic Files 1951–53, RG 218, NARA, 2.

60. Gruenther to JCS, 071820Z Oct., 1953, box 10, JCS Geographic Files 1951–53, RG 218, NARA. See also JCS to ?, Subject: Withdrawal of British and French Forces from Austria, Sept. 29, 1953, ibid.

61. Keyes to DA, Oct. 21, 1947, ibid.

62. Files under G3, 091 Austria TS, box 8, Army Operations Decimal File, RG 319, NARA, 1; *FRUS, 1952–1954,* pt. 2, 7:1729.

63. Gruenther to JCS 011310Z Oct., 1953, box 10, JCS Geographic Files, 1951–53, RG 218, NARA.

64. JCS to Secretary of Defense, memorandum, Subject: United Kingdom and French Forces in Austria, Sept. 11, 1953, box 11, ibid.

65. JCS to Secretary of Defense, memorandum, Oct. 13, 1953; and Collins to Secretary of Subject: Reduction of Forces in Austria, Dec. 24, 1953, ibid.; *FRUS, 1952–1954,* pt. 2, 7:1930–34, 1938.

66. JCS to Secretary of Defense, memorandum, Subject: U.S. Objectives and Policies with Respect to Austria, NSC-164/1, Dec. 9, 1953, box 11, JCS Geographic Files 1951–53, RG 218, NARA 2.

67. Dulles to Wilson, July 3, 1954, Political Advisor and High Commissioner, Top Secret General Records, 1945–55, Box 7, RG 84, NARA; USCINCEUR to CSUSA DEPTAR, 131640Z Oct., 1953, box 10, JCS Geographic Files 1951–53; memorandum, Subject: Discus-

sion of the 216th meeting of the National Security Council, Wednesday, Oct. 6, 1954, Oct. 7, 1954, Declassified Documents Reference System.

68. USCICEUR to JCS, 131426Z Nov., 1953, box 10, JCS Geographic Files 1951–53, RG 218, NARA; Memorandum for Freund, Department of State, Subject: First Report of Working Group, NSC-164/1, Jan. 12, 1954, White House Office, SHAPE Correspondence 1951–53, Central Files, DDE; *FRUS, 1952–1954*, pt. 2, 7:1923–26, 1949–51, 1976–80.

Chapter 8. Secrets

1. Hays to Wedemeyer, Sept. 17, 1948, box 98, Wedemeyer Papers.
2. Military Division to Deputy Commissioner, Subject: Ex CONSTABLE, Exercise Constable, FO1020/3458, PRO.
3. Halvor Ekern, "The Allied Commission for Austria," in *American Experiences in Military Government*, ed. Carl Friedrich, 59; Rauchensteiner, *Sonderfall*, 231.
4. Hqs., USFA, "Implementation of Strategic Control Plan," Dec. 1, 1948; and memorandum, Subject: Austrian Standing Rationing Plans, Dec. 9, 1950, Arthur Compton Files, box 12, Records of the Office of Western European Affairs, 1941–54, Austria, RG 59, NARA; ? to Magruder, Sept. 20, 1950, box 9, Records of the Office of Western European Affairs, 1945–50, RG 59, NARA.
5. Memorandum, Subject: Precautions Against the Isolation of Vienna, July 17, 1948, FO1020/3468, PRO; Erwin Schmidl, "The Airlift that Never Was: Allied Plans to Supply Vienna by Air, 1948–50," *Army History,* fall, 1997/winter, 1998, 18.
6. Erhardt to State Department, memorandum, Subject: Possible Partition of Austria and blockade of Vienna, Oct. 25, 1948, box 188, RG 263, NARA.
7. Memorandum of Conversation, Dec., 1950, Arthur Compton Files, box 12, Records of the Office of Western European Affairs, 1941–54, Austria, RG 59, NARA.
8. *FRUS, 1951*, pt. 2, 4:1046; Christian Stifter, *Die Wiederaufrüstung Österreichs: Die geheime Remilitarisierung der westlichen Besatzungszonen, 1945–1955*, 151–52.
9. Memorandum for Freund, Department of State, Subject: First Report of Working Group, NSC-164/1, Jan. 12, 1954, White House Office, National Security Council Staff Papers 1948–61, OCB Central Files, DDE.
10. *FRUS, 1951*, pt. 2, 4:1047.
11. Ibid., *1952–1954*, pt. 2, 4:1921.
12. Herz, *Understanding Austria*, 454.
13. Stifter, *Die Wiederaufrüstung Österreichs*, 132–33; Franz Hesztera, *Von der "A-Gendarmerie" zur B-Gendarmerie der Aufbau des Österreichischen Bundesheeres 1945 bis Herbst 1952*, 12–21; Wilhelm Svoboda, *Franz Olah: Eine Spurensicherung;* Rauchenteiner, *Sonderfall*, 295, 397n. 28.
14. In 1952, for example, the army requested the transfer of $4,515,000 of MDAP funds to the CIA. See "Index for Army Operations Decimal File," box 8, RG 319, NARA. See also Heimo Segel, "U.S. Waffenposts in Oberösterreich," 71–75; Franz Cede, "Die rechtlichen Aspekte der U.S. Waffendepots in Österreich," 6–23; and Christian Sgur-Cabanac, "Erkenntnisse aus der Verteilung der Depots und Ammerkungen zum militärischen Tiel der Bergung," 53–66, all in *Sorry Guys, No Gold*, ed. Manfried Rauchensteiner and Claudia Ham.
15. Yuri Modin, *My Five Cambridge Friends, Burgess, Maclean, Philby, Blunt and Cairncross*, 67–168, 175.
16. Herz, *Understanding Austria*, 380–81, 495–96; *FRUS, 1952–1954*, pt. 2, 7:1858.
17. Christopher Andrew and Vasili Mitrokhin, *The Sword and the Shield*, 359–60.
18. Rauchensteiner, *Sonderfall*, 305.
19. Alexandre Y. Mansourov, "Stalin, Mao, Kim, and China's Decision to Enter the Korean War, September 16–October 15, 1950: New Evidence from the Russian Archives," *Cold War International History Project Bulletin*, nos. 6 and 7 (winter, 1995/96), 94–118; Kathryn Weathersby, "Korea 1949–1950: To Attack or Not to Attack? Stalin, Kim Il Sung, and the

Prelude to War," *Cold War International History Project Bulletin,* no. 5 (spring, 1995), 8–9; idem., "New Findings on the Korean War," *Cold War International History Project Bulletin,* no. 3 (winter, 1993), 17.

20. Memorandum, Subject: Establishment of Checkmate Project, Mar. 31, 1951, Arthur Compton Files, box 12, Records of the Office of Western European Affairs, 1941–54, Austria, RG 59, NARA.

21. Bolte to EUCOM, June 7, 1949, box 10, JCS Geographic Files 1948–50, RG 218, NARA. For a discussion of the Aufgebot see, Stifter, *Wiederaufrüstung Österreichs,* 164–71.

22. Hays to JCS, 110Z Oct., 1952, box 10, JCS Geographic Files 1951–53, RG 218, NARA; memorandum by the Chief of Staff, U.S. Army, Subject: Austrian Peace Treaty Negotiations, box 11, JCS Geographic Files, RG 218, NARA, 2. See also ibid., 1.

23. Civil Affairs Division Special Staff, DA, "Austria: Problems of U.S. Army in Occupation," NDUL, 12.

24. Memorandum of the Executive Secretary, National Security Council, Subject: Proposal for a Volunteer Freedom Corps, Feb. 14, 1953, box 4, White House Office, Office of the Special Assistant for National Security Affairs, NSC Series, Policy Papers Subseries, DDE, 6–7; "Top Secret Supplement, Annual Historical Report, Headquarters, U.S. Army, Europe (U), 1 Jan. 1953–30 June 1954," n.d., CMH, 75. For a comprehensive history of the proposal, see James Jay Carafano, "Mobilizing Europe's Stateless: America's Plan for a Cold War Army," *Journal of Cold War Studies* 1 (spring, 1999): 61–85.

25. Galambos, *Papers of Dwight David Eisenhower,* 12:340.

26. Memorandum, Subject: Discussion at the 132nd meeting of the National Security Council on Wednesday, Feb. 18, 1953, Feb. 19, 1953, box 1, Dwight D. Eisenhower: Papers as President, NSC series, DDE, 3–4; "Top Secret Supplement, Annual Historical Report, Headquarters, U.S. Army, Europe (U), 1 Jan. 1953–30 June 1954," 74–75, CMH; "Narrative Summary of Major Events and Problems, OACofS, G3," 20–2.3 AA, CMH, 2.

27. Carafano, "Mobilizing Europe's Stateless," 68. Lodge was not the only one to popularize this proposal. See, e.g., Alvin O'Konski, "Foreign Legions for the USA," Demobilization including Rehabilitation and Redeployment Survey Prepared by the Analysis Branch, War Department Bureau of Public Affairs, May 4, 1946, no. 56, MHI, 1.

28. Edgar P. Allen, Department of State, to Ambassador Donnelly, Feb. 1, 1952, Arthur Compton Files, box 12, Records of the Office of Western European Affairs, 1941–54, Austria, RG 59, NARA; *FRUS, 1952–1954,* pt. 2, 7:1730–32.

29. H. W. Brands incorrectly concluded that the proposal for the corps originated with C. D. Jackson. See H. W. Brands Jr., "A Cold War Foreign Legion? The Eisenhower Administration and the Volunteer Freedom Corps," *Military Affairs* 52 (Jan., 1988): 7. Lodge's role as the first advocate to suggest the program to the new president and as the drafter of the initial proposal is confirmed in Cutler to Lodge, Jan. 26, 1953; Lodge to Cutler, Feb. 9, 1953; and Lodge to Cutler, memorandum, Feb. 4, 1953, P-373, reel 3, Lodge-Eisenhower Correspondence, Henry Cabot Lodge II Papers, MHS.

30. "USFA History, 5 July to 30 Sept 1945," box 1, USFA Historical File, RG 260, NARA. See also "The Displaced Persons Problem in Germany and Austria," Intelligence Review no. 43, Dec. 5, 1946, MHI, 32–38.

31. "Apr.–June 1946 USFA Report," box 1, USFA Historical File, RG 260, NARA, 157.

32. Pieter Lagrou, *The Legacy of Nazi Occupation: Patriotic Memory and National Recovery in Western Europe, 1945–1965,* 31–32. For a contemporary assessment of the threat stateless communities represented to European stability, see the analysis by Lawrence Frenkel, who worked as the UNRAA's chief public health officer for Austria in, "Typed Manuscript," folder 1, Lawrence Frenkel Papers, HI.

33. Memorandum, Subject: Discussion at the 150th Meeting of the National Security Council, Thursday, June 18, 1953, June 19, 1953, box 4, Dwight D. Eisenhower Papers, NSC series, DDE.

34. Memorandum for Crittenberger, Subject: State Department Comments on the Volun-

teer Freedom Corps, Apr. 13, 1953, White House Office, National Security Council Staff Papers, 1953–61, DDE, 6, 10.

35. Secret telephonogram by V. Semenov and V. Sokolovski in Berlin to V. M. Molotov, June 18, 1953, morning, available at http://cwihp.si.edu/cwihplib.nsf.

36. Christian Ostermann, "New Documents on the East German Uprising of 1953, Intro-duction and Commentary," available at http://cwihp.si.edu/cwihplib.nsf; Christian Ostermann, "Keeping the Pot Simmering, the United States and the East German Uprising of 1953," German Studies Review 19 (Mar., 1996): 61–89.

37. Memorandum for Cutler, Nov. 3, 1954, box 8, White House Office, National Security Council Staff Papers, 1948–61, Special Staff File Series, DDE.

38. "Implementation of Paragraph 8 of NSC-143/2," Aug. 20, 1954, White House Office, National Security Council Staff Papers, 1948–61, DDE.

39. ACofS, G3, "Annual History Report, USAREUR, 1 Jan 1954–30 Jun 54," CMH, 26–27; idem., "Summary of Major Events and Problems, Fiscal Year 1954," file 20–2.3 AA 1954, CMH, 11–12.

40. "Part B—Detailed Development of Major Actions, Progress Report NSC-164/1," OCB Files, DDE.

Chapter 9. Arming Austria

1. Williamson to Perkins, Oct. 14, 1952, box 25, Miscellaneous Office Files of the Assistant Secretary European Affairs, 1943–57, RG 59, NARA.

2. "A Short Report on the Austrian Battalion," Jan. 24, 1945, Formation of the Gen-darmerie, FO1020/2265, PRO; Allied Commission for Austria (British Element), Subject: Soviet Suspicions on Demilitarization Issues, Feb. 25, 1946, Alleged Austrian Army, FO1020/888, PRO; "Allied Commission for Austria, 13th Meeting, Jan., 1946," Jan. 10, 1946, box 1, Record of the Allied Commission for Austria, HTPL; Stifter, Wiederaufrüstung Österreichs, 43–44.

3. Stifter, Wiederaufrüstung Österreichs, 33–34.

4. Periodical Intelligence Digest no. 22, Feb. 15, 1946, "Alleged Austrian Army," app. A, FO1020/888, PRO, 2.

5. Ibid.

6. Subject: Austrian Army, Sept. 15, 1945, Alleged Austrian Army, FO1020/888, PRO.

7. Stifter, Wiederaufrüstung Österreichs, 45.

8. Keyes to JCS, Jan. 6, 1949, box 11, JCS Geographic files 1948–50, RG 218, NARA.

9. "Alliierte Kommission für Österreich Alliiertes Sekretariat, an den Österreichen Bundes-kanzler," May 11, 1946, HM; "Einstellung der Tätigkeit, Aufteilung des Personals," May 21, 1946, HM.

10. Keyes to JCS, Jan. 6, 1949.

11. See, e.g., Department of State, Austria, "The Issue of the State Police Developments in the South Tirol," Apr. 17, 1947, box 185, RG 263, NARA.

12. Allied Commission for Austria (British Element), Subject: Arms for Police and Gen-darmerie, May 13, 1948; ibid., Subject: Transfer of British Military Commitments to the Gen-darmerie, Feb. 11, 1948; ibid., Subject: Arms for the Austrian Police and Gendarmerie; and ibid., Subject: Arms for Police and Gendarmerie, Feb. 10, 1948, FO1020/126, PRO; Intelli-gence Organization, Allied Commission for Austria (BE), Subject: The Austrian Frontier ser-vices, July 23, 1947, Formation of Gendarmerie, FO1020/2265, PRO.

13. Subject: Post-Occupation Forces in Austria, Jan., 1947, Post-Occupation Security Forces, FO1020/112, PRO.

14. Marjoribanks to Cheetham, Mar. 9, 1948, Exercise Constable, FO1020/3458, PRO.

15. Keyes to DA, Jan. 6, 1949, Box 11, JCS Geographic Files 1948–50, RG 218, NARA; Military Government Austria, "Report of the High Commissioner," no. 17, Mar., 1947, CMH, 201.

16. Douglas to Secretary of State, Apr. 17, 1948, box 11; and Keyes to JCS, May 7, 1948, box 10, JCS Geographic Files 1948–50, RG 218, NARA; Cheetham to Marjoribanks, Apr. 29, 1948, Exercise Constable, FO1020/3458, PRO; Counselor, His Majesty's Legation, to Deputy Commissioner, Subject: Austrian Army, Exercise Constable, Apr. 28, 1948, FO1020/3458, PRO.

17. Stifter, *Wiederaufrüstung Österreichs*, 78–90.

18. Hqs., USFA, Subject: Interview between General Balmer and General Deutsch, Apr. 21, 1948, Future Austrian Army, FO1020/3461, PRO; Minutes, June 29, 1948, Exercise Constable, FO1020/3458, PRO.

19. Subject: Organization of the Austrian Army, June 18, 1948, box 107, RG 263, NARA.

20. COMGENUSFA to DA, message P 3575, July 9, 1949, box 11, Joint Chiefs of Staff Geographic Files 1948–50, RG 218, NARA; Cheetham to Marjoribanks, Aug. 18, 1948; and Winterton to Kirtpatrick, Feb. 27, 1949, Exercise Constable, FO1020/3458, PRO; Allied Commission for Austria (British Element), Subject: Austrian Security Forces, May 3, 1949; and Deutsch to Winterton, Nov. 24, 1948, Future Austrian Army, FO1020/3461, PRO; memorandum for Deputy High Commissioner, Subject: Special Gendarmerie Regiment (Precis of correspondence and Action to date), May 31, 1949, Exercise Constable, FO1020/3458, PRO; American Legation, Subject: Organization of the Austrian Army, June 18, 1948, box 187; and ibid., Subject: The Security of Austria, July 9, 1948, box 188, RG 263, NARA.

21. *FRUS, 1949*, 3:415.

22. Keyes to JCS, Sept. 14, 1948; Keyes to DA, Sept. 25, 1948; and Keyes to JCS, Nov. 16, 1948, box 10, JCS Geographic Files, 1948–50, RG 218, NARA.

23. Keyes to DA, Aug. 5, 1948; Keyes to JCS, Sept. 13, 1948; and Keyes to JCS, Apr. 22, 1948, box 10, JCS Geographic Files 1948–50, RG 218, NARA; Stifter, *Wiederaufrüstung Österreichs*, 100.

24. Keyes to DA, July 9, 1949, box 11, JCS Geographic Files 1948–50, RG 218, NARA.

25. "Quarterly Military Survey," Feb. 20, 1949, box 10, ibid., 12. Figl believed that it would take twelve years to build the army up to its authorized strength under the treaty. This was a far more conservative estimate than that offered by Keyes, who believed that the fifty-three-thousand-man ceiling could be reached within a year. The proposed locations for the Austrian units were Tirol-Vorarlberg-Salzburg (headquarters, Innsbruck), Upper Austria (headquarters, Linz), Carinthia (headquarters, Klagenfurt), Styria (headquarters, Graf); Lower Austria (headquarters, Saint Poelten) and Vienna/Burgenland (headquarters, Vienna).

26. Foreign Office, Vienna, to Foreign Office, Mar. 25, 1949; and Keyes to Galloway, Mar. 10, 1949, Exercise Constable, FO1020/3458, PRO; Outgoing Foreign Office Telegram, Apr. 2, 1950; and "Program for Developing Austrian Army," Future Austrian Army, FO1020/3462, PRO; *FRUS, 1951*, pt. 2, 4:1047; Erhardt to State Department, Mar. 24, 1949; Acheson to Erhardt, Mar. 18, 1949; and London to State Department, Aug. 5, 1949, Arthur Compton Files, box 12, Records of the Office of Western European Affairs, 1941–54, Austria, RG 59, NARA.

27. Keyes to DA, June 29, 1949, box 11, JCS Geographic Files 1948–50, RG 218, NARA; memorandum for Ohly, Subject: MAP Planning to Cope with the Austrian Problem, box 53, RG 330, NARA; Joint Strategic Plans Committee, "Future Course of Military Action with Respect to Austria—Military Aid," Oct. 26, 1949; and London to Secretary of State, Aug. 5, 1949, box 11, JCS Geographic Files 1948–50, RG 218, NARA; Winterton to Commander in Chief, message, Subject: Special *gendarmerie* regiment, 271600 (June, 1947), Exercise Constable, FO1020/3458, PRO.

28. Deputy Commissioner to Commander in Chief, June 27, 1949, Exercise Constable, FO1020/3458, PRO.

29. Galloway to Mallet, June 1, 1949, Exercise Constable, FO1020/3458, PRO. See also MIL/1066/G, Military Division, May 23, 1949, ibid.

30. Lyman L. Lemnitzer Oral History, MHI, 10–11.

31. Quoted in Phil Williams, *The Senate and U.S. Troops in Europe*, 28.

32. Arthur Vandenberg Jr., ed., *The Private Papers of Senator Vandenberg*, 508.

33. Lovett to ?, Dec. 7, 1948, JCS Geographic File 1948–50, RG 218, NARA.

34. Memorandum for Ohly; Joint Strategic Plans Committee, "Future Course of Military Action"; London to Secretary of State, Aug. 5, 1949.

35. Joint Strategic Plans Committee, "Future Course of Military Action," 2.

36. Hqs., EUCOM/USAREUR, "Command Report," 1952, file 8–3.1 CH 5 C1, CMH, 309; "Top Secret Supplement, Annual Historical Report," 26–27.

37. Untitled document dated Sept. 18, 1952, *HM*. The organization, responsibilities, and activities of the committees are described in *Memorandum an den Vorsitzenden des Wiener Komitees*, May 9, 1952, *HM*.

38. "Alarmierung," *HM*; "Gendarmeriealarmbataillon Steiermark—Kärten," *HM*.

39. Brigitte Fiala, "Die Errichtung der B-Gendarmerie, Bibliothek des Staatsarchivs," *ÖSA*, 23.

40. "Bericht, über die IS-Manöver 1952 in Oberösterreich," Nov., 1952, *HM*; "Bemerkungen zu den Organisationvorschlägen," May 24, 1954, *HM*; "Die Frage der Verteidigung Kärentes," *HM*; "Gedächtnisschrift, 03.7.1953, Besprechung zwischen General Dr. Liebitzky und Colonel Stevens," *HM*.

41. *Gruppe 04, Inneres/Justiz*, BMI/5Sch, 1953, 228.001–228.250, *ÖSA*. The B-Gendarmerie came under the *Bundesministerium für Inneres, Generaldirektion für öffentliche Sicherheit, Abteilung 5, Gendarmeriezentralkommando*.

42. *FRUS, 1951*, pt. 2, 4:1026.

43. *FRUS, 1952–1954*, pt. 2, 4:1824–25.

44. Ibid., 4:1822. See also ibid., 4:1833, 1834, 1841–44.

45. *Auslands-Presseschau Nr. 31, Wein am 30. Dezember 1953*, *HM*.

46. *FRUS, 1952–1954*, pt. 2, 4:1858.

47. Memorandum of conversation, Subject: Internal Differences in the Socialist Party, June 3, 1955; ibid., Apr. 8, 1955, participants: Interior Minister Oskar Helmer, Alexander C. Johnpoll; ibid., Apr. 21, 1955, participants: Interior Minister Oskar Helmer, Alexander C. Johnpoll; and ibid., Aug. 19, 1955, participants: Interior Minister Oskar Helmer, Alfred Puhan, Embassy, all in Lot 58D, RG 59, NARA, 3.

48. Sven Allard, *Russia and the Austrian State Treaty: A Case Study of Soviet Policy in Europe*, 107.

49. Vojtech Mastney, "The Soviet Union and the Origins of the Warsaw Pact in 1955," 6, available at http://www.isn.ethz.ch/php/documents/3A/introduction/introduction.htm.

50. Memorandum of conversation, Subject: Internal Differences in the Socialist Party, Apr. 19, 1955, participants: State Secretary of Interior Ferdinand Graf, Alexander C. Johnpoll, Lot 58D, RG 59, NARA.

51. Memorandum of Conversation, Subject: Austrian Matters, Sept. 22, 1955, Lot 58D, RG 59, NARA; "Sowjettische Waffenlieferungen an Österreich, Bundeskanzleramt," *HM*.

52. James R. Stephens Papers, pt. 3, MHI.

53. "Progress Report on NSC-164/1," Dec., 1955, 1; and memorandum for the Board Assistants, Subject: Detailed Development of Major Actions Relating to Austria (NSC-164/1) from Apr. 7, 1955 through Nov. 14, 1955, Nov. 10, 1955, box 15, Records Relating to State Department Participation in OCB, RG 59, NARA, 24; *FRUS, 1951*, pt. 2, 4:1134.

54. "Outline Plan of Operations with Respect to Austria," Oct. 17, 1956, box 15, Records Relating to State Department Participation in OCB, RG 59, NARA.

55. "Progress Report on NSC-164/1," Apr. 6, 1955, box 15, Records Relating to State Department Participation in OCB, RG 59, NARA, 3. See also "U.S. Background Toward Austria, Briefing Notes for the Planning Board Meeting, 12/1/60," Nov. 30, 1960, Papers of Dwight D. Eisenhower as President, DDE.

56. Manfried Rauchensteiner, "Das Amt für Landesverteidigung: Die Anfänge des Bundesheeres 1955/56," *Truppendienst* 19 (Oct., 1980): 443–46.

57. Clausewitz, *On War*, 595.

Epilogue

1. For a detailed discussion of final negotiations and the motivations and activities of the participants see, Stourzh, *Um Einheit und Freiheit,* 335–524. Günter Bischof, "The Making of the Austrian Treaty and the Road to Geneva," in *Cold War Respite: The Geneva Summit of 1955,* ed. Günter Bischof and Saki Dockrill, 117–60.

2. Trachtenberg, *A Constructed Peace,* 125–27.

3. The account of the treaty signing is taken from the Llewelyn Thompson Oral History, SL.

4. The JCS's response to the treaty is summarized in Kenneth Condit, *History of the Joint Chiefs of Staff and National Policy, 1955–1956,* 107–11.

5. *FRUS, 1952–1954,* pt. 2, 7:1976; Special National Intelligence Estimate no. 11-8-56, "Likelihood of Soviet Violation of Austrian Neutrality," Nov. 6, 1956, file 193, NSA.

6. Odd Arne Westad, "The New International History of the Cold War: Three (Possible) Paradigms," *Diplomatic History* 24 (fall, 2000): 551–66.

BIBLIOGRAPHY

Archives and Manuscript Collections

Center of Military History, Fort Lesley J. McNair, Washington, D.C.
    Archive Files
        "Austria Military Government Handbook." 1945.
        Integration of Negro and White Troops in the U.S. Army Europe, 1952–54.
        Military Government Austria. Reports of the High Commissioner.
        Reports of the General Board. United States Forces, European Command.
        Supreme Headquarters Allied Expeditionary Force. "Provisional Handbook for Military Government in Austria." 1945.
        William P. Yarborough Oral History.
Cold War International History Project. Available at http://cwihp.si.edu
Declassified Documents Reference System, Primary Source Media. Available at http://www.ddrs.psmedia.com
Dwight David Eisenhower Presidential Library, Abilene, Kans.
    Alfred M. Gruenther Papers
    C. D. Jackson Papers
    Eleanor Lansing Dulles Papers
    J. Lawton Collins Papers
    Papers of Dwight D. Eisenhower as President
        Ann Whitman Diary Series
        Dwight D. Eisenhower Diary Series
        International Series
        National Security Council Series
        Dulles-Herter Series
        White House Office: Office of the Staff Secretary Files
        Office of the Special Assistant for National Security Affairs Files
Franklin Delano Roosevelt Presidential Library, Hyde Park, N.Y.
    Charles Fahy Papers

John G. Winant Papers
President's Alphabetical File
President's Official File
President's Secretary's File
George C. Marshall Center, Lexington, Va.
George C. Marshall Collection
Harry S. Truman Presidential Library, Independence, Mo.
Papers of Dean Acheson
Papers of Charles P. Kindleberger
Papers of Harry S. Truman
President's Secretary Files
Heeresgeschichtliches Museum, Vienna, Austria
Gendarmerie Files
Hoover Institution, Stanford University, Stanford University, Palo Alto, Calif.
Albert C. Wedemeyer Papers
Charles Arthur Roberston Papers
David Harris Papers
Franklin A. Lindsey Papers
George P. Hays Papers
John Doane Hartigan Papers
Lawrence Frenkel Papers
Imperial War Museum, London
Fred Warner Papers
Lieutenant Martin-Smith Papers
Montgomery Papers
P. H. Layton Papers
R. L. Crimp Papers
Lauinger Memorial Library, Georgetown University, Washington, D.C.
Diplomatic Oral History Collection
Harry Hopkins Papers
Martin F. Herz Papers
Manuscripts Division, Library of Congress, Washington, D.C.
George S. Patton Jr. Papers
W. Averell Harriman Papers
Massachusetts Historical Society, Boston
Henry Cabot Lodge II Papers
Military History Institute, U.S. Army War College, Carlisle Barracks, Pa.
Demobilization including Rehabilitation and Redeployment Survey
Prepared by the Analysis Branch, War Department Bureau of Public
Affairs
Frank J. McSherry Papers

Halley G. Maddox Papers

Intelligence Review, no. 10, April 18, 1946

Intelligence Review, no. 18, June 13, 1946

Intelligence Review, no. 30, September 5, 1946

James R. Stephens Papers

Lester D. Flory Papers

Lyman L. Lemnitzer Oral History

Matthew B. Ridgway Papers

OSS Files

Paul W. Caraway Papers

Paul L. Freeman Oral History

Perry Family Papers

Ralph E. Pearson Papers

Richard B. Moran Papers

Thomas Stewart Brush Papers

Thomas F. Hickey Papers

Thomas T. Handy Oral History

Walter T. Kerwin Oral History

Willis D. Crittenberger Papers

U.S. Forces in the European Theater, G3. "Plan TOTALITY: Alert Plan for Defense in the Event of Aggression." Germany. January, 1946.

Mugar Library, Boston University, Boston

William Yarborough Papers

National Archives and Records Administration, College Park, Md.

Records Group 59, Records of the Department of State

Records Group 84, Records of the Foreign Service Posts, Department of State

Records Group 165, Records of the War Department, General and Special Staffs

Records Group 169, Records of the Foreign Economic Administration

Records Group 218, Records of the Joint Chiefs of Staff

Records Group 226, Records of the Office of Strategic Services

Records Group 260, Records of U.S. Occupation Headquarters, World War II

Records Group 263, Records of the Central Intelligence Agency

Records Group 319, Records of the Army Staff

Records Group 330, Records of the Office of Secretary of Defense

Records Group 335, Records of the Office of Secretary of the Army

Records Group 353, Records of the Interdepartmental and Intradepartmental Committees

Records Group 389, Office of the Provost Marshal General

Records Group 407, Records of the Adjutant General's Office
National Defense University Library, Fort McNair, Washington, D.C.
Civil Affairs Division Special Staff, Department of the Army. "Problems in U.S. Army Occupation, 1945–1947." January 1, 1948.
Fahey, Daniel Cox, Jr. "Findings, Conclusions, Recommendations, and Analysis Concerning U.S. Civil Affairs/Military Government Organization." February, 1951.
Komer, Robert W. "Civil Affairs and Military Government in the Mediterranean Theater." 1950.
National Security Archive, George Washington University, Washington, D.C.
The United States Intelligence Community Collection
Savranskaya, Svetlana, trans. *O deiatelnosti organov Severo-atlanticheskogo Soiuza v sviazi s sozdaniem atlanticheskoi armii i remilitarizatsiei zapadnoi Germanii.* February, 1951.
Österreichisches Staatsarchiv, Archiv der Republik, Vienna, Austria
Fiala, Brigitte. "Die Errichtung der B-Gendarmerie. Bibliothek des Staatsarchivs."
Gruppe 04, Inneres/Justiz
Public Records Office, London
FO 371, Foreign Office Correspondence and Minutes
FO 898, Political Warfare Executive
FO 1020, Occupation Records
HS 6, SOE Records
Seeley G. Mudd and Firestone Libraries, Princeton University, Princeton, N.J.
Allen Dulles Papers
H. Alexander Smith Papers
George Meader Oral History
J. Lawton Collins Oral History
John Foster Dulles Papers
James W. Riddleberger Oral History
Llewelyn E. Thompson Oral History
Loris Norstad Oral History
Mark W. Clark Oral History

Unpublished Papers and Dissertations

Anton, Walter. "Die Österreichische Bundesgendarmerie, 1945–1955: Ein Beitrag zur Geschichte Österreichs in der Besatzungszeit." Ph.D. diss., University of Vienna, 1984.
Beer, Siegfreid. "OSS and SSU in the American Occupation of Austria:

Intelligence Between War and Cold War." Paper presented at the Society for Military History Conference, Arlington, Va., 1996.

————. "Early CIA Reports on Austria, 1947–1949." In *Austrian Historical Memory and National Identity* Ed. Günter Bischof and Anton Pelinka. New Brunswick, N.J.: Transaction, 1997.

————. "Target Central Europe: American Intelligence Efforts Regarding Nazi and Early Postwar Austria." Working Paper no. 97–1. Center for Austrian Studies, University of Minnesota, Minneapolis, August, 1997.

————, and Eduard Staudinger. "Die 'Vienna Mission' der Westalliieren im June 1945." Studien zue wiene Geschichte Jahrbuch des Vereins für Geschichte der Stadt Wien. Band 50.

Bischof, Günter. "Between Responsibility and Rehabilitation: Austria in International Politics, 1940–1950." Ph.D. diss., Harvard University, 1989.

Bohman, Eric James. "Rehearsals for Victory: The War Department and the Planning and Direction of Civil Affairs, 1940–1943." Ph.D. diss., Yale University, 1984.

Brown, Ralph W., III. "A Cold War Army of Occupation: The U.S. Military Government in Vienna, 1945–1950." Ph.D. diss., University of Tennessee, 1995.

Hutton, Carl I. "An Armored Artillery Commander in the European Theater." Unpublished manuscript. U.S. Army Field Artillery School, Fort Sill, Okla.

Knight, Robert Graham. "British Policy towards Occupied Austria 1945–1950." Ph.D. diss., London School of Economics, London University, 1986.

Kretzman, Edwin. "Four Powers in Three-Quarter Time: Tales of the Austrian Occupation, 1945–1948." Unpublished manuscript. Author's collection.

Leidenfrost, Josef. "Die amerikanische Besatzungsmacht und der Wiederbeginn des Politischen Lebens in Österreich." Ph.D. diss., University of Vienna, 1986.

Mark, Eduard. "Revolution By Degrees: Stalin's National-Front Strategy for Europe, 1941–1947." Working Paper no. 31. Cold War International History Project, Washington, D.C., February, 2001.

Pechatnov, Vladimir. "'The Allies are Pressing on You to Break Your Will . . .' Foreign Policy Correspondence Between Stalin and Molotov and Other Politburo Members, September 1945–December 1946." Trans. Vladislav M. Zubok. Working Paper no. 26. Cold War International History Project, Washington, D.C., September, 1999.

————. "The Big Three After World War II: New Documents on Soviet

Thinking about Post-War Relations with the United States and Great Britain." Working Paper no. 13. Cold War International History Project, Washington, D.C., July, 1995.

Samouce, Alexander. "I Do Understand the Russians." Unpublished manuscript. Author's collection.

Books and Articles

Ableitinger, Alfred, Siegfried Beer, and Edward Stavdinger, eds. Österreich Unter Alliierter Besatzung, 1945–1955. Vienna: Böhlau, 1998.

Acheson, Dean. *Present at the Creation. My Years in the State Department.* New York: W. W. Norton, 1969

Albrich, Thomas, et al., eds. *Österreich in den Fünfzigern.* Innsbruck: Österreichischer Studien Verlag, 1995.

Alcock, Antony Evelyn. *The History of the South Tyrol Question.* Geneva: Graduate Institute for International Studies, 1970.

Allard, Sven. *Russia and the Austrian State Treaty: A Case Study of Soviet Policy in Europe.* University Park: Pennsylvania State University Press, 1970.

American Military Government of Occupied Germany, 1918–1920: Report of the Officer in Charge of Civil Affairs and Armed Forces in Germany. Washington, D.C.: GPO, 1943.

American Military Government of Occupied Germany. Vol. 11, *American Occupation of Germany.* The U.S. Army in the World War, 1917–1919. Reprint ed. Washington, D.C.: Center of Military History, 1991.

Andrew, Christopher, and Vasili Mitrokhin. *The Sword and the Shield.* New York: Basic Books, 1999.

Bassford, Christopher. *Clausewitz in English: The Reception of Clausewitz in Britain and America, 1815–1945.* Oxford: Oxford University Press, 1994.

Bader, William. *Austria Between East and West, 1945–1955.* Stanford: Stanford University Press, 1966.

Banac, Ivo. *With Stalin Against Tito: Cominformist Splits in Yugoslav Communism.* Ithaca, N.Y.: Cornell University Press, 1988.

Beer, Siegfried, and Stefan Kramer. *Der Kreig aus der Luft: Kärnten und Steiermark, 1941–1945.* Graz: Wieshaupt, 1992.

Binder, L. James. *Lemnitzer: A Soldier for His Time.* London: Brassey's, 1997.

Birtle, Andrew. *U.S. Army Counterinsurgency and Contingency Operations Doctrine, 1860–1941.* Washington, D.C.: Center of Military History, 1998.

Bischof, Günter. *Austria in the First Cold War, 1945–55: The Leverage of the Weak.* New York: St. Martin's Press, 1999.

———. "Der Marshallplan und Österreich," *Zeitgeschichte* 17 (1990): 463–74.

———. "Die Instrumentisierung der Moskauer Erklärung nach dem 2. Weltkrieg." *Zeitgeschichte* 20 (November-December, 1993): 245–365.

———. "The Making of a Cold Warrior: Karl Gruber and Austrian Foreign Policy, 1945–1953." *Austrian History Yearbook* 26 (1995): 99–127.

———. "Anglo-amerkanische Planungen und Überlegungen der österreichischen Emigration während des Zweiten Weltkrieges für Nachkriegs-Österreich." In *Österreich 1945: Ein Ende und viele Anfänge.* Ed. Manfried Rauchensteiner and Wolfgang Etschmann. Graz: Styria, 1997.

———. "Der Nationale Sicherheitsrat und die Amerkanische Österreichpolitik im frühen Kalten Kreig." In *Österreich Unter Alliierter Besatzung, 1945–1955.* Ed. Alfred Ableitinger, Siegfried Beer, and Edward Stavdinger. Vienna: Böhlau, 1998.

———. "Eine historiographishe Einführung: Die Ära des Kaltenkrieges und Österreich." In *Österreich im frühen Kalten Krieg, 1945–1958: Spione, Partisanen, Kriegs Plane.* Ed. Erwin Schmidl. Vienna: Böhlau, 2000.

———, and Stephen E. Ambrose, eds. *Eisenhower and the German POWs: Facts Against Falsehood.* Baton Rouge: Louisiana State University Press, 1992.

Bishof, Günter, and Saki Dockrill, eds. *Cold War Respite: The Geneva Summit of 1955.* Baton Rouge: Louisiana State University Press, 2000.

Bischof, Günter, and Josef Leidenfrost, eds. *Die Bevormundete Nation: Österreich und die Alliierten, 1945–1949.* Vienna: Haymon Verlag, 1988.

Bischof, Günter, and Anton Pelinka, eds. *Austria in the Nineteen Fifties.* London: Transaction Publishers, 1995.

———, eds. *Austrian Historical Memory and National Identity.* New Brunswick: Transaction, 1997.

———, and Ferdinand Karlhofer, eds. *The Vranitzky Era in Austria.* New Brunswick, N.J.: Transaction, 1999.

Bischof, Günter, Anton Pelinka, and Dieter Stiefel, eds. *The Marshall Plan in Austria.* New Brunswick, N.J.: Transaction, 2000.

Biscombe, Perry. *Werewolf: The History of the National Socialist Guerrilla Movement, 1944–1946.* Toronto: University of Toronto Press, 1998.

Bjelakovic, Nebojsa. "Comrades and Adversaries: Yugoslav-Soviet Conflict in 1948: A Reappraisal." *East European Quarterly* 33 (spring, 1999): 97–114.

Blumenson, Martin. *Mark Clark.* New York: Congdon and Weed, 1984.

Boehling, Rebecca. "Commentary: The Role of Culture in American

Relations with Europe: The Case of the United States's Occupation of Germany." *Diplomatic History* 33 (winter, 1999): 57–69.

Borhi, Lásló. "Rollback, Liberation, Containment, or Inaction? U.S. Policy and Eastern Europe in the 1950s." *Journal of Cold War Studies* 1 (fall, 1999): 67–110.

Bradsher, Greg. *Holocaust-Era Assets: A Finding Aid to the National Archives at College Park.* College Park: National Archives and Record Administration, 1999.

Brands, H. W. *The Specter of Neutralism: The United States and the Emergence of the Third World, 1947–1960.* New York: Columbia University Press, 1989.

———. "A Cold War Foreign Legion? The Eisenhower Administration and the Volunteer Freedom Corps." *Military Affairs* 52 (January, 1988): 7–11.

Brusatti, Alois, and Gottfried Heindl, eds. *Julius Raab Eine Biographie in Einzeldarstellungen.* Linz: Verlag Rudolf Trauner-Druck, 1986.

Bushell, Anthony, ed. *Studies in Political and Cultural Re-emergence.* Cardiff: University of Wales, 1996.

Carafano, James Jay. "Mobilizing Europe's Stateless: America's Plan for a Cold War Army," *Journal of Cold War Studies* 1 (spring, 1999): 61–85.

———. "'Waltzing into the Cold War': U.S. Army Intelligence Operations in Postwar Austria, 1944–1948." In *The Vranitzky Era in Austria.* Ed. Günter Bischof, Anton Pelinka, and Ferdinand Karlhofer. New Brunswick, N.J.: Transaction, 1999.

Clark, Mark. *A Calculated Risk.* New York: Harper and Brothers, 1950.

Clausewitz, Carl von. *On War.* Ed. and trans. Michael Howard and Peter Paret. Princeton, N.J.: Princeton University Press, 1974.

Clay, Lucius. *Decision in Germany.* Garden City, N.Y.: Doubleday, 1950.

Coakley, Robert. *The Role of Federal Military Forces in Domestic Disorders, 1789–1878.* Washington, D.C.: Center of Military History, 1988.

Cold War International History Project Bulletin, no. 3 (winter, 1993).

Cold War International History Project Bulletin, no. 5 (spring, 1995).

Cold War International History Project Bulletin, nos. 6 and 7 (winter, 1995/96).

Cold War International History Project Bulletin, no. 10 (March, 1998).

Cole, Ronald, et al. *The History of the Unified Command Plan, 1946–1993.* Washington, D.C.: Joint History Office, Office of the Chairman of the Joint Chiefs of Staff, 1995.

Coles, Harry, and Albert Weinberg. *Civil Affairs: Soldiers Become Governors.* Washington, D.C.: Office of the Chief of Military History, 1964.

Collins, J. Lawton. *Lightning Joe: An Autobiography.* Baton Rouge: Louisiana State University, 1979.

Condit, Doris. *The Test of War, 1950–1953*. Vol. 2. Washington, D.C.: Historical Office, Office of the Secretary of Defense, 1988.

Condit, Kenneth. *History of the Joint Chiefs of Staff and National Policy, 1955–1956*. Washington, D.C.: Office of the Joint Chiefs of Staff, 1998.

Converse, Elliot, III. *Forging the Sword: Selecting, Educating, and Training Cadets and Junior Officers in the Modern World*. Chicago: Imprint, 1998.

Cronin, Audrey Kurth. *Great Power Politics and the Struggle over Austria, 1945–1955*. Ithaca, N.Y.: Cornell University Press, 1986.

Dalfiume, Richard. *Desegregation of the Armed Forces: Fighting on Two Fronts, 1939–1953*. Columbia: University of Missouri Press, 1969.

Daly, Hugh, ed. *42nd "Rainbow" Infantry Division*. Baton Rouge: Army and Navy, 1946.

Department of State. *Foreign Relations of the United States: Diplomatic Papers: Conferences at Malta and Yalta, 1945*. Washington, D.C.: GPO, 1955.

———. *Foreign Relations of the United States: Diplomatic Papers, 1945*. Vols. 1–4. Washington, D.C.: GPO, 1963–69.

———. *Foreign Relations of the United States: Diplomatic Papers, 1946*. Vol. 2. Washington, D.C.: GPO, 1970.

———. *Foreign Relations of the United States: Diplomatic Papers, 1947*. Vol. 2. Washington, D.C.: GPO, 1972.

———. *Foreign Relations of the United States: Diplomatic Papers, 1948*. Vol. 3. Washington, D.C.: GPO, 1973.

———. *Foreign Relations of the United States: Council of Foreign Ministers: Germany and Austria, 1949*. Vol. 3. Washington, GPO, 1974.

———. *Foreign Relations of the United States. Europe: Political and Economic Development, 1951*. Vol. 4. 2 pts. Washington, D.C.: GPO, 1998.

———. *Foreign Relations of the United States: Germany and Austria, 1952–1954*. Vol. 7. 2 pts. Washington, GPO, 1986.

———. *Foreign Relations of the United States: Austrian State Treaty: Summit and Foreign Ministers Meetings, 1955*. Vol. 5. Washington, D.C.: GPO, 1988.

———. *Foreign Relations of the United States: Emergence of the Intelligence Establishment*. Washington, D.C.: GPO, 1996.

Dimitrijevic, Bojan. "Soviet Security Relationships: Yugoslav-Soviet Military Relations, 1945–1948." *Journal of Slavic Military Studies* 9 (September, 1996): 581–93.

Dinardo, Richard. "Glimpse of an Old World Order? Reconsidering the

Trieste Crisis of 1945." *Diplomatic History* 21 (summer, 1997): 365–81.

Dixon, Joe. *Defeat and Disarmament. Allied Diplomacy and the Politics of Military Affairs in Austria, 1918–1922* Newark: University of Delaware Press, 1976.

Donnison, F. S. V. *Civil Affairs and Military Government: Central Organization and Planning.* London: HMSO, 1966.

Dower, John. *Embracing Defeat: Japan in the Wake of World War II.* New York: W. W. Norton, 1998.

Dulles, Eleanor Lansing. *Eleanor Lansing Dulles: Chance of a Lifetime.* New York: Prentice Hall, 1980.

Eister, Klaus. *Französische Besatzungspolitik: Tirol und Vorarlberg 1945/46.* Innsbruck: Haymon, 1991.

Feis, Herbert. *From Trust to Terror: The Onset of the Cold War, 1945–1950.* New York: Norton, 1970.

Fitzpatrick, George, et al. *A Survey of the Experiences and Opinions of U.S. Government Officers in World War II.* Chevy Chase, Md.: Operations Research Office, Johns Hopkins University, 1956.

Foot, M. R. D. *Resistance: European Resistance to Nazism, 1940–45.* London: Butler and Tanner, 1976.

Ford, Kirk, Jr. *OSS and the Yugoslav Resistance, 1943–1945.* College Station, Texas: Texas A&M University Press, 1992.

Friedrich, Carl, ed. *American Experiences in Military Government.* New York: Rinehart, 1948.

Gabriel, R. H. "American Experiences with Military Government." *American Historical Review* 49 (1944): 630–44.

Gaddis, John Lewis. *The United States and the Origins of the Cold War, 1941–1947.* New York: Columbia University Press, 1972.

———. *Strategies of Containment: A Critical Appraisal of Postwar American National Security Policy.* New York: Oxford University Press, 1982.

———. *We Now Know: Rethinking Cold War History.* Oxford: Clarendon Press, 1997.

———. "The Emerging Post-Revisionist Synthesis on the Origins of the Cold War." *Diplomatic History* 17 (summer, 1993): 171–90.

———. "The Tragedy of the Cold War History," *Diplomatic History* 17 (winter, 1993): 1–16.

Galambos, Louis, et al., eds. *The Papers of Dwight David Eisenhower.* Vol. 5, *Occupation, 1945.* Baltimore: Johns Hopkins University Press, 1978.

———. *The Papers of Dwight David Eisenhower.* Vol. 7, *The Chief of Staff.* Baltimore: Johns Hopkins University Press, 1978.

————. *The Papers of Dwight David Eisenhower.* Vol. 12, *NATO and the Campaign of 1952.* Baltimore: Johns Hopkins University Press, 1989.

Garson, Robert. "American Foreign Policy and the Limits of Power, Eastern Europe, 1946–50." *Journal of Contemporary History* 21 (July, 1986): 347–66.

Gehler, Michael. "Austria and European Integration 1947–60: Western Orientation, Neutrality and Free Trade." *Diplomacy & Statecraft* 9 (November, 1998): 154–210.

————, and Rolf Steininger, eds. *Österreich und Die Europäische Integration, 1945–1993.* Vienna: Böhlau, 1993.

————, ed. *Karl Gruber: Reden und Dokumente, 1945–1953. Eine Auswahl.* Vienna: Böhlau, 1994.

Goode, Petra. "From Villains to Victims: Fraternization and Feminization of Germany, 1945–1947." *Diplomatic History* 23 (winter, 1999): 1–20.

Gorman, Paul. *The Secret of Future Victories.* Reprint ed. Fort Leavenworth, Kans.: U.S. Army Command and General Staff College Press, 1994.

Grose, Peter. *Operation Rollback: America's Secret War Behind the Iron Curtain.* Boston: Houghton Mifflin, 2000.

Gruber, Karl. *Between Liberation and Liberty: Austria in the Post-War World.* New York: Frederick A. Praeger, 1955.

Hannl, Margarete. "Mit Den Russen Leben: Besatzungszeit im Mühlviertel, 1945–55." *Zeitgeschichte* 16 (1989): 147–66.

Hammond, Thomas, ed. *Witnesses to the Origins of the Cold War.* Seattle: University of Washington Press, 1982.

Harper, John Lamberton. *American Visions of Europe: Franklin D. Roosevelt, George F. Kennan and Dean G. Acheson.* Cambridge: Cambridge University Press, 1996.

Heideking, Jürgen, and Christof Mauch, eds. *Geheimdienstkrieg gegen Deutschland: Subversion, Propaganda und politische Planungen des amerikanischen Geheimdienstes im Zweiten Weltkrieg.* Göttingen: Vandenhoeck and Ruprecht 1993.

Heinemann, Winfried. "The West and Yugoslavia in the 1950s." *Army History* 40 (winter, 1997): 12–15.

Herz, Martin F. *Understanding Austria: The Political Reports and Analyses of Martin F. Herz, Political Officer of the U.S. Legation, 1945–1948.* Ed. Reinhold Wagnleitner. Salzburg: Wolfgang Neugebauer, 1984.

Hesztera, Franz. *Von der "A-Gendarmerie" zur B-Gendarmerie der Aufbau des Österreichischen Bundesheere 1945 bis Herbst 1952.* Mattighofen: Aumayer, 1998.

Heuser, D. B. *Western Containment: Policies Towards Yugoslavia, 1948–1953.* New York: Routledge, 1989.

Hills, Alice. *Britain and the Occupation of Austria, 1943–45.* New York: St. Martin's Press, 2000.

Hogan, Michael, ed. *America in the World: The Historiography of American Foreign Relations Since 1941.* Cambridge: Cambridge University Press, 1995.

———. *A Cross of Iron: Harry S. Truman and the Origins of the National Security State, 1945–1954.* Cambridge: Cambridge University Press, 1998.

Holborn, Hajo. *American Military Government: Its Organizations and Policies.* Washington, D.C.: Infantry Journal Press, 1947.

Huston, James. *Outposts and Allies: U.S. Army Logistics in the Cold War, 1945–1953.* London: Associated University Press, 1988.

Howard, Robert, and Sakamoto Yoshikaz, eds. *Democratizing Japan: The Allied Occupation.* Honolulu: University of Hawaii Press, 1987.

Hunt, Michael. *Ideology and U.S. Foreign Policy.* New Haven, Conn.: Yale University Press, 1987.

Infantry in Battle. Richmond: Garret and Massie, 1939.

Ingimundarson, Valur. "The Eisenhower Administration, the Adenauer Government, and the Political Uses of the East German Uprising in 1953." *Diplomatic History* 20 (summer, 1996): 381–410.

Jackson, Robert. *High Cold War: Strategic Air Reconnaissance and the Electronic Intelligence War, 1949–97.* Wellingborough, UK: Patrick Stephens, 1998.

Kennan, George. *Measures Short of War: The George F. Kennan Lectures at the National War College, 1946–1947.* Ed. Giles Harlow and George Maerz. Washington, D.C.: National Defense University Press, 1991.

———. *Memoirs, 1925–1950.* Boston: Little, Brown, 1967.

Keyserlingk, Robert. *Austria in World War II: An Anglo-American Dilemma.* Montreal: Kingston, 1988.

———. "Arnold Toynbee's Foreign Research and Press Service, 1939–43, and Its Post-war Plans for Southeast Europe." *Journal of Contemporary History* 21 (October, 1986): 539–58.

Koch, Scott. "The Role of U.S. Army Attaches Between the World Wars." *Studies in Intelligence* 38 (1995): 111–15.

Kolko, Joyce, and Gabriel. *The Limits of Power: The World and United States Foreign Policy, 1945–1954.* New York: Harper and Row, 1972.

Krenn, Michael. *Black Diplomacy: African Americans and the State Department, 1945–1969.* Armonk, N.Y.: M. E. Sharpe, 1999.

Lagrou, Pieter. *The Legacy of Nazi Occupation: Patriotic Memory and Na-*

tional Recovery in Western Europe, 1945–1965. Cambridge: Cambridge University Press, 2000.

Laurie, Clayton, and Ronald Cole. *The Role of Federal Military Forces in Domestic Disorders*. Washington, D.C.: Center of Military History, 1997.

Leffler, Melvyn P. *A Preponderance of Power: National Security, the Truman Administration, and the Cold War*. Stanford: Stanford University Press, 1992.

———. "The American Conception of National Security and the Beginnings of the Cold War." *American Historical Review* 89 (April, 1984): 246–81.

Lindsey, Franklin A., and John Kenneth Galbraith. *Beacons in the Night: With the OSS and Tito's Partisan in Wartime Yugoslavia*. Stanford, Calif.: Stanford University Press, 1993.

MacDonald, Charles B. *The Last Offensive*. Washington, D.C.: Center of Military History, 1973.

MacGregor, Morris, Jr. *Integration of the Armed Forces, 1940–1965*. Washington, D.C.: Center of Military History, 1981.

Mähr, Wilfried. *Der Marshallplan in Österreich*. Graz: Styria, 1989.

Mansourov, Alexandre Y. "Stalin, Mao, Kim, and China's Decision to Enter the Korean War, September 16–October 15, 1950: New Evidence from the Russian Archives." *Cold War International History Project Bulletin*, nos. 6 and 7 (winter, 1995/96): 94–119.

Mantl, Wolfgang, ed. *Politik in Österreich Die Zweite Republik: Bestand und Wandel*. Vienna: Böhlau, 1992.

Marchio, Jim. "Resistance Potential and Rollback: US Intelligence and the Eisenhower Administration's Policies Toward Eastern Europe, 1953–1956." *Intelligence and National Security* 10 (April, 1995): 219–41.

Marrus, Michael. *The Unwanted: European Refugees in the Twentieth Century*. Oxford: Oxford University Press, 1985.

Mastny, Vojtech. *Russia's Road to the Cold War: Diplomacy, Warfare, and the Politics of Communism, 1941–1945*. New York: Columbia University Press, 1979.

———. *The Cold War and Soviet Insecurity: The Stalin Years*. New York: Oxford University Press, 1996.

———. "The Soviet Union and the Origins of the Warsaw Pact in 1955." Available at http://www.isn.ethz.ch/php/documents/3A/introduction/introduction.htm.

May, Ernest R., ed. *American Cold War Strategy: Interpreting NSC 68*. Boston: Bedford Books of St. Martin's Press, 1993.

McMahon, Robert J. "Credibility and World Power: Exploring the Psychological Dimension in Postwar American Diplomacy." *Diplomatic History* 15 (fall, 1991): 455–72.

Meissl, Sebastian, Klaus-Dieter Mulley, and Oliver Rathkolb, eds. *Verdrängte Schuld, verfehlte Sühne: Entnazifizierung in Österreich, 1945–1955: Symposion des Instituts für Wissenschaft und Kunst, Wien, März 1985*. Munich: R. Oldenbourg, 1986.

Milano, James, and Patrick Brogan. *Soldiers, Spies and the Rat Line*. Washington, D.C.: Brassey's, 1995.

Miller, Francis Trevelyan. *The Complete History of World War II*. Armed Services Memorial ed. Chicago: Progress Research, 1947.

Mitrovich, Gregory. *Undermining the Kremlin: America's Strategy to Subvert the Soviet Bloc, 1947–1956*. Ithaca, N.Y.: Cornell University Press, 2000.

Modin, Yuri. *My Five Cambridge Friends, Burgess, Maclean, Philby, Blunt and Cairncross*. New York: Farrar, Straus, Giroux, 1994.

Molden, Fritz. *Exploding Star: A Young Austrian against Hitler*. London: Weidenfeld and Nicolson, 1978.

———. *Fires in the Night: The Sacrifices and Significance of Austrian Resistance*. Boulder, Colo.: Westview Press, 1989.

Moore, Jason Kendell Moore. "Between Expediency and Principle: U.S. Repatriation Policy toward Russian Nationals, 1944–1949." *Diplomatic History* 24 (summer 2000): 381–404.

Naimark, Norman. *The Russians in Germany: A History of the Soviet Zone of Occupation, 1945–1949*. Cambridge, Mass.: Harvard University Press, 1997.

Nalty, Bernard, and Morris MacGregor, eds. *Blacks in the Military: Essential Documents*. Wilmington, Del.: Scholarly Resources, 1981.

Nevins, Alan. *He Walked Alone: A Biography of John Gilbert Winant*. The Hague: Mouton, 1968.

Oakley, Robert, Michael Dziedzic, and Eliot Goldberg, eds. *Policing the New World Disorder: Peace Operations and Public Security*. Washington, D.C.: National Defense University Press, 1999.

Olah, Franz. *Die Erinnerungen*. Vienna: Amalthea, 1995.

Ostermann, Christian. "Keeping the Pot Simmering, the United States and the East German Uprising of 1953." *German Studies Review* 19 (March, 1996): 61–89.

———. "New Documents on the East German Uprising of 1953, Introduction and Commentary." Available at http://cwihp.si.edu/cwihplib.nsf.

Pach, Chester. *Arming the Free World: The Origins of the United States Mil-*

itary Assistance Program, 1945–1950. Chapel Hill: The University of North Carolina Press, 1996.

Pelinka, Anton. "Karl Renner: A Man for All Seasons." *Austrian History Yearbook* 23 (1992): 111–19.

Pick, Hella. *Guilty Victim: Austria from the Holocaust to Haider.* London: Tauris, 2000.

Peterson, Edward. *The American Occupation of Germany: Retreat into Victory.* Detroit: Wayne State University Press, 1977.

Polika-Treunesee, Adolf. "Die Abzeichen der B-Gendarmerie." *Truppendienst* 1 (1977): 6–8, 110–12.

Postwar Foreign Policy Preparation. Washington, D.C.: GPO, 1949.

Pratner, Robert. *Leopold Figl: Ansichteneines eines grossen Österreiches.* Vienna: Österreichische Staatsdruckerie, 1992.

Rathkolb, Oliver. *Washington ruft Wien: U.S.-Grossmachtpolitik und Österreich, 1953–1963.* Vienna: Böhlau, 1997.

————. "Professorenpläne für Österreichs Zukunft. Nachkriegsfragen im Diskurs der Forschungsabteilung Research and Analysis." In *Geheimdienstkrieg gegen Deutschland: Subversion, Propaganda und politische Planungen des amerikanischen Geheimdienstes im Zweiten Weltkrieg.* Ed. Jürgen Heideking and Christof Mauch. Göttingen: Vandenhoeck and Ruprecht 1993.

————, ed. *Gesellschaft und Politik am Beginn der Zweiten Republik, Vertauliche Berihte der U.S. Militäradministration aus Österreich 1945 in englischer Originalfassung.* Vienna: Böhlau, 1985.

Rauchensteiner, Manfried. *Die Zwei: Die Grosse Koalition in Österreich, 1945–1966.* Vienna: Bundesverlag, 1987.

————. *Der Sonderfall: Die Besatzungszeit in Österreich, 1945 bis 1955.* Vienna: Styria, 1995.

————. *Der Krieg in Österreich in '45.* Graz: Styria, 1995.

————. "Das Amt für Landesverteidigung: Die Anfänge des Bundesheeres 1955/56." *Truppendienst* 19 (October, 1980): 443–46.

————, and Claudia Ham, eds. *Sorry Guys, No Gold.* Vienna: Heeresgeschichtliches Museum, 1998.

Rauchensteiner, Manfried, and Wolfgang Etschmann, eds. *Österreich 1945: Ein Ende und viele Anfänge.* Graz: Styria, 1997.

Rauscher, Otto. "Gendarmerie, B-Gendarmerie, Bundesheer." *Truppendients* 5 (1985): 481–83.

Rauer, Michael. "Order out of Chaos: The United States Constabulary in Postwar Germany." *Army History* 45 (summer, 1998): 29–35.

Rauscher, Walter. *Karl Renner: Ein Österreichischer Mythos.* Wein: Uberreuter, 1995.

Report of the Proceedings of the Committee on the Armed Services, S.273. Executive Session, July 11, 1949. Vol. 1. Washington, D.C.: GPO, 1949.

Report to Congress on United States participation in operations of UNRRA. Vols. 1–12. Washington, D.C.: GPO, 1944–45.

Resis, Albert, ed. *Molotov Remembers: Inside Kremlin Politics: Conversations with Felix Chuev.* Chicago: Ivan R. Dee, 1993.

Ridgway, Matthew B. *Soldier: The Memoirs of Matthew B. Ridgway.* Westport, Conn.: Greenwood Press, 1974.

Riefenstahl, Leni. *The Sieve of Time: The Memoirs of Leni Riefenstahl.* London: Quartet, 1992.

Rose, Lisle A. *The Cold War Comes to Main Street, America in 1950.* Lawrence: University Press of Kansas, 1999.

Ross, Steven. *American War Plans, 1945–1950.* London: Frank Cass, 1997.

Rudgers, David. *Creating the Secret State: The Origins of The Central Intelligence Agency, 1943–1947.* Lawrence: Kansas University Press, 2000.

Sale, Sara. *The Shaping of Containment: Harry S. Truman, the National Security Council, and the Cold War.* Saint James, N.Y.: Brandywine Press, 1998.

Sarantakes, Nicholas. *Keystone: The American Occupation of Okinawa and U.S.-Japanese Relations.* College Station: Texas A&M University Press, 2000.

Schaller, Michael. *The American Occupation of Japan: The Origins of the Cold War in Asia.* New York: Oxford University Press, 1985.

Schmidl, Erwin, ed. *Österreich im frühen Kalten Krieg, 1945–1958: Spione, Partisanen, Kriegspläne.* Vienna: Böhlau, 2000.

———, ed. *Peace Operations Between War and Peace.* London: Frank Cass, 2000.

———. "Rosinenbomer' über Wien? Alliierte Pläne zur Luftversorgung Wiens im Falle einer sowjetischen Blockade, 1948–1953." *Österreichische Militärische Zeitschrift* 36 (April, 1998): 411–18.

———. "The Airlift that Never Was: Allied Plans to Supply Vienna by Air, 1948–1950." *Army History,* fall, 1997/winter, 1998, 12–23.

Schmidt, Hans. ed. *U.S. Occupation in Europe After World War II.* Lawrence: Regents Press of Kansas, 1976.

Schwab, Gerald. *OSS Agents in Hitler's Heartland: Destination Innsbruck.* Westport, Conn.: Praeger, 1996.

Schwartz, Thomas. *America's Germany: John J. McCloy and the Federal Republic of Germany.* Cambridge, Mass.: Harvard University Press, 1991.

Simons, William. *Liberal Education in the Service Academies.* New York: Bureau of Publications, Teachers College, Columbia University, 1965.

Smith, Bradley. *The Shadow Warriors: O. S. S. and the Origins of the C. I. A.* New York Basic Books, 1994.

Smith, Harry Alexander. *Military Government.* Fort Leavenworth, Kans.: General Service School Press, 1920.

Smith, Jean Edward, ed. *The Papers of General Lucius D. Clay: Germany, 1945–1949.* Vol. 1. Bloomington: Indiana University Press, 1974.

Soffer, Jonathan. *General Matthew B. Ridgway: From Progressivism to Reaganism, 1895–1993.* Westport, Conn.: Praeger, 1998.

Sparrow, John. *History of Personnel Demobilization in the United States Army.* Washington, D.C.: Center of Military History, 1994.

Srodes, James. *Allen Dulles Master of Spies.* Washington, D.C.: Regency, 1999.

Stadler, Karl. *Adolf Schärf: Mensch Politiker Staatsman.* Vienna: Europaverlag, 1982.

The State Department Policy Planning Staff Papers, 1949. Vols. 2 and 3. New York: Garland, 1983.

Stearman, William Lloyd. *The Soviet Union and the Occupation of Austria: An Analysis of Soviet Policy in Austria, 1945–1955.* Bonn: Siegler, 1961.

Steinacher, Gerald. *Südtirol und die Geheimdienste, 1943–1945.* Wien: Studien Verlag, 2000.

Stever, James. "The glass firewall between military and civil administration." *Administration and Society* 31 (Mar., 1999): 28–49.

Stewart, I. D. *Thunderbolt.* 11th Armored Division Association, 1948.

Stiefel, Dieter. *Entnazifizierung in Österreich.* Vienna: Europaverlag, 1981.

Stifter, Christian. *Die Wiederaufrüstung Österreichs: Die geheime Remilitarisierung der westlichen Besatzungszonen, 1945–1955.* Innsbruck: Studien Verlag, 1997.

Stillman, Richard, II. *The Integration of the U.S. Armed Forces.* New York: Frederick A. Praeger, 1968.

Stone, David. "The Balkan Pact and American Policy." *East European Quarterly* 28 (September, 1994): 393–407.

Stourzh, Gerald. *Um Einheit und Freiheit, Staatsvertrag, Neutralität und das Ende der Ost-West-Besetzung Österreichs, 1945–1955.* Wein: Böhlau, 1998.

———. *Geschichte des Österreichischen Staatsvertrages, 1945–1955: Österreichs Weg zur Neutralität.* 3d ed. Graz: Styria, 1985.

Svoboda, Wilhelm. *Franz Olah: Eine Spurensicherung.* Vienna: Promedia, 1990.

———. *Die Partei, Die Republik und Der Man mit den vielen Gesichtern Oskar Helmer und Österreich II.* Vienna: Böhlau, 1993.

Thayer, Charles. *Bears in the Caviar*. Philadelphia: J. B. Lippincott, 1950.
———. *Hands Across the Caviar*. Philadelphia: J. B. Lippincott, 1952.
Trachtenberg, Marc. *A Constructed Peace: The European Settlement, 1945–1963*. Princeton, N.J.: Princeton University Press, 1999.
Trask, David. *The AEF and Coalition Warmaking, 1917–1918*. Lawrence: University Press of Kansas, 1993.
Tweraser, Kurt. *U.S. Militarriegierung Oberösterreich, 1945–1950, Band 1: Sicherheitspolitische Aspekte der amerikanischen Besatzung in Oberösterreich-Süd*. Linz: Oberösterreichisches Landesarchiv, 1995.
———. "Military Justice as an Instrument of American Occupation Policy in Austria 1945–1950: From Total Control to Limited Tutelage," *Austrian History Yearbook* 24 (1993): 153–78.
U.S. Army. *Basic Field Manual 27–5: Military Government*. Washington, D.C.: War Department, 1940.
U.S. Army. *Field Service Regulations*. Washington, D.C.: War Department, 1924.
Vandenberg, Arthur, Jr., ed. *The Private Papers of Senator Vandenberg*. New York: Houghton Mifflin, 1952.
Wagnleitner, Reinhold. *Coca-Colonization and the Cold War: The Cultural Mission of the United States in Austria After the Second World War*. Trans. Diana Wolf. Chapel Hill: University of North Carolina Press, 1994.
Wala, Michael. *The Council on Foreign Relations and American Foreign Policy in the Early Cold War*. Oxford: Berghahn Books, 1994.
Weathersby, Kathryn. "New Findings on the Korean War." *Cold War International History Project Bulletin*, no. 3 (winter, 1993): 14–18.
———. "Korea 1949–1950: To Attack or Not to Attack? Stalin, Kim Il Sung, and the Prelude to War." *Cold War International History Project Bulletin*, no. 5 (spring, 1995): 1–9.
Weinstein, Allen, and Alexander Vassiliev. *The Haunted Wood: Soviet Espionage in America, the Stalin Era*. New York: Modern Library, 2000.
Westad, Odd Arne. "The New International History of the Cold War: Three (Possible) Paradigms." *Diplomatic History* 24 (fall, 2000): 551–66.
Whitehorne, Joseph. *The Inspector General of the United States Army*. Washington, D.C.: Office of the Inspector General and the Center of Military History, 1998.
Whitnah, Donald R., and Edgar L. Erickson. *The Occupation of Austria: Planning and Early Years*. Westport, Conn.: Greenwood Press, 1995.
Whitnah, Donald, and Florentine Whitnah. *Salzburg Under Siege: U.S. Occupation, 1945–1955*. New York: Greenwood Press, 1991.
Wilkinson, Peter. *Foreign Fields: The Story of an SOE Operative*. London: I. B. Tauris, 1997.

Williams, Phil. *The Senate and U.S. Troops in Europe.* New York: St. Martin's Press, 1985.

Willoughby, John. *Remaking the Conquering Heroes: The Social and Geopolitical Impact of the Post-War American Occupation of Germany.* New York: Palgrave, 2001.

Wohlforth, William. "New Evidence on Moscow's Cold War: Ambiguity in Search of a Theory." *Diplomatic History* 21 (spring, 1997): 237–40.

Wolfe, Robert. ed. *Americans as Proconsuls: United States Military Government in Germany and Japan, 1944–1952.* Carbondale: Southern Illinois University Press, 1984.

Woodbridge, George. *UNRRA: The History of the United Nations Relief and Rehabilitation Administration.* Vol. 2. New York: Columbia University Press, 1950.

Woods, Randall Bennett. *Fulbright: A Biography.* New York: Cambridge University Press, 1995.

Zegart, Amy. *The Evolution of the CIA, JCS, and NSC.* Stanford: Stanford University Press, 1999.

Zubok, Vladislav, and Constantine Pleshakov. *Inside the Kremlin's Cold War.* Cambridge, Mass.: Harvard University Press, 1997.

INDEX

James Jay Carafano is a graduate of West Point and earned his M.A. and Ph.D. at Georgetown University. A retired Army officer, and the former editor of *Joint Force Quarterly*, he is a senior fellow at the Center for Strategic and Budgetary Assessments and an adjunct professor at Georgetown. His publications include the Military Book Club main selection, *After D-Day: Operation Cobra and the Normandy Breakout.*

ISBN 1-58544-213-5